Contents

Introduction

Foreword

Like the athletic fortunes of most major institutions, Stanford's football history has had many moments and years of great exhilaration for students and fans alike. It has had equally despairing moments of great disappointment. Yet withal, its history is very possibly a unique one in this country.

Stanford is a very distinguished academic institution. It has drawn its student-athletes in thirteen men's intercollegiate sports from a relatively small undergraduate male student body of approximately 4,000. Yet it continues to be nationally competitive and successful in many sports—including football—while competing in one of the strongest intercollegiate conferences in the country (the Pacific-8). And, in recent years, it has done this with far fewer athletic scholarships than almost any other major athletic power in the country.

Stanford believes in diversity of talents within its student body—and exceptional athletic talent is given equal recognition with other talents—music, leadership, etc., in its admission process, assuming, of course, that any student is academically qualified for admission. Since 1949, it has followed the progress of its student-athletes compared to their classmates in their respective grade point averages, range of academic majors, graduation records and, in recent years, career aspirations. It has found that intercollegiate athletes equal or do slightly better in all these categories than their classmates. This strongly indicates that its student-athletes have been a truly representative sample of the general student body.

These studies confirm a long-held belief by Stanford that there is no inherent conflict between maintaining a strong athletic and academic program side by side in the same institution for a student who happens to have athletic talent.

Stanford intends to continue to compete in football and other major sports, for both men and women, against the best competition in the country. It does so in the strong belief that sports competition against the best is healthy, is a unique learning experience in educational institutions for young men and women interested in participating, and that its importance to the student-athlete and the institution rests on the integrity and personal qualities of the coach (or teacher) it employs to assist young people in their personal development as well as in the development of their athletic talent.

Fred Merrick's book highlights the highs and lows of Stanford's most visible sport—football. It is an excellent history. Underlying the highs and lows is this unique philosophy that Stanford holds as basic to a sound and sane athletic program.

Stanford has had several of the nation's most distinguished mentors as its coaches—innovators in the field—men such as "Pop" Warner, Clark Shaughnessy, Chuck Taylor, and John Ralston. Its roster of players has included some of the best and most exciting individuals in football—Ernie Nevers, Bob Reynolds, Frankie Albert, Bill McColl, John Brodie, Jim Plunkett, Jeff Siemon. It is a proud history and heritage that Stanford will be trying to uphold in future years.

Joseph H. Ruetz
Stanford Director of Athletics

Introduction

It was only natural that Leland Stanford Jr. University should be known as the Farm. Founded in 1885 at Palo Alto, California, by Senator and Mrs. Leland Stanford, the university is located on 8,800 acres which prior to that time had served as a breeding and training grounds for Senator Stanford's trotting horses. Stanford, who was governor of California in 1862-63 and U. S. Senator from 1885 until his death in 1893, was highly regarded for his trotting champions.

The death in 1884 of their only child, Leland Stanford, Jr., while traveling in Italy at the age of 15, caused Senator and Mrs. Stanford to turn their thoughts to founding a university. A founding grant was obtained in 1885, and the doors of this new institution, located in mid-peninsula some 35 miles south of San Francisco, were opened in 1891 to 559 students. David Starr Jordan was the first president of the university. Today the enrollment totals 11,374, of which 6,412 are undergraduates, and 4,962 are doing graduate work.

Stanford is a unique university in that it strives for No. 1 recognition nationally each year in both scholarship and sports. It has done well in both fields. Academically Stanford ranks among the top five or six schools in the country in a survey by the American Council on Education. While many great institutions such as Harvard, Yale, and the University of Chicago have de-emphasized or abandoned football, Stanford anticipates no such retreat. Stanford has football games scheduled through 1984 with such intersectional rivals as Penn State, Michigan, Army, Colorado, Tulane, Illinois, Oklahoma, Boston College, Purdue, Ohio State, and the Air Force Academy.

In this century Stanford has had a remarkable balance of 39 Rhodes Scholars and 36 All America football players. In the past 15 years Stanford has had 16 Rhodes Scholars and six All Americans. Since 1960 only Harvard, Yale, and Princeton have produced more Rhodes winners than has Stanford. Each year Stanford sends a number of its top football players into the National Football League. However, more of its gridders have gone into graduate school than into the pro football ranks.

Football players must be able to make it in political science, economics, engineering, human biology, psychology, premed, pre-law, or some other such field. There is no physical education major at Stanford. There also is no overabundance of financial help for athletes. Stanford offers only 63 full-ride scholarships in football, all of which are funded by the Buck Club, an organization of some 4,000 alumni and friends of the university. By means of selective recruiting, hard work, and the desire of a number of blue ribbon athletes to obtain a first class education at an outstanding institution, Stanford has been able to hold its own in the tough Pacific-8 Conference while also playing top intersectional opponents outside the conference.

According to Joe Ruetz, Stanford athletic director, there are no future plans to cut back to an Ivy League type of football because of the tough academic program faced by the student athletes. "We really don't have a choice," Reutz said. "There aren't enough schools in our geographical area willing and able to compete in an Ivy type league. We can either accept the challenge of major intercollegiate competition or get out, and we think there are more than enough values in the challenge to meet it. From a financial point of view it would be disastrous for us to de-emphasize football. Receipts from football support 70 percent of the Stanford program in all sports on all levels—intercollegiate, club, and intramural."

Warner Influence

Under a sprawling oak tree at the northwest corner of Stanford Stadium is a stone drinking fountain, and next to it is a pedestal with a bronze profile of Glenn S. Warner. Underneath is the inscription "In memory of Glenn S. 'Pop' Warner, 1870-1954, Whose contributions to the game of football and other intercollegiate sports are legendary."

One of football's all-time great coaches, Glenn Scobey Warner guided Stanford to national prominence during his nine years of coaching on the Farm.

Until Warner took over the duties, Stanford had had a variety of football coaches, amounting at times to a yearly turnover. It was at this stage, shortly after the resumption of American football following the end of World War I, that the Board of Athletic Control decided to obtain a football coach of proven ability and national prominence.

Glenn Scobey "Pop" Warner was their man.

Prior to coming West he had served as head coach at Georgia, Cornell, Carlisle, and University of Pittsburgh. When he signed to coach the Cardinals, his salary was $20,000, but an even more important part of the agreement was that he receive two round-trip tickets per year from Palo Alto to the East. During his nine years at Stanford Warner compiled a record of 71 victories, 17 defeats, and 8 ties. His teams scored 1,974 points while allowing only 594, and three of his teams went to the Rose Bowl.

Until Warner's arrival in 1924, the Cardinals' football success had been limited to the Pacific Coast. But Warner struck it rich at Stanford and enjoyed instant success by winning the

Pacific Coast Conference championship his first year and earning an invitation to the Rose Bowl. The assignment was against Notre Dame and its famed "Four Horsemen" on January 1, 1925.

Warner took Stanford back to the Rose Bowl on New Year's Day in 1927 and 1928, and also launched the Cardinals on a program of intersectional games which resulted in transcontinental trips to play games with Army, Minnesota, Dartmouth, and Pittsburgh. The national exposure earned recognition for Stanford players with the result that end Jim Lawson and fullback Ernie Nevers became the first All America players produced by Stanford.

Although Warner enjoyed success against California, the Cardinals' traditional rival, he never was able to master Howard Jones and the University of Southern California. Warner beat Jones the first two years of their rivalry (1925 and 1926) and earned a tie the following year (1927), but the Trojans dominated the series the next five years, registering shutouts against the Cardinals in four of these games.

Warner's feeling that he never would be able to develop promising freshman talent because of the desire of President Ray Lyman Wilbur to make Stanford a graduate school, and thus never would be able to compete against Southern California, helped Warner decide to accept an offer to coach at Temple. He left Stanford after the 1932 season.

"I believe this is a wonderful opportunity, and I am satisfied I am bettering my position," Warner said in announcing his decision to move to Temple. "After all, nine years is enough for a coach to stay in one place. I was at Pittsburgh that long. Every move I have made has been an advancement."

When word got out that "Pop" was leaving, a group of some 80 football players called on him and begged him to stay at Stanford. They promised to do anything he asked if he would stay, but to no avail.

The history of Stanford football is one of eras, several of which were successful. Claude E. "Tiny" Thornhill, one of Warner's assistants, assumed the head coaching role in 1933 following "Pop's" departure and stayed seven seasons. Warner had thought he lacked the material to compete with USC, but Thornhill's first three teams went to the Rose Bowl. Thornhill had a 35-25-7 record before giving way to Clark Shaughnessy.

Shaughnessy, whose T formation revolutionized college

12

football on the Coast, took over in 1940 and, like Thornhill, went to the Rose Bowl his first year. But he stayed only two seasons before resigning at the outbreak of World War II. Shaughnessy could have stayed on at Stanford, but he wanted to be active as a coach instead of handling an assignment in the physical education department. Knowing that Stanford would be abandoning football for the duration, Shaughnessy accepted an offer from Maryland to serve as coach and athletic director.

Some lean years followed World War II, and Marchamont "Marchie" Schwartz, a former Notre Dame All America, suffered through them, breaking even in six seasons with a 28-28-4 record.

Charles A. "Chuck" Taylor, an All America guard under Shaughnessy, returned to the Farm as head football coach in 1951, and, like Warner, Thornhill, and Shaughnessy, went to the Rose Bowl with his first team. Taylor chalked up a 40-29-2 mark during seven years at the helm before resigning to become assistant athletic director to Al Masters.

Colorful Jack Curtice succeeded Taylor and led Stanford for five seasons during which the Cardinals slipped to a low mark of 14-36. Curtice had his best year in 1962 when he broke even with a 5-5 record before being replaced by John Ralston, an energetic coach who rejuvenated the Cardinals. He capped his stay with two sensational Rose Bowl victories before he was lured into the professional football ranks by the Denver Broncos of the NFL. Ralston had a record of 55 wins, 36 losses, and 3 ties.

Jack Christiansen, a former All-Pro player with the Detroit Lions and coach of the San Francisco 49ers for five years, stepped up from Ralston's staff to take over the duties of head man in 1972. His three year record is 18-13-2.

How It All Began

Stanford's first intercollegiate game was played on March 19, 1892, against California, and the Cardinals unexpectedly won the game 14-10. Since that time Stanford's annual meeting with the University of California has been the "Big Game." The name was a natural because for several years it was the only game the Cardinals played against another college team. The other contests on the schedule were merely warm-ups against club or town teams to prepare for the clash with the Golden Bears from Berkeley. California had been playing football since 1882, albeit against a bunch of club teams.

Only a short time after the opening registration at Stanford in 1891, the wheels were set in motion for the organization of the Cardinals' first football team. A group of students interested in playing the game called on John R. Whittemore, a senior transfer student from Washington University in St. Louis. Because Whittemore had played football at Washington and knew the game, the group approached him to ask if he would help them organize a team and serve as captain.

Whittemore went to work devising plays and coaching the team, and after three months of practice decided that the squad was ready for some competition. California had approached the Cardinals earlier and had proposed a Thanksgiving Day game, but Whittemore had declined knowing his team was not ready. This time when Stanford contacted the Bears a game was arranged for March 19, 1892, the first meeting between the two Bay area universities.

To prepare for the meeting with California, Whittemore lined up a series of practice games, and Stanford won its very

14

first start by defeating Hopkins Academy 10-6. The Cards followed up with a 22-0 victory over the Berkeley Gym, a team which included several California players. The final tuneup was against the San Francisco Olympic Club and resulted in a 10-6 loss for Stanford.

With a very light team and without too much experience Stanford went into the game with California without much hope of winning. The Bears were big, and more experienced, and had beaten both Hopkins Academy and Berkeley Gym by larger margins than had Stanford. However, California also had lost to the Olympic Club by a score of 6-0.

Although collegiate football was unknown in San Francisco at that time, the contest between the Cardinals and the Golden Bears attracted surprising interest. Tickets had been printed for 10,000, but a crowd estimated at 20,000 showed up at the Haight Street Grounds. This created a number of problems. Don E. Liebendorfer, former Stanford sports information director and sports historian, says in his book *The Color of Life is Red* that these were solved by Herbert C. Hoover, student manager of the Stanford team who later became the 31st president of the United States. According to Liebendorfer, Hoover rounded up wash boilers and dish pans in which to deposit the gold and silver paid by the spectators for their tickets. There was little paper money in circulation in those days.

Cardinal had been adopted as the official color for Stanford and new uniforms purchased for the Big Game. In the excitement, however, everyone forgot to bring a football. When referee Jack Sherrard called Captain Whittemore of Stanford and Captain George Foulks of California to the middle of the field for the pregame coin toss, it was discovered that no one had a ball with which to start the game. The contest was delayed for more than an hour while the owner of a sporting goods store, who was in the crowd, rode his horse into town to get a ball.

Stanford capitalized on a California fumble to register an early touchdown. Using an early version of the reverse, right halfback Paul Downing slipped the ball to fullback Carl Clemans who, unnoticed by the Bear defense, scooted 45 yards for a touchdown. Three minutes after the first score, Clemans tallied again on another 45-yard run. Whittemore, who played left half, accounted for the third touchdown on a 30-yard dash after Dowling had ripped through the Bears for a 25-yard gain. With

Whittemore converting one of the scores, the half-time score-board showed Stanford in front by a 14-0 margin. Touchdowns counted only four points in those days while conversions were good for two points.

California's superior weight began to tell in the second half, but the best the Bears could do was to score two touch-downs. How California scored its other two points, whether by a conversion or a safety is subject to controversy, but the records agree that Stanford was the winner, 14-10.

All 11 starters on both teams played the entire game, which lasted 100 minutes, another switch from the modern game. In addition to Whittemore, Clemans, and Downing, the Stanford lineup was made up of M. D. Grosh, right end; Claud S. Downing, right tackle; C. C. Adams, right guard; Arthur H. Barnhisel, center; Stewart D. Briggs, left guard; Ellsworth L. Rich, left tackle; Charles H. Hogg, left end; and Thomas K. Code, quarterback.

With the arrival of "Pop" Warner on the Stanford campus the annual meeting with the Trojans of the University of Southern California took on added meaning, gradually advancing in importance until it rivaled the Big Game. Stanford's "Vow Boys" added to this rivalry with the Trojans, and in recent years the game with USC, probably, has carried more importance, as far as the Stanford players are concerned, than the contest with the Bears. One of the reasons for the prestige of the Stanford-USC game has been that its outcome usually decides the Cardinals' chances of winning the conference championship.

Walter Camp Helps Out

Despite the success of the first season, Whittemore felt that Stanford needed an experienced coach to direct its football team. Accordingly, he wrote to Walter Camp, famous Yale graduate, asking if he would recommend a coach. Camp, who later was to be called "The Father of American Football," surprised Whittemore by offering to take the assignment without salary. The only catch was that he would not be available until after Yale had completed its season. As a result, a second game for 1892 between Stanford and California could not be scheduled until December 17.

For warm-up games the Cardinals lined up Oakland High School and the Olympic Club, winning both contests handily. A rematch with the Olympic Club resulted in a 14-14 tie. With two minutes left to play the game was called by the referee because of darkness. The Olympic Club entered a vigorous protest concerning Stanford's second touchdown, made by William H. Harrelson on a 70-yard run. The clubmen protested on the grounds they had called time out for an injured player, but the referee ruled that he had not been notified of the injury and allowed the score to stand. Harrelson also scored two other touchdowns for Stanford that day.

As had been the case in the spring game, Stanford's team was much lighter than California's, and again the backers of the redshirts did not have much hope for success. Although Camp had made some position changes upon his arrival at Stanford, injuries had weakened the team to some extent. But with quick play similar to that displayed in the spring game the Cardinals managed to gain a 10-10 tie with the Bears.

Walter Camp, Stanford's first "name" coach.

The game again was scheduled for the Haight Street Grounds and attracted a lot of attention from San Francisco residents. Crowd estimates range from 15,000 to 18,000, and the game, like a majority of those to follow in this great rivalry, proved exciting.

Even in the early days of this traditional rivalry between Stanford and California there was mischievous goings-on between the students, a practice which has expanded in recent years to include such things as painting the rival campus with the colors of the opposing team, and attempting to steal the "Axe" which has been the trophy awarded the winner of the Big Game.

Harry Phillips, a clerk in the office of Carnell-Hopkins Company, had a huge horn built to use at the second 1892 game. It was 12 feet long and 6 feet across. On Friday night before the game a group of California students pirated it away and displayed it at the game the following day.

H. A. Walton, who had not played in the first game, proved an important addition to the Stanford lineup. A series of fumbles by both teams marred the early action before Walton scampered 30 yards around left end. Martin Kennedy made 10 yards and Clemans, behind good interference, swept for another 10, but California recovered a fumble to halt this threat.

A few minutes later Stanford pounced on a California fumble, and the Cardinals baffled the Bears with a Walton to Clemans reverse that gained 15 yards. But Stanford lost the ball on downs at the California 12.

Stanford put on an explosive offensive show late in the first quarter, however, to score. The Cards covered 100 yards in just three plays, starting from their own 10 yard line. The field was 110 yards long at that time. Walton, who was playing right halfback, started the drive with a 40-yard gain. Clemans, who had been moved from fullback to left half, added another 40 yards on a reverse from Walton around left end behind the interference of Walton, Kennedy, and quarterback Code. Then Walton, behind good interference, circled right end for the final 20 yards and the touchdown. Kennedy added the conversion for a 6-0 lead.

California capitalized on a Walton fumble to get on the scoreboard. Loren Hunt, Percy Benson, George Foulks, and Morse alternated carrying the ball to the Stanford 17. Hunt carried on five of the next six plays, including the final two on

19

which he gained 12 and 3 yards for the touchdown. However, Oscar Taylor missed the conversion, leaving the score 6-4.

Stanford's swiftness led to another touchdown after the Cardinals recovered a fumble on their own 20. Clemans ran for 10, Walton added 25, Kennedy 5, and then Clemans swept around right end behind the blocking of Code and Julius Frankenheimer, Jr., for 40 yards and a touchdown. Kennedy missed this conversion.

The superior weight of the California team began to tell in the second half, and the Bears mounted another scoring march with less than 10 minutes left in the game. California powered 76 yards in 11 plays with fullback Hunt covering the final 20 yards. Taylor kicked the conversion to tie the score at 10-10. An unusual thing about this game was that Camp, the Stanford coach, refereed the first half, and Thomas McClung, California's coach, refereed the second.

An account of the game by Robert L. Porter, an ex-college player, said: "It was strength and weight against quickness and skill, and each offset the other. Stanford played a snappy and reasonably fast game, but they were light, woefully light at center.

"Berkeley almost ignored one of its strongest cards, Taylor's punting. Again and again a well placed punt, well followed, would have won them the game. While on the other hand, had Stanford men used their interference plays oftener on the second down more points would stand to their credit. The Stanford wedge was used for the first time on any field, and its originator, Mr. Camp, must feel well satisfied with its practicability. It enabled the comparatively light team to slide Kennedy through time after time for eight and ten yard gains."

Camp's evaluation of the game was "that it was fully as interesting and well played as the Eastern game. The only exception that both teams seemed to make to the regulation play was that neither had any fancy for punting."

An Undefeated Season

C. D. "Pop" Bliss, a famous Yale halfback, was critical of the Stanford players before the start of the 1893 season. Bliss was hired to replace Camp who had returned to the East. Attempts were made to bring John Hartwell or Charles Gill, a couple of other former Yale stars, to the Farm, but they could not be tempted away from the coaching positions they held with Eastern teams.

"There is Thompson, a candidate for center," Bliss said. "He is not aggressive enough by any means. He doesn't work hard enough, and doesn't follow a man when he gets through the line. Code, the quarterback, is slow in passing the ball, while Downing and Whitehouse, the tackles, overrun their men. The tackling generally is weak, and the center men are slow and awkward. I have no doubt these faults will all be corrected as we go along. It won't be my fault if they are not."

Bliss apparently corrected the faults. Stanford registered its first undefeated season, winning eight games and being tied by California. Perhaps even more impressive was the fact that the Cardinals held seven of their nine opponents scoreless. The only teams to score against Stanford were the Olympic Club, which lost 24-11 in the second game after losing the first time by a 46-0 margin, and California, which battled to a 6-6 tie.

The engagement of Bliss opened an athletic, diplomatic, and financial struggle between Stanford and California for football supremacy and perhaps all athletics. The University Club offered a silver football trophy to the winner of the Big Game, and it was expected that this would help attract athletes of all kinds.

As had been the custom, Stanford played three warm-up games before meeting California. However, this time the season did not end with the Big Game. The Cardinals played five more games, winding up with a New Year's Day contest against Multnomah A. C. in Portland. Not one of the nine games was played at Stanford. Of the so-called home games one was played in San Jose and four in San Francisco.

Bliss, who was on hand before school opened, had whipped his team into shape for the opening game with the Olympic Club, and the Cards romped to a smashing 46-0 win. Stanford scored within four minutes of the opening kickoff. Guy Cochran contributed the most spectacular play of the game with a 95-yard punt return for a touchdown.

Stanford football players enjoyed the luxury of their first training table in 1893. Rea E. Maynard, who had been elected manager of the football team by the Board of Athletic Directors, reported: "Thanks to the efforts of the president, the steward at Encina Hall is setting a very satisfactory training table. The fare is plain and composed largely of rare meats, vegetables, and fresh fruits. Seventeen players are on training table, and others will be added when they show ability."

Players were required to sign a pledge to retire and rise at certain hours, report for duty when called upon, and abstain from the use of tobacco and alcoholic drinks in order to qualify for training table.

Football rules prior to the turn of the century called for the loss of the ball for certain penalties, such as offensive holding. It was a couple of situations such as this that cost Stanford scoring opportunities in the first half of the Big Game. Once the Cardinals reached the California five, and another time recovered a blocked kick on the Bears' two, only to lose the ball on penalties. California took advantage of a fumbled punt to go in front 6-0 in the first half, marking the first time California had led in three meetings with Stanford.

The Cardinals staged a 42-yard drive to score in the second half with Kennedy getting the touchdown from the two yard line. He also kicked the conversion to give Stanford a tie in the contest which was played in the rain and mud.

Stanford concluded its season with a four-game tour of the Northwest, winning all four games by shutouts. Included was a 40-0 win over University of Washington, the first game played by the Huskies against another college team. This game was played on December 30, and on January 1 the Cards finished their season by beating Multnomah A. C. 18-0 at Portland. Stanford finished the season with 284 points, the most ever to be scored by a Cardinal football team until Andy Kerr came along to tie that figure in 1923.

Football Comes
To The Campus

Stanford played its first football game on campus in 1894 as Walter Camp returned to direct the Cardinals to a 6-3 season. The occasion was a 20-0 victory over Reliance Club after the Cardinals had lost two earlier games to the same team. The season also was to feature the first real intersectional game for Stanford when it split two games with the University of Chicago, losing the first in San Francisco, 24-4, but winning the second game in Los Angeles 12-0. Aside from the one home game with Reliance, the Cardinals played four games in San Francisco, two in Los Angeles, one in Santa Cruz, and one in Sacramento.

Moving players to different positions was one of Camp's favorite diversions. Paul Downing had been a halfback on Stanford's first team in the spring of 1892. Camp had moved him to guard in the fall, and Bliss had shifted him to center in 1893. Now Camp assigned Downing to a fourth position, shifting him to tackle.

California was a solid favorite for the Thanksgiving Day game on November 29 with Stanford, but the Cardinals scored a 6-0 upset, the lone score coming on a blocked kick. Charlie Ficket, Stanford left guard, broke through to block Wolf Ransome's punt somewhere around the Card's 43 yard line. As the ball bounded towards midfield, Stanford tackle Guy Cochran outran Ransome, scooped up the ball, and dashed 45 yards for a touchdown. Kennedy converted to end the scoring.

There were numerous other threats, however. Prior to the score, Stanford had advanced to the Bears' three yard line on one occasion and to the fifteen on another. Late in the game

California pulled a maneuver which almost resulted in a touchdown. Rules of that time permitted a player on the offensive team, who was behind the kicker at the time the ball was punted, to field the ball if he were fast enough to do so. With the end of the game drawing near, Percy Benson, California quarterback, lofted a punt diagonally across the field where Eddie Sherman, a Bear end who had been onside, caught it. Sherman apparently was on his way to a touchdown, but Al Spalding, Stanford end, caught him just before he reached the goal line. Spalding's tackle knocked the ball out of Sherman's grasp, and Bill Harrelson, Stanford quarterback, recovered for a touchback to preserve the Cardinals' 6-0 victory.

Camp became the first Stanford coach to stick around for a second season when he stayed for the 1895 campaign, which was sharply curtailed in comparison with the previous year. The Cards played only five games, and three of those were against the Olympic Club. Stanford went into the Big Game with California undefeated and had allowed only two points to the opposition. The Bears had lost one of their four warm-up games. Camp, in a surprising move, had attended one of the Bears' games in what may have been the first scouting maneuver in the West.

The game, played in a new location at Central Park in San Francisco, wound up in a 6-6 tie, the third deadlock in five meetings between the teams. Wet and windy weather limited attendance for the Big Game to 10,000.

Stanford capitalized on the recovery of a California fumble with Tom Williams, Card center, falling on the ball on the Bears' eight yard line. Three plays later Captain Guy Cochran slipped over the goal line to score. Nat Carle converted.

California took advantage of a short Stanford punt to tie the score in the final two minutes of the game.

The first five Big Games had been closely contested, but the 1896 meeting turned out to be a rout, Stanford winning by a score of 20-0. Harry P. Cross, who had been an outstanding center at Yale, had replaced Camp as coach of the Cardinals and had followed some of his predecessor's tactics by moving Steuart Cotton from tackle to fullback. Cotton collected Stanford's first touchdown against California by scoring on a short plunge to cap a 60-yard drive midway in the first quarter as the Cardinals dominated action from the start. Jack Rice, a 158-pound Cardinal tackle, recovered a fumbled punt in the end zone for another score, and Chet Murphy, freshman quarter-back, dashed 17 yards for a third. Cotton tallied the final touch-down from eight yards out after alternating with Ben Searight to advance the ball into scoring territory.

Lining up a schedule proved extremely difficult for George H. Brooke, who had been an All America halfback at Pennsylvania in 1894 and an All America fullback in 1895, when he took over the Stanford coaching duties in 1897. Brooke's selection snapped a monopoly held by Yale graduates since 1892. The only opposition available was the Reliance Club which the Cardinals played four times in preparation for the meeting with California.

Stanford was a big favorite for the Thanksgiving Day game at Recreation Grounds in San Francisco, and the Cardinals did not take long to prove the odds were right. Stanford scored three times in the first half and went on to register a 28-0 triumph, the second straight lopsided victory and the second consecutive shutout of the series.

Chet Murphy, now a sophomore, kept California in a hole with his kicking. Stanford made effective use of the guards-back formation, featuring Nat Carle and Charlie Fickert, to march 65 yards to score. A second touchdown was achieved in the same fashion, with Cotton accounting for both scores. The gridiron still was 110 yards long, and the Cardinals drove 108 yards for their third score after stopping a California threat on the Stanford two.

A 20-yard run by left halfback Jack Daley and a third touchdown by Cotton featured the second half scoring. Murphy set up the final score with a 60-yard punt return.

Stanford and California drew up a pact in February, 1897, which outlined some basic rules of eligibility. Among the new regulations adopted at this time were the limitation of athletes to four years of competition in one sport, establishment of a minimum number of hours of classroom work for an athlete to be eligible, and a ruling that students of other institutions would be ineligible to compete for either university. The pact also called for annual meetings between Stanford and California in football, baseball, track and field, tennis, and boat racing.

There also were a number of changes in the football rules, among them being an altering of the scoring to make a touch-down worth five points instead of four and the conversion one point instead of two. Thus the total of six remained the same.

An expanded schedule with several new opponents, including Washington, Kansas, and the Iowa Volunteers, greeted Harry Cross on his return as Stanford coach in 1898. Key to the entire season was a 22-0 loss to California, ending a seven-year stretch in which Stanford had not lost to the Bears.

California was the favorite on the strength of its undefeated season which included six wins, two ties, and seven shutouts. Stanford threatened only once and that was the result of an unusual play made by Chet Murphy when he recovered his own punt on the Stanford one yard line and ran to the California 28 before being hauled down. The Cardinals were able to reach only the Bears' 16 before losing the ball. California drove 94 yards in 18 plays to claim a 5-0 half-time lead. Except for the fact that Murphy averaged 42 yards on 12 kicks, California might have won by an even bigger score than the final 22-0.

The 1899 season was one of disappointment from the beginning. Burr Chamberlain, an All America tackle at Yale in 1897 and 1898, had a nucleus of only three veterans, and the nine-game schedule included five games with the Olympic Club, a team usually made up of former college stars.

Going into the Big Game California had a record of six wins and a tie and had not been scored upon. Stanford, with a 1-3-2 mark, was unable to change the pattern. The Bears scored four times in the first half to pile up a commanding 24-0 advantage. Stanford did a much better job on defense in the second half, holding California to a single touchdown. The Bears somewhat made amends for their four previous losses in the series with this 30-0 victory.

Yost, A Coach And A Rival

At the turn of the century Stanford's football fortunes took an upward turn with the selection of Fielding H. Yost as head coach. Yost, who later was to acquire the nickname of "Hurry Up" and become one of the most famous coaches in the college ranks with his high scoring Michigan teams, was a graduate of Lafayette College in Easton, Pennsylvania. There he had earned All America honors in 1896 on a team unbeaten in a 12-game schedule, including victories over Princeton and Navy.

Prior to coming to Stanford Yost had coached at Ohio Wesleyan where he compiled a record of 7-1-1 in 1897, beating Ohio State and tying Michigan while losing only to Oberlin. Moving to Nebraska in 1898 he fashioned a 7-3 mark, losing the final two games of the season to Drake and Iowa by scores of 6-5. In 1899 at Kansas, Yost put together a team that went undefeated in 10 games, holding eight opponents scoreless. Thus Stanford was getting its most experienced coach until that time. Most of the previous Card coaches had been either fresh out of college or with only a year or two of experience.

Even at this early stage in his career Yost was a man in a hurry, and in addition to his duties at Stanford he took on the assignment of coaching two other teams. He directed Stanford in the afternoon, handled a San Francisco high school in the morning, and worked with San Jose Normal (now San Jose State University) at night under gas lights.

One of the unusual features of the season, which produced a 7-2-1 record, was the appearance of San Jose Normal on the Stanford schedule for two games. It was Yost vs. Yost since he was coaching both squads. Stanford won both contests handily,

35-0 and 24-0. Perhaps even more important from Yost's point of view was his discovery at San Jose of Willie Heston, an outstanding back who was to follow Yost to Michigan the next year and become one of football's immortal backs, twice earning All America honors as a member of the Wolverines' famous "point-a-minute" teams.

Under Yost the Stanford team developed early, slipped a little, and then improved again. One observer noted that the team "showed excellent fighting spirit, but lacked the cohesion of the freshman squad." With the exception of Sheeley and Ralph McFadden the line was slow in both offense and defense, and it was "plainly every man for himself" in the backfield with the exception of Frank Slaker.

The Cardinals blanked eight of their ten opponents, but the two teams who were able to score were responsible for the two defeats. The season must be considered a success, however, for Yost succeeded in restoring Stanford to its position of supremacy over California. The Cards' 5-0 victory in the Big Game was the result of a field goal by Bill Traeger, Stanford left tackle who later gained prominence as sheriff of Los Angeles County, in the final two minutes of an evenly fought defensive struggle.

A report of the game praised the play of ends Kenneth Cooper and Tom McFadden who "clearly outclassed those of Berkeley in every department of the game, and Harrison Hill, who outpunted Moore of California." Traeger's place-kick for the winning goal was regarded as routine. "It was a play which he had reduced to a practical certainty by faithful practice throughout the season," said an account of the game.

With Yost's departure for Michigan, where he served as coach from 1901 until 1923 and after that as athletic director, Stanford brought Charlie Fickert back to the Farm. Fickert, a star guard from the 1894-97 era and captain of the 1896 team, was the first Stanford graduate to become head coach. California scored a 2-0 victory over the Fickert-coached Cardinals in the Big Game with the only points coming just before the end of the first half when the Bears blocked a Stanford kick. The ball rolled over the goal line where it was recovered by Frank Slaker, Stanford fullback, for a safety.

The crusher, however, was to come on January 1, 1902, when Stanford was beaten by Yost and his Michigan team 49-0 in the forerunner of the now famous Rose Bowl. In some quarters this contest is considered the first Rose Bowl game, probably because it was staged by the Tournament of Roses Association. However, Don Liebendorfer, Stanford sports historian, never has recognized it as such for a variety of reasons. Supporting Liebendorfer's theory is a reference to the 1964 Rose Bowl game by Joe Hendrickson, Pasadena newspaperman, in his book *The Tournament of Roses, A Pictorial History*. Hendrickson says, "The parade (1964) was the 'Diamond Anniversary' event in Tournament history, the 75th anniversary of the festival. The game was thus the 50th."

There also was some question as to why Stanford was selected to face Michigan, which had won 10 straight games and had outscored its opponents 501-0.

The Rose tournament had adopted blue and gold as its official colors, and the city of Pasadena was decorated with pennants of these colors. This aroused the ire of Stanford followers because it closely resembled the blue and maize colors of Michigan, and perhaps even more significant was the fact that these also were the colors of arch-rival University of California.

There were 1,000 seats at Tournament Park, located on what now is part of the campus of the California Institute of Technology. However, it is estimated that more than 8,500 showed up for the game, the crowd overflowing around the playing field.

Michigan's high-scoring team was unable to dent the Stanford defense in the early going, and the game developed into a kicking duel between Sweeley of Michigan and Fisher, McGilvray, and Traeger of Stanford. Heston, the great Michigan back who was to wind up with 170 yards for 18 carries during the afternoon, finally cracked the Cardinals defense with a 21-yard sprint to the Stanford eight yard line on a naked reverse. The remainder of the Michigan team ran to the right, drawing the Stanford defense in that direction. Meanwhile, Heston, without any interference, ran to his left and had reached the eight yard line before the Cards recovered and caught him. Neil Snow, the Wolverine fullback, scored four plays later.

Stanford trailed only 17-0 at the half but was no match for Michigan in the final two quarters. Heston, of course, was the star of the game, but Michigan had other outstanding performers too. Snow scored five times and A. E. Redden twice on 25-yard punt returns. One of the Stanford players was William

K. Roosevelt, a second cousin of Theodore Roosevelt. The Stanford guard gave an exhibition of gritty work which long will be remembered. "With his leg fractured he continued playing the best quality of football for another 10 minutes giving way to a substitute only after having received additional injuries which made it impossible for him to play," according to an account of the game.

Stanford, going into the game with Michigan, had a new combination of backs with McGilvray at fullback and Fisher and Slaker at halfback. The unit proved greatly superior to the arrangement in the Big Game. Although there was some confusion by the substitution of Paul Tarpey from the end position to quarterback only a few days before the game, they worked well together. McGilvray was especially effective in his line plunges. Traeger was opposed to B. C. Shorts, who was ranked as the greatest Western tackle. Pregame reports said that Yost expected Shorts to "eat up Traeger." However, Stanford backers felt that if Traeger did not clearly outplay Shorts he "clearly knocked the cannibalistic appetite out of him."

In the early days of Stanford University a group advertised itself as the "Stanford Football Team" and journeyed to San Jose to play a picked team from that community. This situation raised the first question of amateur status of athletes because each of the players was reported to have received $12 for participating in the game. When it became evident that amateur rules would be enforced, the concept of expenses was rapidly and freely developed. One player informed the investigating committee that it had cost him $1 for transportation to San Jose, and that he had had to pay $11 for a broken appointment with a dentist, adding up to the $12 he had received for playing.

31

The Lanagan Era

Stanford and California both went into the 1902 Big Game undefeated. The Bears also were unscored on in six games while the Cardinals had given up only 10 points. There had been some charges and counter-charges on ineligibility, and this game became known as the "Locomotive Smith" contest. Smith was the California star, but he was declared ineligible on a technicality just before the game.

However, Bobby Sherman, who was Smith's substitute, returned a punt 105 yards for a touchdown, and the Bears went on to win 16-0. Sherman's run, with the interference of almost the entire Berkeley team, was considered the finest play ever seen on a Western gridiron at that time.

Carl "Clem" Clemans, who had been manager and a halfback for the first Stanford team in 1892 and had captained the team in the fall, returned to coach the Cardinals in 1902. A review of the season in the *Quad*, Stanford's yearbook, cited the renewed spirit of the Cardinal athletic teams. "During the past few years Stanford has been fighting not only Berkeley, but also a force within herself which is more powerful than the State University—the breaking of training rules," said the *Quad* article. "But last year saw the beginning of the death of this force and the revival of the old 'Stanford Spirit.' The two men to whom most credit is due are Dr. Frank Angell and Capt. McCaughran of the track team."

Accounts of the Big Game indicate that the score did not show how close the contest really was. "Rarely have two teams been more evenly matched," one story said. "Alfred Cole was a star at halfback for Stanford while George Clark was outstanding at left end, never allowing the Bears to gain around his side of the line, and time after time breaking up the opponent's play before it started." Orval Overall kicked two field goals for California to supplement Sherman's touchdown.

The game with California was played November 8. On Thanksgiving Day the Cardinals traveled to Salt Lake City on their longest intersectional venture to date. There they defeated the University of Utah in the snow, 35-11. McGilvray starred for Stanford with touchdown runs of 45 and 65 yards.

James F. Lanagan assumed the Stanford coaching duties in 1903 and launched one of the most successful eras in the early history of Cardinal football. Lanagan, who had graduated from Stanford in 1900, was extremely popular with the students. During his years at Stanford he established a spirit of fair play and a determination to win which was aptly characterized as the "Lanagan Fighting Spirit."

He also issued a plea for a place where a man of average skills could participate in sports and stressed a need for a thorough organization of college athletics. Lanagan proposed class teams as a means towards achieving this goal. "Every man ought to be given a fair chance to show his ability," Lanagan said. "What we need is a place to play."

When Lanagan resigned in 1908 to enter law practice, the students showed their regard for Lanagan by dedicating the *Quad* to him.

Lanagan produced an undefeated team in 1903, his first year. "The season was a success and would have been regarded as such had Stanford lost to California," the *Quad* said. "Stanford men knew that discipline was more needed than victory, and discipline we had, vigorous and wholesome, resulting in perhaps the most successful football season in matter of spirit since the days of Walter Camp."

California was the only team to score on Stanford during the 1903 season as the Cardinals registered 10 shutouts and wound up scoring 199 points while allowing 6 points. But that touchdown and conversion gave California a 6-6 tie in the November 4 Big Game at Richmond Field in San Francisco. Stanford finished the year with eight victories and three ties. Reliance A. C. and Nevada played scoreless ties with the Cardinals.

California's record was almost equal to Stanford's going into the Big Game. The Golden Bears had lost only one game and had given up only one touchdown before facing the Cardinals, losing to Nevada, 6-2. A 45-yard run by Louis "Dutch" Bansbach, captain and quarterback, on a fake reverse gave Stanford an early lead. Wilfred Dole's conversion made it 6-0. A blocked kick and conversion in the closing minutes allowed California to tie the score. In a switch of their earlier habits, the Cardinals played the first nine games on the Stanford campus.

First staging of the Big Game on college grounds highlighted the 1904 season as the Cardinals and Bears met at Berkeley on November 12 with Stanford scoring an 18-0 win. There was some anxiety over the plan to switch the game to the campus, but these worries proved groundless as the game drew a larger crowd than ever before, and approximately $20,000 was cleared to be split between the two schools.

Stanford was conceded to have a better team than California, but the Bears, largely due to the punting of Bill Heitmuller, battled the Cardinals to a 0-0 deadlock in the first half. Stanford played better in the second half, and better physical condition was apparent as quarterbacks Edmund "Stump" Stott and Bansbach, halfbacks Dole and Alexander "Bull" Chalmers, and fullback Milo "Sunny Jim" Weller led the Cardinal offensive assault for an 18-0 victory. Stanford rooters celebrated their first Big Game win since 1900 by staging a torchlight parade up Market Street in San Francisco.

Lanagan wound up his second season with a 7-2-1 record with the Stanford defense again proving tough to score against. The Cards had eight shutouts but in turn were blanked three times. These three failures to score prevented Lanagan from having back-to-back undefeated seasons. Stanford completed the campaign with 206 points while giving up only 10. The only teams to score on the Cards were the Olympic Club and the Sherman Indians, both of whom registered 5-0 victories.

Lanagan, with only three lettermen returning for the 1905 season, produced the first undefeated and untied team in Stanford history when the Big Game made its first appearance on the Stanford campus.

Dr. Angell, a professor of psychology and a champion for the Stanford athletic program, and the Training House Corporation were responsible for construction of bleachers which would accommodate 15,000 spectators at the Stanford Field.

Captain Forrest Fisher of the 1898 team had suggested that each class leave as large a sum as possible for a parting gift

34

with the understanding that when $5,000 was obtained, a training house should be built. The Class of 1899 left $195, the Class of 1900 added nothing, but the Class of 1901 contributed $427. In 1904 the Board of Trustees set aside a new tract of 40 acres for athletic fields. In 1905 with $10,000 raised somehow, the corporation proceeded with grading of grounds and construction of training quarters and the football grandstands. There was some concern that the bleachers would not be completed in time for the game, but Dr. Angell and his crew came through.

The first half of the game produced little excitement until the closing minutes when Stanford suddenly came to life and marched 50 yards in five plays for a touchdown. Captain Chalmers scored from seven yards out, and Dole converted for a 6-0 Stanford lead at the intermission. Following the Stanford score Ollie Snedigar, California's great back, returned the kickoff for 75 yards and an apparent touchdown, but the score was nullified because he had stepped out of bounds on the Stanford 28.

Early in the second half when Snedigar ran 42 yards for a touchdown, it stood up, but the Bears missed the conversion. Late in the game the Cardinals staged a 75-yard march, capped by a 15-yard scoring dash by Ted Van Dervoort, Cardinal right halfback. That made the final count 12-5 for Stanford.

Because the many injuries and fatalities were causing concern about American football, and because public resentment was growing, President Roosevelt in mid-season called representatives of Yale, Harvard, and Princeton to the White House and told them to remove every objectionable feature in order to save the game.

The season had ended in an uproar of protest against the brutality of play. An article by Amos Alonzo Stagg, then coach at the University of Chicago, said a survey showed 18 deaths and 159 more or less serious injuries had resulted from football. On January 12, 1906, under the leadership of Walter Camp and Capt. Palmer E. Pierce of West Point, the American Intercollegiate Football Rules Committee was organized, and a program effecting far-reaching changes to open up the game and save football was adopted.

At the end of the 1905 season President David Starr Jordan of Stanford and President Benjamin Wheeler of California met and decided football at the two universities should be replaced by rugby.

The Rugby Years

Stanford enjoyed unusual success during its 12 years of rugby competition (1906-1917) thanks in a large part to the addition of two talented players from Australia and New Zealand, and the arrival of the Templeton brothers, Robert L. "Dink" and his 150-pound "big" brother Rick. Led by Danny Carroll, Jim Wylie, and the Templeton brothers, the Cardinals were undefeated in 1914 and 1915 with a scoreless tie against the Olympic Club the latter year being the only game Stanford failed to win in that stretch.

Lanagan, whose three-year record as football coach showed 23 wins, 2 losses, and 4 ties, knew nothing about rugby, but he was retained because of the respect with which he was held by the students and the university. To prepare himself for his new duties Lanagan made a trip to Vancouver, British Columbia, and spent the summer picking up as much knowledge as possible about rugby. Encouraged by reports that rugby was "any man's game," one of the largest squads ever to turn out at Stanford confronted Lanagan for the start of practice for the 1906 season. When he resigned at the end of the 1908 season to enter law, Lanagan had compiled a record of 26-8-1.

George Presley, who had played for Lanagan in 1906 and helped coach the next two seasons, took over the coaching reins and quickly demonstrated that he could handle the position. In four seasons Presley's teams won 30 games while losing 8 and tying 1.

Floyd Brown, another former Stanford player, returned to the Farm as rugby coach in 1913 and after an 8-3 record that year, produced unbeaten teams in 1914 and 1915. Brown received a big lift with the addition of Carroll, who had been an outstanding performer with the Australian Waratahs when they had played at Stanford in 1912. Carroll liked the school and the people he met so much that he decided to enroll at Stanford instead of returning to Australia. A year later he was joined by Wylie, a standout for the New Zealand All Blacks, who had handed Stanford a pair of lacings in 1913. Like Carroll, Wylie decided to take up life on the Farm, and this pair led the Cardinals to an undefeated season, winning 10 straight games and defeating California 26-8.

That was the end of athletic relations between the Cards and the Bears for five years. California had been seeking a rule to prohibit freshmen from participating in varsity sports. Stanford resisted, arguing that it took 15 recommended units to gain admission to the university and, therefore, freshmen should be eligible. The appearance of Carroll and Wylie at Stanford may have helped bring the disagreement to a head. At any rate when the five-year pact between the two universities expired January 1, 1915, California officials demanded that any renewal must ban freshmen from varsity teams. When an agreement could not be worked out, athletic relations between the two arch-rivals were suspended.

Santa Clara stepped in to fill California's spot as the "big game" on the Stanford schedule in 1915. Meanwhile, the Bears were unable to find such a replacement and returned to American football.

The Templetons joined Carroll and Wylie on the 1915 squad, and the Cards swept to 10 straight victories after a 0-0 tie with the Olympic Club in the season opener. Don Liebendorfer, Stanford sports information director and sports historian who watched the Cardinals for more than 50 years as a student and publicist, rated the Templeton brothers as two of the greatest kickers in Stanford history. Dink, who later became famous as Stanford track coach and developer of champions and world record holders, played football in 1919 and 1920. In later years he taught some of his kicking tricks to Ernie Nevers, one of Stanford's all-time football greats.

A mandate of the Stanford board of trustees led to a complete reorganization of the athletic and physical training program in the fall of 1916. The aim of the new plan, to become effective October 1, 1916, was to effect cooperation between the university and the students.

Henceforth all physical exercise, whether merely for exercise or for intercollegiate contests, was to be directed by a new Board of Athletic Control. The BAC, an amalgamation of the old Board of Control of Athletic Fields and the Advisory Athletic Committee, was made up of three faculty members, three alumni, and three students.

The Pacific Coast Conference was created in 1916 with California, Oregon, Washington, Washington State, and Oregon State as original members. Stanford joined the group in 1917, although the Cardinals did not return to football until 1919. Idaho and Southern California were added to the conference in 1922; Montana gained membership in 1924, and UCLA was admitted in 1928.

Prior to 1936 there was no schedule arranged to determine a conference champion. However, after the 1935 season, a ruling reduced the conference to eight members by requiring that members play seven conference games within a seven-week period.

As members of the new Pacific Coast Conference, Stanford and California resumed athletic relations in 1919 with the Bears winning by a score of 14-10. Stanford went into the game full of confidence despite discouraging reports from Berkeley about the strength of the Bears. Templeton, making good use of his rugby talent, dropkicked a 45-yard field goal in the first quarter while Frederic Adams caught a pass for a Stanford touchdown. The Cardinals carried the ball to the California five yard line in the closing minutes, but John Patrick's attempt to get a winning touchdown was stopped, and a pass fell incomplete as the final gun sounded.

A 13-0 loss to Southern California dropped Stanford's record to 4-3, a disappointment for Bob Evans who had started the season in an optimistic mood. Templeton's educated toe played a major role in victories over Oregon Agricultural College (later to become Oregon State University) and St. Mary's. His kicking kept Oregon State at bay in the fourth quarter to give Stanford a 14-6 win after Adams had scooped up a fumble and sprinted 75 yards for a touchdown. Against St. Mary's, Templeton and Robert Pelouze worked an onside kick to perfection for a pair of touchdowns in a 34-0 victory. In the opening minutes of play, Templeton got off a long kick which carried over the head of Gael quarterback Correa. Before the St. Mary's man knew what had happened, Pelouze had put the ball down between the goalposts for a touchdown. Templeton and Pelouze worked the same play again the next time Stanford had the ball.

Evans was a good coach, but he irritated many of the Stanford alumni, and as a result he was replaced as coach in 1920 by Walter Powell, who had played at Wisconsin. Powell had the misfortune to come along at the time of Andy Smith's "Wonder Teams" at California, and the Cards took a 38-0 lacing in the 1920 Big Game. California took a 10-0 lead in the first quarter, but the Cardinals held their rivals scoreless in the second period. Stanford gave up another touchdown in the third quarter, but then the Bears rolled up three touchdowns in the final period against an exhausted Cardinal team.

Highlight of the 1921 season was the playing of the Big Game for the first time in the newly constructed Stanford Stadium, which boasted a seating capacity of 60,000. The stadium had been started in 1919, using mule power for the excavating, and was completed in 1921 at a cost of $573,470. Stanford claimed the honor of scoring the first touchdown in the stadium, but that was about the only solace for the Cardinals that day. Andy Smith's Golden Bears completed an undefeated season with a smashing 42-7 victory over Stanford.

California fumbled the opening kickoff which Patrick, the Cards' captain and fullback, recovered on the Bears' four yard line. Stanford took four downs to cover those four yards, but halfback Chet Wilcox made it over the goal line on the last play, and Bob Shlaudman converted. The rest of the day belonged to California.

Andy Kerr Paves The Way

A new era was about to dawn on Stanford football. The feeling among Cardinal alumni was that Stanford should hire a coach of proven talent instead of bringing in a recently graduated player each year. The result was the launching of a search for an established coach, a project which led to Glenn Scobey "Pop" Warner who was then coaching the University of Pittsburgh where he had turned out five undefeated teams since taking over the Panthers in 1915.

Warner also had turned in outstanding jobs at Georgia, Cornell, and Carlisle Indian School before moving to Pittsburgh. When he was contacted by Leland Cutler, a member of the Stanford Board of Athletic Control, he expressed interest in the idea of developing a team at Stanford.

However, Warner, who had two years remaining on his contract with Pitt, declared he would not break it. Nor would he ask to be relieved of fulfilling the pact. He agreed, instead, to send two of his assistants—Andy Kerr and Claude "Tiny" Thornhill—to install his system and set the stage for his arrival after he had fulfilled his Pitt contract. Kerr had been a member of Warner's staff for six years, and Thornhill had been a star tackle for the Panthers from 1914 to 1916. Both knew "Pop's" style very well. Kerr was to be the head coach and also coach basketball while Thornhill was to coach the line.

In this manner the wheels were set in motion that would lead Stanford to a position of national prominence and also attract national recognition for its players. Kerr had a good foundation on which to start building a team with such veterans as Dudley DeGroot, an outstanding center who later coached at

San Jose State and in the professional ranks with the Washington Redskins; guards Bob Cravens and Dick Faville; and halfbacks Art Wilcox and Paul Murray. Also a number of promising new men included Jim Lawson, an end who became Stanford's first All American; tackle Harry Shipkey; quarterback "Scotchy" Campbell; and fullbacks Norm Cleaveland and Murray Cuddeback. The latter was the star of the 1924 game with California.

Kerr, who was a perfectionist, had to display a lot of patience while teaching the fine points of the reverses and blocking assignments of the Warner system to this group of players who never had seen this style of play. To make matters worse for Kerr, Stanford opened its season against a big and experienced Olympic Club team led by John Patrick, captain and fullback of the 1921 Stanford team. Coach of the Olympic Club was Bob Evans who had been fired by Stanford at the end of the 1919 season. It was a situation which could only mean trouble for Stanford. The Cardinals scored first on a field goal by Cuddeback, but the Olympians were in charge of the game the rest of the way and won handily by a 27-9 margin.

Things began to go together a lot better after the opening setback, and Stanford won four games in a row, the first three by shutouts. But the Cards managed only single touchdowns in their victories over Santa Clara and Oregon State and had to

Coaches Andy Kerr (center, back row) and Claude (Tiny) Thornhill (left, back row) with 1922 Stanford varsity.

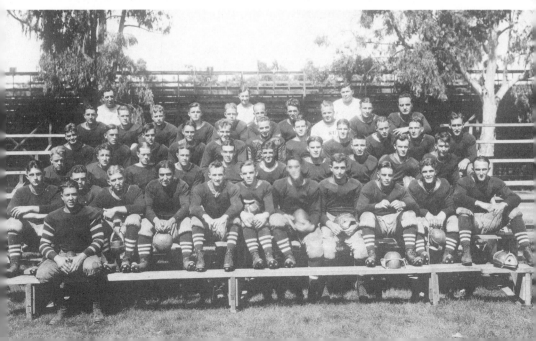

depend on three field goals by Cuddeback for a 9-0 win over St. Mary's. After a 17-7 triumph over Nevada, Stanford came up empty handed the rest of the season, losing the last four games.

Even with a new system the Cardinals were no match for California's "Wonder Team" and suffered a 28-0 mauling. Warner, possibly anxious to see how Kerr and Thornhill were progressing, brought his Pittsburgh team to Palo Alto on December 20 and gave the fans a look at the real Warner system by defeating the Cardinals 16-7. The appearance of Warner in the first intersectional game ever played in Stanford Stadium failed to attract much attention, however, as only 6,000 fans showed up for the contest.

As a result of the late season failures, "Little Andy's Fighting Gridders," as Stanford was known, wound up with a 4-5 record, which probably was not too disappointing when the problems and the schedule were considered.

A renewal of the Stanford spirit, an attitude towards football distinctly different to that of the two previous years, accompanied the start of the 1923 season. Kerr cautioned against high hopes, but with the benefit of a year's experience with the Warner system the team appeared to be much stronger. The season also marked the first appearance in a Stanford uniform of Ernie Nevers, who was destined to become one of Stanford's greatest athletes.

Lopsided victories marked the start of the season as the Cardinals romped over Mare Island 82-0, Nevada 27-0, Santa Clara 55-6, and Occidental 42-0. Tackle Charles Johnston blocked a kick and fell on the ball for a touchdown in the Nevada game, and a little later scored again when he recovered after Nevers had blocked a Wolfpack punt.

The shoe was on the other foot against Southern California. Two blocked punts resulted in a 14-7 victory for the Trojans, who had lost to Washington the previous week and were fighting mad when they invaded Stanford Stadium for the October 27 game.

Paul Murray, Nevers, and Cleaveland featured a Stanford drive from midfield to the USC 6, but the scoring bid fell one foot short when Murray received a short pass on fourth down and stumbled over a teammate before he could make it to the goal. A few minutes later the Cardinals started to march again, and this time Murray scored. Later in the half Harold Adams of the Trojans blocked a Nevers punt, and Hally Adams scored to

Stanford's first All America, Jim Lawson.

make it 7-7. Adams also scored USC's second touchdown when he scooped up the ball and ran for a score after Norman Anderson blocked another Stanford punt on the Cards' 15 yard line.

Stung by the USC loss Stanford developed a fighting spirit and rebounded to whip the Olympic Club 40-7 although four regulars were out of the game with injuries. Cuddeback ran 75 yards for one touchdown, and Campbell ran 30 yards and then took a pass from Fred Solomon to score. Merrill Armour blocked a punt, and McDermott recovered and ran 15 yards for still another Stanford score.

Blocking kicks for touchdowns was becoming one of Stanford's best plays at this stage. Art Thomas blocked a punt and ran the ball in for a score as Stanford defeated Oregon 14-3 on November 10 at Portland, but it was an intercepted pass by Campbell that turned the tide when the Cardinals beat Idaho 17-7 in its next start. Idaho was undefeated and untied, but Stanford played one of its best games of the season. Following

Campbell's interception the Cards scored on a fourth down gamble when Solomon hit Campbell on a screen pass, and the Stanford captain scooted 43 yards for a touchdown.

The 1923 Big Game was the first contest played in the new California Memorial Stadium, and the Bears dedicated it with a 9-0 victory over Stanford. California missed two field goals in the second quarter, but got the first break of the game when Stanford fumbled a punt and Charles Mell recovered for the Bears on the Cardinals' 41. California was unable to capitalize on the situation, and Bill Blewett kicked out of bounds on the Stanford five. On a well executed play Edwin "Babe" Horrell blocked Nevers' kick and fell on the ball for the only touchdown of the game.

Stanford threatened just before the end of the half, marching from its own 25 to the California 25. But on third down, with 20 seconds left in the half, Cuddeback's pass was intercepted by Don Newmayer of the Bears and returned to the 42. California stalled the Cardinals with two more interceptions in the second half and collected its other two points as the result of a missed field goal.

The Bear field goal attempt was low and hit a Stanford player. Campbell recovered the ball in the end zone and tried to run it out but was tackled for a safety. Nevers, the leading ground gainer of the season for Stanford, was selected on the All Coast team and named on Walter Camp's All America third team, the first national recognition for a Stanford football player.

Bears Almost "Stole" Nevers

Ernie Nevers earned All America fame and became one of the greatest football players in Stanford history, but he might not have come to the Farm except for the persistency of a devoted alumnus by the name of Findlay Geary, a prominent Santa Rosa attorney. Nevers almost wound up at California, but Geary and some other Stanford followers succeeded in sneaking him away from the Bears. With a little more time to think things over, and knowing that "Pop" Warner was coming to Stanford, Nevers cast his lot with the Cardinals.

"I never had met Findlay Geary until he stopped me one rainy night in Santa Rosa," Nevers recalled as he sat in the dining room of his home in Tiburon, overlooking San Francisco Bay. "He told me then that I was going to go to Stanford. He had seen me play football and basketball at Santa Rosa High School."

Nevers was born in a small town of Willow River, Minnesota, in 1902 and had attended high school in Superior, Wisconsin, until his senior year when he moved to Santa Rosa. "I was so lousy I didn't get a uniform my freshman year," Nevers said. "They put me in a sawdust pit and used me as a tackling dummy, me and a friend named Ole Haugsrud. He's part owner of the Minnesota Vikings now. I was a 168-pound tackle my sophomore year and a 175-pound end as a junior.

"But I was a helluva basketball player. That was my game. We won the state championship one year and were runnersup another. They didn't have a football team at Santa Rosa until the year I got there. The coach never had played football so I gave him the plays we had used at Superior, and I played full-

45

Stanford's all-time great Ernie Nevers. A consensus All America in 1925.

back. I had grown to 190 pounds then and was beginning to get coordinated. I always could throw the ball and kick."

Since he had played only one year at Santa Rosa, not too many people knew about Nevers and his talent. Scouting of high school players had not been developed to the science it is now. But Geary was aware of him, and so was California.

"California had started to work on me," Nevers said. "They had seen me play. 'Brick' Muller (an All America end for the Bears in 1920-21-22) had been a great idol of mine, and I had gotten to know him. But I knew 'Pop' Warner was coming to Stanford, and that sold me. I sent my credits to Stanford, but I lacked a half unit of getting in. When I heard that, I didn't know what to do.

"After a couple of days I packed my suitcase and went down to Berkeley, but I didn't register. Some Stanford guys found me and hid me out for a week or so. California always started classes ahead of Stanford, and once school had started I went back to Santa Rosa and went to junior college and got the half unit I needed. I organized a football team at Santa Rosa junior college, and coached it and played. We only had 13 players on the squad."

After he had obtained the necessary half unit, Nevers

transferred to Stanford in 1922, and it was during spring practice in 1923 that Ernie first met Warner. "He told me then that I was going to play fullback the next season," Nevers said.

"Many people thought the Warner system was all reverses and fakes," he continued. "But actually the main thing about it was the straight ahead power he could generate between the tackles. The reverses were used when he had the defense pulled in to stop the attack inside the tackles. 'Pop' liked the unbalanced line for a good many reasons, but it made it easier to do the obvious, attack the strong side, and it made it seem less likely that we wouldn't do the obvious. Yet we could strike just as hard on the weak side because the defense had to shift over to compensate for the unbalanced line.

"The basic defense of that era was a seven man line because the forward pass was not the factor it is now. There were several reasons for the lack of emphasis on the pass. For one, the passer had to be five yards behind the line of scrimmage when he threw the ball, which tipped his hand. There also was a five-yard penalty for two incomplete passes in the same series of downs, and the football was shaped differently. It was fatter and harder to control.

"There are all kinds of little tricks in kicking a football. You can kick it out of bounds or kick it high and make the receiver handle it. You can kick it high so that it will bounce back, or kick it low so it will run. 'Dink' Templeton taught me a lot of things about kicking. But Warner was the one who taught me the 'rocker' step. Most kickers took three or four steps forward which put them close to the line. With the 'rocker' step you take a step back before kicking. You get just as much distance."

Nevers thinks field position was a lot more important in his day than it is now when modern rules call for the ball to be brought in to a hash mark 15 yards from the sideline. "They've taken a lot of the strategy out of the game," he said. "In those days the quarterback had to watch his position on the field. There were a lot of times when the only player on one end of the line was the center because the ball was put in play where the previous play stopped. It wasn't brought in from the sideline."

One Of Greatest Big Games

When Warner arrived to take over the Stanford coaching duties in 1924, he inherited a team with such talent as Nevers, Jim Lawson, Ted Shipkey, Fred Swan, George Bogue, and Cuddeback. It also was well groomed in the Warner system by Kerr and Thornhill.

The Cardinals moved through their regular season undefeated, though tied by California, the first time Stanford had accomplished this feat since 1905. As a result the Cardinals were rewarded with an invitation to play in the 1925 Rose Bowl game against Notre Dame and its famous "Four Horsemen."

It did not amount to much of a season for Nevers, however, except for the Rose Bowl game. "I broke my left ankle in a scrimmage with a navy team before the first game and was on crutches for most of the season," Nevers said. "Then I played against Montana the week before the Big Game and was only in the game a few minutes when I broke the other ankle. I got caught in a pileup and was lying flat on my back when some guy jumped on my toes. He didn't do it on purpose, of course. The ankle hurt when I got up, but we had to kick on the next down. I didn't know whether I should or not, but I decided to go ahead. When I kicked I felt something snap. The ankle must have been cracked, and that kick busted it.

"So now I was on crutches from late November until 10 days before the Notre Dame game, and then when they took the cast off I had to wait five days before I could run. They had orthopedic people trying to make a brace inside my shoe and all kinds of things, but nothing seemed to work. 'Pop' took me up to his workshop, and he pounded out a piece of aluminum to fit

48

Glenn (Pop) Warner arrives to take over in 1924 with assistants Charles Winterburn (left) and Claude (Tiny) Thornhill.

my foot. Then he put an innertube from the back of my heel up to the back of my leg and taped it. The thing that was bad was that the tendons had been torn and the foot was weak from being in the cast that long. Hell, I had a great day. The doctor told me not to play, that if I broke the ankle again I might be crippled for life. But nothing happened. I always was crazy about the game, maybe too crazy.''

The loss of Nevers was a serious setback for Warner, who took over a squad which included 10 veterans of the previous Big Game. "Pop" moved Bogue and Cliff Hey to fullback for the opening game with Occidental. The Cards rolled up 455 yards to 48 for Oxy with power the keynote of Stanford's 20-6 victory.

Warner set out to find a quarterback in the game with the strong Olympic Club team and finally centered on Howard Mitchell and Fred Solomon. Stanford squeezed past the clubmen, 7-0, and then rolled to a 28-13 win over Oregon. The Webfoots scored first on an 80-yard run, but the Cardinals bounced back for four touchdowns before Oregon could score again on a long pass. Warner used Cleaveland on plays requiring speed and shiftiness, and Norm responded with 129 yards in 10 carries.

For some unexplained reason Stanford played University of Idaho at Multnomah Stadium in Portland in its next game and escaped with a 3-0 victory in a rain-soaked, muddy field. Idaho fumbled on the Stanford one-foot line, and in the fourth quarter Cuddeback kicked a field goal after Idaho had held the Cardinals at the 16. Stanford got its scoring opportunity when Chuck Johnston blocked an Idaho punt and Hey recovered on the 26. This game was considered the turning point of the season for Stanford.

Warner played his reserves liberally in a 20-0 victory over Santa Clara with the idea of having his regulars rested for the USC game the following week. These plans were made useless by the sudden announcement of the severance of athletic relations with the Trojans. Stanford and California had been having a dispute with USC over eligibility rules, and the situation came to a showdown immediately after the Trojans had lost to California 7-0 at Berkeley, November 1. The Stanford-USC game was cancelled by action of the USC student body, leaving the Cardinals with an open date late in the season. A certain laxity in standards, culminating in the unfortunate disqualification of one of the USC players just before the California-USC game, appeared to have had a direct bearing on the relations between the Trojans and the two northern schools.

The situation created quite a problem. Special trains had been chartered for the game in Los Angeles. Hotel rooms had been reserved and an elaborate schedule of events planned for Los Angeles. All of these had to be cancelled. However, a reconciliation was effected later in the winter quarter.

Graduate Manager Paul Davis of Stanford scouted around and found University of Utah willing to fill in the open date. Another problem developed, however, because the Stanford and California freshmen football teams were scheduled to play that

50

weekend in Stanford Stadium. Instead of moving the frosh game to Berkeley, Stanford and Utah played at Cal's Memorial Stadium with the Cards winning 30-0 on a wet field.

Nevers saw action for the first time during the 1924 season on November 15 when Stanford entertained Montana, then a member of the Pacific Coast Conference, but the 41-3 victory over the Grizzlies was to be a costly one. Nevers played less than three minutes before being taken from the field with a broken right ankle. The win gave Stanford the PCC lead, and optimism ran high on the Farm.

The loss of Nevers for the Big Game was a blow, but two days before the contest Cleaveland, around whom much of Warner's attack was centered, was declared ineligible. California officials called to the attention of Stanford authorities that Cleaveland had played two minutes in a game against Nevada in 1921 as a sophomore. Although time for a legal protest had

End Ted Shipkey, a 60-minute man.

passed and several California administration officers urged that the case be dropped, Stanford did not play him and offered to forfeit all of the conference games it had won. The other schools waived all forfeit claims, however.

Warner had to do some last minute switching in his plans and assigned Jim Kelly, a big but not too swift halfback, to take Cleaveland's place for this game, which many fans list among the all-time great Big Games. The finish certainly rates among the most exciting in the history of the series.

Stanford's line was solid and tough. In fact, all but one linesman would play the entire 60 minutes. Center George Baker, guard Fred Swan, tackles Chuck Johnston and Harry Shipkey, and ends Capt. Jim Lawson and Ted Shipkey were joined by halfback Cuddeback in playing without substitution on that November 22, 1924, afternoon at Berkeley. Warner used only 16 players during the game.

California also came into the Big Game undefeated, although tied by Washington. The two teams battled through a scoreless first quarter, but Stanford got on the scoreboard early in the second period. A 20-yard pass from Cliff Hey to Ted Shipkey helped the Cardinals advance to the Bears' seven-yard line before they stalled and Cuddeback kicked a field goal.

Later in the quarter Cuddeback intercepted a pass and led a march from the Stanford 27 to the California three before losing the ball on downs. Just before the end of the half Stanford advanced to the Cal 32 but ran short of time, so Cuddeback kicked a field goal from the 43-yard line to give the Cards a 6-0 advantage at the half.

California's offense came to life in the third quarter, and the Bears took a 7-6 lead after marching 81 yards to score with the help of a 47-yard run by Tut Imlay. Bert Griffin punched over for the touchdown. Late in the period the Bears started another drive from the Stanford 42 and grabbed a 14-6 edge on the third play of the final quarter, this score coming on a Jim Dixon to Imlay pass. The Bears made it 20-6 a few minutes later by scoring in four plays after recovering a fumble on the Stanford 29. This time, however, Cal missed the extra point, although it did not seem too important at the moment.

Coach Andy Smith of the Bears took Imlay and Dixon out of the game at this point, apparently feeling that the 14-point lead was sufficient against a team that had managed only a pair of field goals. But Smith overlooked a rule which was in effect

Murray Cuddeback, star of 1924 tie with California.

in those days. Players were not permitted to return to the game in the same quarter they were taken out. Thus, Imlay and Dixon were through for the afternoon.

Ed Walker, an unheralded halfback, went into the Stanford lineup at this point and helped spark the offense on a day when the defense dominated action. Walker was helped by Cuddeback, who came through brilliantly when the chips were down. There were 10 minutes to play when Fred Solomon returned a punt 15 yards to the California 35. Walker flipped a pass to Solomon for 15 yards, and Jim Lawson made 7 on an end around. After a couple of running plays lost three yards, Walker took to the air again and hit Ted Shipkey, who had outmaneuvered the California defenders, in the end zone. Cuddeback kicked the extra point to make the score 20-13 with five minutes left to play.

Stanford's chances did not look too bright when the Bears intercepted a pass and drove to the Cardinals' 19 yard line before yielding the ball. But Hey made 32 yards on a fake reverse, and Cuddeback fired a long pass to Ted Shipkey to reach the Cal 38. Time was running short, but the Cardinals did not need too much. Walker dropped back again and hit Cuddeback with a toss at the Bears' 20, and the Cards' senior halfback ran the remaining distance to score with just two seconds left on the clock. As 77,000 fans roared in disbelief at this amazing comeback, Cuddeback calmly stepped back and kicked the extra point to produce a 20-20 tie.

Stanford was invited to the Rose Bowl, over the objections of USC, which had forfeited its chance to claim the bid by cancelling its game with the Cardinals. The West team was given the option of selecting its opponent, and Graduate Manager Davis of the Cards announced the selection of Notre Dame, setting the stage for a meeting between Warner and Knute Rockne, two of the greatest coaches in the history of college football.

Nevers Vs. "Four Horsemen"

Capacity of the Rose Bowl in 1925 was 53,000, and with the selection of Notre Dame and the "Four Horsemen" the game was sold out two weeks in advance.

Notre Dame won the game from Stanford 27-10, but it was not the fault of Ernie Nevers. Although he had been able to run for only five days after having the cast taken off his ankle, and with the brace designed by Warner limiting his maneuverability, Ernie still managed to almost match the entire Notre Dame backfield. As it was, Nevers set a Rose Bowl record by carrying the ball 34 times. He gained a net 114 yards while Elmer Layden, Jim Crowley, Harry Stuhldreher, and Don Miller, the legendary Four Horsemen, combined for a total of only 127 yards.

Stanford made 17 first downs to 7 for the Fighting Irish, and outgained the Notre Dame team 298 yards to 179. But Nevers suffered two pass interceptions, both of which were run back by Layden for touchdowns, something that probably would not have happened if Ernie had been able to run normally and cover his passes.

Baker, Swan, Johnston, Harry Shipkey, Lawson, Ted Shipkey, and Cuddeback, all of whom had played 60 minutes against California, went the entire game against Notre Dame without substitution, as did Nevers. Warner used only 14 men against Notre Dame's 28 that day. Rockne started his shock troops but quickly replaced them with his regulars to meet the fury of the Stanford attack.

The Cardinals took a 3-0 lead on a 17-yard field goal by Cuddeback after Johnston recovered a fumble by Miller. After

55

Ernie Nevers and Warner prepare for Rose Bowl game.

that bobble on their first offensive play, however, the Irish uncorked their vaunted speed. Crowley got Notre Dame untracked as he followed the blocking of Miller and Layden for a 27-yard gain, and the lads from South Bend marched to the Stanford nine yard line before Nevers and the Cardinal line led by Ted Shipkey and Johnston could halt the advance. A short punt went out of bounds on the 32 yard line, and the Irish had another scoring opportunity. This time they did not pass it up.

Notre Dame advanced to the seven as the quarter ended, and on the second play of the second period Layden slammed over for the first of his three touchdowns from the three yard line. Crowley's extra point try was blocked by Swan, the Stanford left guard.

Starting from its own 20 after Layden's 72-yard punt carried over the goal line, Stanford marched to the Notre Dame 31 with Lawson gaining 14 on an end around and Nevers doing most of the rest of the work. On fourth down, with six yards to go, Solomon called for a flat pass to Ted Shipkey. Layden sensed the play, and Nevers' throw never reached Shipkey. Layden tipped the ball into the air, caught it on the run, and scampered 75 yards down the sidelines to score. Crowley's conversion made it 13-3.

The Notre Dame defense was set for straight ahead power, for which the Warner system was famous, but the Cardinals adopted different tactics in a bid to close ground on the Irish. Using Shipkey and Lawson on end around plays, and mixing in Nevers' powerful rushes with some reverses, Stanford began to move. Nevers passed to Solomon, who apparently was off to a touchdown until he was caught from behind by Chuck Collins after a 25-yard gain. The Cards reached the Notre Dame 10 before they were halted by a fumble which center Adam Walsh recovered on the Irish 17 as the first half ended.

Cuddeback missed field goals from the 32 and 45-yard lines early in the third quarter before Notre Dame capitalized on a break for its third touchdown. Layden lofted a 50-yard punt, which Solomon lost in the sun and fumbled. He grabbed for the ball but missed, and Ed Huntsinger, Notre Dame right end, grabbed the loose ball and ran 20 yards for a touchdown. Crowley made it 20-3.

Nevers and his Stanford teammates were not ready to concede. Ernie intercepted a Stuhldreher pass and returned to the Irish 29. Three straight rushes by the big fullback produced a first down on the 16, and three more attempts made it fourth and one at the 7. With the Irish defense bunched to stop another plunge by Nevers, the Cards switched tactics. Walker, who had teamed with Cuddeback to spark the fourth quarter rally to tie California, stepped back and passed to Ted Shipkey for a touchdown. Cuddeback's extra point made it 20-10.

Another pass interception, this time by center George Baker who ran it back eight yards to the Notre Dame 31, gave Stanford another opportunity to score. Shipkey made five and Nevers carried half of the Notre Dame team as he fought for eight yards and a first down at the 18. Shipkey contributed another five, but the next two plays failed to gain anything. Solomon called on Nevers on fourth down, and he hammered out seven yards for a first down on the six yard line.

Three more times the Cards called on Nevers, and he

pushed the pigskin to the two foot line, where it was fourth down and goal. Stanford followers who were at the 1925 Rose Bowl game still argue that Nevers scored on the next play. The two lines collided, and Nevers drove straight ahead for what he and the rest of the Stanford team thought was a touchdown.

Referee Ed Thorp ruled otherwise and put the ball down inches from the end line. "I know I was over," says Nevers. "I had the ball, and I was way over the goal line. (Walter) Eckersall, who was the head linesman and whose job it was to call the touchdowns, signalled a touchdown. When they unpiled, both ball clubs were piled up in one heap, I was still over the goal line. They thought I had pushed the ball over. (But) I was just trying to breathe under there. No, I think we got gypped out of that. It would have made a big difference too. But it was a great game."

Even after that disappointing turn of events the Cardinals fought back. With Nevers carrying the ball and passing to Shipkey, and Cuddeback throwing to Lawson, they moved deep into Notre Dame territory only to have Crowley intercept on the 10 yard line. Layden's short punt gave Stanford another chance, but time was short and the Cards took to the air. Nevers tried a flat pass, and again Layden diagnosed the play perfectly, racing in front of Lawson to grab the ball and dashing 70 yards for the final touchdown with 20 seconds remaining. Crowley converted to make the final score 27-10.

Later, in recounting outstanding individual feats, Rockne praised Nevers as one of the greatest players and thrill makers he had seen. "He could do everything," said Rockne. "Smash the line, run the ends, pass and kick." In 1930 the great Notre Dame coach named Nevers on his all-time backfield along with Morley Drury of USC, Jim Thorpe of Carlisle, and Elmer Oliphant of Army.

A Rebuilding Job

Warner was forced to do a major rebuilding job in 1925 because of heavy losses to graduation. The line was especially hard hit with center George Baker, guard William Neill, tackles Harry Shipkey and Chuck Johnston, and end Jim Lawson missing. The only returning veterans were end Ted Shipkey and guard Fred Swan. The backfield was better equipped with Nevers, Solomon, and Bogue on hand.

The Cardinals lost their opening game to the Olympic Club 9-0 and were knocked out of the conference title by a 13-0 loss to Washington, but the season had to be considered a success because of victories over USC and California. "Pop" was doing some experimenting in the early games in an effort to find the best combination and used 22 players against the Olympians and 25 in the second game against Santa Clara. Stanford scored a 23-3 win over the Broncos as Nevers turned in a fine performance, averaging five yards per carry. Stanford used the huddle for the first time the following week while beating Occidental 28-0. Mike Murphy, a sophomore halfback, set up the first score with a 50 yard run, while Nevers accounted for 100 yards in 19 carries and scored twice. Solomon also tallied a pair of touchdowns. Stanford made 21 first downs to 2 for Occidental.

That set the stage for the meeting with Southern California in Los Angeles, and the Cardinals scored a 13-9 victory, their first win over the Trojans since the resumption of American football in 1919. Nevers tallied the first touchdown after Ted Shipkey recovered a fumbled punt on the USC 12 yard line. The Cards got their other score just before the end of the first half when Murphy returned a punt 55 yards for a touchdown.

1925 Stanford varsity gave Warner his first win over USC. Team was led by Nevers (third from right in front row).

Stanford had to hold off a Trojan comeback in the second half.

"One play stands out in my memory about that game," Nevers said. "I was punting from behind the goal line, and Brice Taylor, a USC guard, broke through and blocked the kick. I saw the ball bouncing back to the left behind me, and I knew there was no way I could get to the ball before Taylor, but that he could beat me. So I blocked him. Don Hill saw the action and fell on the ball for a safety. Otherwise it would have been a touchdown. That was one of the best plays I made in all my life."

Warner often would think of plays while playing golf and always carried an envelope or a note pad along. When an idea came to him, he would whip out his envelope and scribble down the maneuver for future reference. Such a thought came to him when Stanford was apparently facing annihilation from Oregon State on October 24, 1925. Warner told his team to pass on every down from the opening kickoff, no matter where the ball was on the field.

The Aggies, now known as the Beavers, got on the scoreboard first with a field goal, but Nevers completed passes to Don Hill and Dick Hyland, and Hill added a 16-yard run to advance the ball deep into Oregon State territory, and Nevers

60

plunged over for the score. Ted Shipkey accounted for the second Cardinal score on an end around, but Oregon State stayed close with a score of its own in the third quarter.

Ward Poulson, a junior tackle, had been out of action for several days and was under doctor's orders not to play. But things began to look bad so Poulson was sent to the rescue. A few minutes later he intercepted a pass and ran it to the OSU 19. Nevers hit the end zone in two plays. Nevers, who gained 126 yards on 24 carries, was relieved by Ernie Patchett at this stage, and the sophomore back tallied the final touchdown for Stanford, to make it 26-10.

Warner used his second team in the first half of the Oregon game the following week, and they managed to punch out a 14-13 lead at the intermission. Hyland, who acquired the nickname of "Tricky Dick" because of his shifty style of running, returned the opening kickoff 70 yards to set up a touchdown, which was scored by Patchett. Hyland set up the second score with a long pass to Joel "Tex" Middleton. Nevers, Murphy, Bogue, and Shipkey ran the Ducks ragged in the second half for a 35-13 win.

Stanford invaded Seattle on November 7 to meet the University of Washington for the Pacific Coast Conference title, but the Cardinals could not function in the mud and lost 13-0. Stanford got down to the Huskies' nine yard at one stage. Murphy gained three yards, and Nevers picked up two. But Nevers was stopped on the next play, and an incomplete pass ended the threat. Washington drove to one score in the first quarter and added a second when Louis Tesreau intercepted a pass and raced to a touchdown. Stanford lost tackle Ward Poulson for the rest of the season with a severe dislocation of his left arm at the elbow.

"I lost my memory for three days after that game," Nevers said. "I don't remember a penalty being called, not even an offsides. It wasn't dirty, but it wasn't exactly clean either. There was just a lot of hard hitting. It was a gravel field, and 'Pop' used to dress us pretty light with no hip pads and such. We came back from Seattle, and we were picking pebbles out of our skin for days. George Wilson, who played in the Washington backfield that year, was one of the best running backs in football. He was tough. Elmer Tesreau, who was in the same backfield, was another good one."

UCLA, then known as the University of California, Southern Branch, made its appearance on the Stanford football schedule for the first time in 1925 and quickly found out it was not ready for such competition. Stanford used only a couple of members of its first team, but even the reserves ran wild to pile up an 82-0 win. Hyland, Patchett, and Hill had field days. Hyland ran a punt back 35 yards to score, Patchett had four touchdowns, and Hill had three.

Warner was not even around for the game, having turned the squad over to Thornhill while he went to Berkeley to scout California against Washington. "'Pop' took about half of the first team over to see the Cal game," Nevers recalled. "'Pop' was pretty sure what was going to happen with the opponent coming up when he did this. When UCLA started they were pretty weak. 'Tiny' used everybody on the bench. A contest like that doesn't do anybody any good."

Stanford had not beaten California in American football since 1905, but the 1925 Big Game was to usher in a new era of winning Cardinal teams. It would be six more years before the Golden Bears would again enjoy a victory over Stanford. The game was a dazzling array of Warner's plays, perfectly executed, a great deal of them by Nevers, and a great line that outplayed and outguessed its more experienced opponents. It also marked the departure from intercollegiate football of Nevers, All-America fullback and Stanford's greatest athlete. Nevers carried the ball for 117 yards, averaged 42 yards for eight punts, and led Stanford to a 20-0 lead in the first half.

"I wanted to beat the hell out of them," Nevers said. "We could have slaughtered them. We had a 20-0 lead at the half, but 'Pop' started the second team except for myself and the quarterback in the second half, and they got a couple of quick touchdowns. We had terrific momentum going but I don't think 'Pop' wanted to beat his old friend Andy Smith that bad. That taught me a good lesson. Why humiliate an opponent if you don't have to? I wanted to beat them bad, and so did two or three other guys on the team because as freshmen they had beaten us 56-0, and all of them were playing on the Cal team."

Nevers recovered a fumble on the California 30, and the Cardinals scored their first touchdown in three plays. Bogue made six, Nevers hit for seven, and then as the Bear defense closed in to stop a Nevers plunge, Murphy swung wide and raced 17 yards to score. California drove to the Stanford 27 a short time later, but three plays picked up only five yards and Nevers batted down Perrin's pass and the Cardinals took over on the 22. From here Stanford marched 78 yards to score again. Nevers made one run of 14 yards, and Bogue went the final 11 yards on a double reverse as some Bears chased Nevers and others scrambled after Murphy.

Stanford drove to the Cal four in the second quarter only to lose the ball but got another opportunity when the Bears punted out to only their 29 yard line. The Cards scored in four plays with Nevers going over from the five. California managed to register two touchdowns in the fourth quarter, but Stanford added another when Ed Walker blocked a Cal punt and recovered on the two yard line. Nevers collected his third touchdown. Murphy's final conversion attempt was blocked, but two California linemen were offsides on the play and Stanford was awarded the point. Head linesman Dudley R. Clarke notified referee George Varnell of the infraction, and he allowed the point. Some of the fans attending the game left the stadium thinking the final score was 26-14 when it actually was 27-14.

Tops In The Country

Stanford swept through 10 straight opponents in 1926 to earn the Rissman National Trophy awarded to the top college team in the country. The award was made on the basis of rankings made by Frank G. Dickinson, associate professor of economics at the University of Illinois, who had devised a mathematical formula for his ratings. Stanford had finished fifth in the 1924 ratings and ninth in 1925.

Warner, who always was coming up with some new innovation, added a new wrinkle in 1926 by opening the season with a double header only 10 days after the start of practice. The two games gave Warner a chance to see 51 players in action that afternoon as the Cardinals romped over Fresno State 44-7 and Cal Tech 13-6.

Stanford scored 32 points in the first half against Fresno, but Cal Tech proved to be a tougher assignment. Warner started his reserves against the Engineers, and Cal Tech scored first. Stanford came back to tie the score before yielding to the regulars who added another touchdown for the winning margin. Clifford "Biff" Hoffman, a sophomore fullback who later became one of Stanford's top all-around athletes, made his first appearance in a Cardinal uniform in these games.

Early in the season Warner said he had prospects of a Coast championship team. Then during the first week in October he told the Stanford student body that if the team was doing its best work it possibly could be the poorest team he had coached in 15 years.

Warner's assessment apparently came after the Cardinals had trouble beating Occidental 19-0, managing only a touchdown by Hoffman in the first half. Ed Walker added another score in the third quarter and Tom Work, a star high jumper on the track team, intercepted an Oxy pass and ran 95 yards for a touchdown to wind up the scoring. Work promptly gave up football and returned to his high jumping.

Warner was off scouting the next week when the Cardinals faced the Olympic Club, a team well stocked with former Stanford players. This time the opposition was a lot tougher than anticipated, and Thornhill and Chuck Winterburn, who had taken Andy Kerr's place on the staff when Kerr left at the end of the 1925 season to take the job as Washington and Jefferson's head coach, had their hands full. The Olympians kicked a field goal in the second quarter and hung onto their 3-0 lead until the final two minutes when Hoffman, Murphy, and Bob Sims rallied the Cardinals for a touchdown. Murphy broke a 20-yard run to spark the drive, and Sims went the final five yards. Murphy kicked the extra point for a 7-3 win.

Stanford also had to come from behind in both of its next two games to win. The Cards trailed Nevada 9-0 at the half but quickly got the situation under control in the second half as Sam Joseph, Dick Hyland, and Ted Shipkey registered touchdowns in a 33-9 victory. The following week Oregon took a 12-9 edge in the first two quarters, but the Cardinals again blanked their opponents in the second half while rolling up a 29-12 win. Bogue, Hyland, and Shipkey led the second half surge.

Oregon partially blocked a punt by Hoffman and recovered the ball on the Stanford 15 to set up its second touchdown. A Woodie to Vic Wetzel pass was good for the score. Stanford registered a third quarter score in unusual fashion when Shipkey caught a pass for a 25-yard gain after two Oregon players and a couple of Stanford men batted the ball before Shipkey caught it. Bogue's touchdown also was a bit out of the ordinary. The 230-pound halfback was free in the open field and on his way to a touchdown when the ball popped out of his hands, bounced off the ground, and back into his hands. Bogue did not even have to break stride as he continued his 35-yard dash to score. Hyland had a 75-yard punt return called back because of a penalty before Hoffman scored the final touchdown, his second of the game. Hoffman wound up with 108 yards rushing for the game while Bogue had 86.

Stanford showed its ability to come from behind again

Tricky Dick Hyland, halfback, 1925-27.

when the Cardinals beat Southern California on October 30 by a 13-12 score. Mort Kaer and Manuel Laraneta smashed the Stanford line for big gains in the opening quarter as the Trojans drove to the Card 17 before being stopped. Later in the period USC started another march, and the last play of the quarter brought the ball to the Stanford one inch line. Kaer scored on the first play of the second quarter. Later in the period Lloyd Thomas of USC grabbed a fumble by Hoffman in the air and ran 50 yards for a second touchdown to give USC a 12-0 lead.

Hoffman baffled the Trojans in the second half with fakes and single and double reverses. George Bogue, although injured, replaced Don Hill at halfback, and the Stanford offense came to life. With Hoffman passing to Bogue and Hyland the Cardinals began to march. Hoffman changed the pattern with a 19-yard pass to Ed Walker. Hyland, trying to pass, was unable to find an open receiver so he tucked the ball under his arm and ran to the five yard line. Hoffman made two on a reverse and on the next play scored. Bogue missed the extra point, leaving the score 12-6.

Later in the third quarter Kaer fumbled and Chris Freeman recovered for Stanford on the USC 36. But after getting within short range of the Trojan goal line the Cardinals' advance was halted, and Bogue missed on a field goal attempt. Southern California's passing attack failed, and the Trojans were forced to punt, giving Stanford the ball near midfield. Hoffman spotted Hyland in the clear on the Trojan 15 and whipped the ball to the speedy halfback who continued into the end zone for the tying touchdown. This time Bogue made the conversion to give Stanford a 13-12 win and Warner his second straight victory over Howard Jones.

Hoffman was the only regular to play for Stanford in a 33-14 win over Santa Clara. Bob Sims ran 45 yards on a double reverse for a first quarter score, and Lawrence Lewis, playing quarterback, caught a pass for another. Roland Sellman, Cardinal tackle, blocked a punt by Len Casanova, later to become a highly respected coach at Santa Clara and University of Oregon, and recovered on the Bronco 30. Frank Wilton accounted for the final 18 yards and the touchdown.

Lewis intercepted a Bronco pass on the Santa Clara 40 to set up a touchdown in the second half, and Patchett scored from the three. Casanova passed for one Bronco touchdown and caught a pass for the other. Coach of the Santa Clara team was Adam Walsh, center on the Notre Dame team that had beaten Stanford in the 1925 Rose Bowl.

Stanford scored three touchdowns in an 11-minute span in the fourth quarter to defeat Washington and gain revenge for the previous year's loss in Seattle. It took the Cards just six plays to move 84 yards for their first score. Key plays in the drive were a 22-yard run by Bogue, a Hoffman to Shipkey pass for 33 yards to the Huskies' 27, and Murphy's dash on a reverse from that point to the touchdown. Louis Tesreau punted 71 yards to the Stanford four to put the Cards in a hole, but Hoffman kicked out to the 47 and Washington was unable to capitalize on its field position.

Hyland opened the second half with a 56-yard kickoff return, but Stanford was able to get only three points out of this situation as Bogue kicked a 36-yard field goal when the

Card drive bogged down. Washington had not done much up to this point, but George Guttormsen, the Huskies captain, changed that when he intercepted a Hoffman pass and returned it 70 yards for a touchdown. Guttormsen was hit at the five yard line by Ed Walker but stayed on his feet to score.

Tesreau intercepted another Stanford pass, but this time Washington had to settle for a field goal. Tesreau passed to D. Douglass for 39 yards, but the score was called back and the Huskies penalized 15 yards. Officials ruled that Douglass had hurdled Hyland on his way to the goal. Tesreau passed to Douglass again to reach the Stanford 17, and Gene Cook kicked a 20-yard field goal to tie the score at 10-10.

Early in the final quarter Bogue got away for 15 yards to the Washington 10, but the play was called back on a penalty and Stanford was assessed 15 yards for holding to the Washington 40. The Cards struck back, however, as Hoffman passed 30 yards to Shipkey for a touchdown. Frank Wilton intercepted a pass on the Huskies' 26, and two plays later Bogue raced 22 yards for another score. Washington gambled on fourth down a few minutes later and lost the ball at its own 33. Hoffman punched over for the final score in three plays from the four yard line after Hill had contributed an 18-yard run. Bogue led Stanford ballcarriers with 154 yards. Washington checked him on his first three carries, but he broke loose for 23 yards on his

Lawrence (Spud) Lewis, quarterback-halfback, 1926-28.

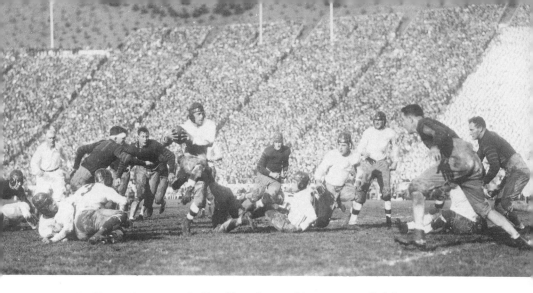

Dick Hyland carries ball off right tackle against California in 1926 Big Game.

fourth try and from then on was unstoppable.

The storm that had been gathering force for three years broke loose in the Big Game November 20 at Berkeley. A crowd of 80,000 was on hand in Memorial Stadium and an estimated 20,000 were jammed on "Tight-Wad Hill" as Warner sent into action a team thoroughly versed in the Warner system and style of play. This team differed in that its power hinged not on one outstanding player but on the coordination of two sets of capable backfield men, operating behind a line of proven strength. There also was no need for Warner to worry about the score since his old friend Andy Smith had departed and Clarence M. "Nibs" Price now was coaching the Bears.

Stanford exploded the first time it handled the ball. California was unable to gain and punted on third down, the ball going out of bounds on the Bears' 48 yard line. The Cards' first play was a perfectly executed reverse with Hyland carrying the ball around right end. Three Cal tacklers had a chance at Hyland, but his speed and deception left the Bear defenders empty handed as he romped 48 yards for a touchdown.

Later in the first quarter Hyland returned a punt 10 yards to the Stanford 47, and the Cardinals set sail again for the goal line. George Bogue, who was playing right half, made 13, and Hyland, the left half, ran for 20, Hoffman added three more, and Bogue carried nine yards to the eight yard line. Bogue made the touchdown on a reverse from the three.

Ed Walker recovered a fumble by Earl Jabs and ran the ball

to the Cal 29 early in the second quarter. After Bogue had lost a yard, Hoffman hit Hyland with a 30-yard pass for a third Stanford touchdown. Walker later pounced on a fumble by Harold Breckenridge, and the Cardinals turned this opportunity into a score to run their advantage to 27-0 as Hoffman passed 20 yards to Shipkey who ran another 16 to the goal line. California got its lone touchdown late in the second quarter when Ned Green of the Bears partially blocked a Hoffman punt and Dick Blewett returned the ball to the Stanford 18. Bert Griffin plunged for seven yards and then made another seven for a first down on the four yard line. Griffin finally scored on fourth down from the one foot line to end California's scoring efforts for the day.

Warner used reserves in a scoreless third period, but the Cardinals added a pair of touchdowns in the final quarter. Bogue intercepted a pass and returned 24 yards to midfield. Bogue contributed a 13-yard gain, and Hyland added 15 to help advance the ball to the Cal eight. Shipkey got the touchdown on a reverse from the six.

Hal McCreery, 1925-27 center.

George Bogue of Stanford is tackled by Earl Jabs of California in 1926 Big Game at Berkeley. Other Stanford players are Capt. Fred Swan (1), Biff Hoffman (34), and Ward Poulson (4).

California tried the "shotgun" formation in an effort to pass against Stanford, but Fred Swan intercepted and ran 30 yards for the final score. Warner commented after the game that if it had not been for the wet field the score might have been bigger. Hyland had runs for 48, 20, 13, and 33 that afternoon as Stanford scored its first win over the Bears in Memorial Stadium.

Hal McCreery, rated by Nevers "one of the finest centers I've ever seen during my years in football" acquired the nickname of "Bad Pass" during the 1926 season. McCreery had great sport pounding his fist on the top of the helmet of the opposing center during the Nevada game. The Nevada man put up with this torture until late in the game when Stanford had the ball deep in its own territory. As McCreery prepared to snap the ball back to the punter on fourth down, the Nevada center gave it a nudge with his foot. The ball sailed over the kicker's head, and Nevada recovered. After that McCreery was known as "Bad Pass."

Back In The Rose Bowl

The smashing victory over California made Stanford an automatic choice for the Rose Bowl since this gave the Cardinals the conference title over Southern California, which missed an undefeated season by only two points. The Trojans, who had lost to Stanford 13-12 but had smashed every other opponent in convincing fashion, wound up their season with a 13-12 loss to Notre Dame.

Alabama, which had beaten Washington 20-19 in a thriller the year before, was selected as Stanford's opponent. The Crimson Tide had been undefeated the previous year and came into the Rose Bowl game with a string of 20 straight victories dating back to the next to last game of the 1924 season.

Stanford dominated the game and led for 59 minutes, but had to settle for a 7-7 tie when Jim Bowdoin, Alabama guard, blocked Frank Wilton's punt with three minutes left to play. Wilton recovered the ball, but since it was fourth down 'Bama took over on the Card 15. The Crimson Tide scored five plays later. Stanford had a big edge in the statistics, gaining 350 yards to Alabama's 117, 12 first downs to 6 and completing 11 of 16 passes for 133 yards while the Tide completed only 1 of 7 attempts for 9 yards.

The Cardinals trotted out in silk pants, which drew a lot of remarks from the Alabama players, but Stanford demonstrated in a hurry that it had come to play football. Hoffman passed to Hyland for a 40-yard gain to the 'Bama 35 on the first play. The Cardinals advanced to the Tide's 18 before bogging down.

Bogue's field goal attempt was wide.

After a fumble had halted another Stanford threat, the Cards finally took the lead when Bogue hooked up with Ed Walker on an 18-yard touchdown pass late in the first quarter.

Hyland's nickname of "Tricky Dick" had been acquired with good reason, and in the second quarter he gave a good exhibition of why the cognomen was a good one. Hyland was a top open field runner and one of the great halfbacks developed by Warner, but he probably caused "Pop" to almost swallow his ever-present cigarette when he fielded a punt on his own five yard line. Hyland started to his left but was hemmed in and could not find any running room so he reversed his field. To get more room he circled behind the goal line and, whether by design or accident, caused one of his Alabama pursuers to run into a goalpost, knocking himself out. Hyland gave the 'Bama team a good run before he finally was tripped up on the 20 yard line.

Fumbles several times killed Stanford threats, and the tough Alabama defense stalled another good opportunity in the fourth quarter. Walker recovered a fumble by Archie Taylor who failed to handle a Stanford punt, and the Cardinals got to the Tide's seven yard line but no farther.

Warner pulled a master stratagem on Alabama. Knowing that the Crimson Tide would be keeping a close watch on Ted Shipkey and Hyland, who had been Stanford's best receivers all year, Warner swapped Hyland and right end Ed Walker. The Alabama safetyman covered Walker, thinking he was Hyland. Meanwhile, Hyland was at end and had a field day. On one play he dashed to the 15 yard line for a pass but had to come back to the 27 to get the toss from Hoffman. Alabama halted that threat, but Stanford later scored to take a 7-0 lead. Alabama blocked a kick to get its touchdown.

Shipkey, Stanford's All America end who had played an outstanding game against Notre Dame two years earlier in the Rose Bowl, had another big day against Alabama. He caught five passes, recovered two fumbles, and made 23 yards on an end around in addition to playing an outstanding defensive game.

Warner had been advocating that each team be given a point for each first down to help in determining the final score, especially in case of ties. With Stanford holding a 2-1 edge in first downs in this case "Pop" was even more inspired to campaign for such a rule.

Gaels, Broncos Score Upsets

The 1927 season yielded an 8-2-1 record and another Rose Bowl appearance as Stanford showed a marked change from its heavy plunging style of past years to a light, fast-charging, deceptive team. The two losses were to St. Mary's and Santa Clara, two small Catholic schools.

Warner blamed the loss to Santa Clara on overconfidence and lack of whole-hearted effort. "This game was a good illustration of how a strong team may be overcome by a supposedly weaker, but harder fighting one," he said.

The Cardinals again opened their season with a double header on September 24 with a 33-0 win over Fresno State and a 7-6 victory over the Olympic Club. Reserves played against Fresno, and Warner started sophomores against the Olympians, and they performed well as the clubs battled to a scoreless first half although the clubmen reached the Stanford 20 with the help of a 45-yard run by "Cowboy" Kietscher before the Cards held. The Olympians drove to the Stanford 10 against the Card regulars in the third quarter, and then Rogers broke through to block Hoffman's punt and fall on the ball in the end zone for a touchdown. However, George Bogue, who had played for Stanford the year before, missed the extra point.

Stanford scored from the six on a reverse to tie the score, capping a 75-yard drive, and Hoffman added the extra point. In the closing minute of the game Bob Sims attempted a field goal from the Olympic Club's 12. The kick was blocked, and Russell Sweet of the club recovered the ball and started trotting leisurely downfield. Sims finally ran Sweet down on the Stanford 25, saving a touchdown.

Warner shook up his lineup before the St. Mary's game, demoting veterans to the second and third teams. Chuck Smalling replaced Hoffman at fullback; Frank Wilton took Hyland's spot while Ralph "Lud" Frentrup and Sims alternated at Don Hill's position. The changes proved ineffective, however, as St. Mary's took advantage of 16 Stanford fumbles to register a 16-0 victory. Both Gael touchdowns were the result of fumble recoveries. Larry Bettencourt, who was named an All America tackle, scooped up a bobble by Wilton and ran 15 yards for the first score in the opening period. Hicks grabbed a fumble by Sims in the second quarter and also scrambled 15 yards for a touchdown.

Stanford twice failed to score on excellent opportunities. The Cardinals had a first down on the two yard line and could not push it over. Later they had a first down on the three and again failed to get any points. The latter opportunity was set up when Wilton ran the kickoff back 75 yards following the second St. Mary's touchdown. Louis Vincenti blocked a St. Mary's kick and Hal McCreery recovered on the Gaels' three, but four plunges by Hyland and Hoffman netted only a one-yard advance and Stanford gave up the ball on the two. "Spud" Harder, Cardinal end, was severely injured when he was hit after catching a pass and falling down out of bounds.

Warner was away scouting Southern California as the Cards beat Nevada 20-2 the following week. Hoffman carried the ball eight times as Stanford marched 75 yards in 14 plays for its first

1927 Stanford varsity, another Rose Bowl team.

score. Hoffman passed 20 yards to Vincenti and 15 yards to Mike Murphy for the big plays in the next drive, and Murphy ran the final 7 yards for the touchdown. Stanford went 70 yards for a third quarter score with Hill contributing a 20-yard run and Herb Fleishhacker carrying three straight plays for the final 15 yards.

Warner changed back to his original backfield before the USC game, installing Lewis at quarterback, Hill and Hyland at halfback, and Hoffman at fullback. The switch proved satisfactory since Stanford managed a 13-13 tie, but the Cardinals had to come from behind in the last few minutes to earn the deadlock. For the best part of three quarters the Trojans, led by Morley Drury, held the upper hand. USC made two early penetrations into Stanford territory, once getting as far as the 13 before the Cardinals managed to dig in and hold for downs.

Near the end of the first quarter, however, Wilton fumbled at the Stanford 27, and Russ Saunders of the Trojans recovered and ran for a touchdown. Stanford received the kickoff and drove from its own 20 to the USC 11 before being stopped when a fourth down pass fell incomplete in the end zone. Southern California came right back with a march that carried all the way to the Stanford 10 where the Cardinals held for downs. This time Stanford got the job done in a hurry, scoring in two plays. Bob Sims reeled off a 16-yard run, and then Hoffman hurled a 30-yard pass which Wilton caught in front of Saunders and ran the remaining 44 yards to score. Hoffman's extra point tied the score at 7-7.

Hyland carried the third quarter kickoff back 45 yards to midfield, but Stanford was unable to take advantage of this good field position. A short time later USC had the ball on its own 46, but the Cardinals stalled the drive by throwing Drury for a two-yard loss and then dumping Saunders for a loss of three. Drury kicked on third down, and the ball rolled into the end zone. But the head linesman ruled that John Preston, Stanford end, had held the USC end while going downfield and gave the ball to the Trojans on the Stanford nine yard line. This opportunity was not passed up by USC as Drury scored from the seven on the second play. Hyland blocked the conversion attempt, however, which turned out to be very important.

Wilton gave Stanford another chance late in the fourth quarter when he pounced on a Drury fumble, and the Cardinals promptly took to the air. Hoffman got off a wild pass that fell into a mass of players and bounced off one of them into the hands of Roland Sellman who ran to the USC 30. A Hoffman to Louis Vincenti pass gained eight, and Warner sent in big Herb Fleishhacker, a sophomore fullback, with instructions to pass to Vincenti. Fleishhacker was so excited when he reported to the referee that he almost tipped off the Cardinal plans. "Fleish-hacker for Hoffman—throw the pass to Vincenti," he said.

The Cardinals stayed on the ground temporarily, and Fleishhacker carried the ball six straight times to set up a third down and three on the USC 3. Frentrup replaced Hill to add more weight to the backfield, and the Trojans apparently took this to mean the Cards planned to run another line plunge. Instead, Fleishhacker, who was a shotputter but not a passer, stepped back and pushed a left-handed pass in the direction of Vincenti, who grabbed it in the end zone to tie the score at 13-13.

"Spud" Lewis usually did the holding on the extra points, but there must have been too much excitement on the Stanford bench because of the score, which came with only 20 seconds left in the game. For some reason no substitution was made. When Stanford lined up for the extra point try Fleishhacker was kneeling in the holding position. This was an entirely new job for Herb, and when the ball came back he planted it with such a firm grip that Mike Murphy was unable to get his kick more than a few feet into the air, and the chance for the Cardinals to take a second straight one point victory over the Trojans went aglimmering. USC could thank Drury for the tie. The All America quarterback had a busy day as he carried the ball 40 times for 161 yards and also intercepted several Stanford passes.

The Cardinals turned in a dazzling display of single and double reverses the following week to beat Oregon State 20-6 on a field that was drying out with a cover of about three inches of mixed sand and sawdust because of heavy rains at Corvallis. Despite the loose top the field was conceded to be reasonably fast. It apparently did not bother the Cardinals, who rushed for 228 yards while gaining only 23 on passes.

Lud Frentrup was outstanding in a 19-0 victory over Oregon. He scored the first touchdown after Don Muller recovered an Oregon fumble and passed eight yards to Muller for the third score. Sam Joseph accounted for the other touchdown with an intercepted pass return.

One of the outstanding features of Stanford's 13-7 win

over Washington on November 6 at Seattle was that the Cardinals did not fumble once despite a wet and slippery field. The Huskies, on the other hand, were guilty of five fumbles with Stanford recovering all five. The Cardinals spent most of the first quarter fighting off Washington threats. The Huskies marched to the Stanford one the first time but fumbled, and Hal McCreery recovered. The next time the Purple and Gold got into a threatening position Hyland stalled them with a pass interception.

Later in the first half Hoffman put Washington in a hole with a fine kick, and a short return punt by the Huskies went out of bounds on the 30. Hyland eluded several charging linemen as he faded to pass and threw to John Preston on the 19, and the sophomore left end ran the rest of the way to score. The extra point was missed, and early in the third quarter Washington marched 71 yards for a touchdown with Chuck Carroll going over from the six inch line. The Huskies converted to take a 7-6 lead.

Stanford missed two scoring opportunities before it managed to tally the winning touchdown. The first time Hoffman tried a field goal from the 36, but the kick was low and the Huskies recovered the ball on their own four. Later Lewis intercepted a pass, and the Cardinals drove to a first down on the Washington six. Four plays left them three yards short of the goal line, but it also left the Huskies in a bad hole. Louis Tesreau went back to punt, but Harder, playing for the first time since he was injured in the St. Mary's game, blocked the kick and Vincenti fell on the ball in the end zone.

Carroll returned the next kickoff to the Stanford 43 before he was tackled by Wilton. This threat ended at the Card 23, however, when Preston recovered another of the Huskies' fumbles. Sellman, Stanford tackle, was selected the outstanding lineman of the game.

Warner did not consider Adam Walsh and his Santa Clara Broncos much of a threat and decided to scout California in its game with Washington the following week. But the only scoring the Cardinals could do that afternoon came on a six-yard run by Fleishhacker after Frentrup had completed passes to Vincenti for 34 yards and to Muller for 22. Bud Cummings broke loose for a 34-yard run to the Stanford 28, and McCormick passed to Cummings for a touchdown to put Santa Clara ahead in the first quarter. The Broncos added a second score on a nine-yard pass from Falk to McCormick, who was standing in the clear in the end zone. The conversion made the final score 13-6.

"Biff" Hoffman was being compared to Ernie Nevers after his performance in the 1927 Big Game. Hoffman, who "played the greatest game of his career" according to Ed R. Hughes in the San Francisco press, was the principle actor in the most spectacular play of the game in the third quarter after California had scored to make it 7-6 in favor of the Cards.

Wilton had returned a punt 37 yards to the Bears' 45, and Hoffman had put Stanford in scoring position with a 23-yard run. Sims made eight yards on the old Statue of Liberty play, and Hoffman decided to try it again. This time he did not find anyone to hand the ball to so he slipped it behind his back and loped around right end for a touchdown. The California defense was fooled, but Benny Lom ran over to check on Hoffman and got a poke on the chin for his curiosity.

Stanford's first score came in the opening five minutes of the game when Hyland, and Hill, and a long pass by Hoffman took the Cardinals to the California two. Hoffman made a yard, and on the next play Hyland was stopped but found only his legs were pinioned, so he stretched out and deposited the ball in the end zone for six points. The conversion gave Stanford a 7-0 lead.

California had the upper hand in the third quarter, but the Stanford defense halted the Bears after they had marched to the Cards' two-yard line. Irving Marcus attempted to run right end on fourth down, but Wilton anticipated the play and threw him out of bounds on the three. Hoffman punted out, but a few minutes later was forced to kick again from his own 21. This time Fritz Coltrin blocked the kick, recovered it at the 15 yard line, and ran for a touchdown. Walt Heinecke, a 5-6, 175-pound center who was one of the fastest, toughest, and hardest hitting men in the Stanford line, broke through to block J. Cockburn's extra point attempt and preserve the Cards' lead.

As a result of its 13-6 win over California, Stanford was named for the Rose Bowl for the third time in four years, and the choice was far from popular with followers of the University of Southern California. The Trojans had tied the Cardinals 13-13, and both teams had identical 4-0-1 records in the conference. In addition, USC had lost only to Notre Dame, 7-6, outside the conference, while Stanford had been beaten by St. Mary's and Santa Clara.

"Master" Vs. "Pupil"

Several teams were mentioned as possible opponents for Stanford in the 1928 Rose Bowl, but the final choice was the University of Pittsburgh, which was undefeated but had been held to a scoreless tie by Andy Kerr's Washington and Jefferson eleven. Led by All America halfback Gilbert Welch, the Panthers had rolled over seven of its other eight opponents by lop-sided scores. The lone close game for Pitt had been against Nebraska. The Panthers also had registered shutouts in seven of their games.

The game offered an interesting sidelight in that it matched Warner "The Old Master" against Dr. John Bain "Jock" Sutherland, who had played for "Pop" in 1919 at Pittsburgh. Warner cooked up a triple play for Pittsburgh with three maneuvers developing off the Statue of Liberty formation. One play had Hoffman handing off to Hyland on a reverse, and from the same movement he had a short pass with Hoffman throwing to the left end. He also installed a line buck with Hoffman hitting at guard. The latter proved effective as the Pitt guard spent most of the afternoon pulling out of the line and backing up when he saw Hoffman raise his arm.

Pittsburgh was made the favorite, but Stanford outplayed the Panthers most of the game with the Cardinal line of Hal McCreery, Seraphim Post, Don Robesky, Roland "Tiny" Sellman, and Chris Freeman drawing a lot of the credit for Stanford's 7-6 victory. Also playing a prominent role was little Walt Heinecke who moved from center to tackle to fill in for Freeman who had been hurt early in the game.

Heinecke, who went on to become one of the greatest

centers in Stanford history, almost did not get a chance to play football for the Cardinals. When he entered Stanford in 1926 as a quarterback, he was ruled physically unfit when a required physical examination uncovered a slight heart murmur. Heinecke was crushed but, with his parents, succeeded in convincing President Ray Lyman Wilbur that he should be permitted to play football. Dr. Wilbur felt that the murmur was a slight one and since Heinecke's parents were willing to take a chance he would go along with them.

All of the game's scoring was concentrated in the third quarter, although Stanford had opportunities in both the first and second quarters. The Cardinals drove to the Pitt seven in the first period and reached the Panthers' one yard line in the second, but lacked the punch to score. Frank Wilton was pegged to be the "goat" of the game after he fumbled on the Stanford 19 in the third quarter and Pitt's Jimmy Hagan scooped up the ball and ran it in for a touchdown. Heinecke rushed in to block

Seraphim (Dynamite) Post and Don Robesky, All America guards of 1928 team.

Allen Booth's conversion attempt, and as it turned out he saved the game for Stanford.

The Cardinals buckled down after Murphy had run the ensuing kickoff back to the Stanford 37. Hoffman connected on a pass to Richard Worden for 31 yards to get things moving, and the Cards moved to a first down on the Pitt 8. Here things got tougher, and Hoffman managed only two yards. Wilton added another two, and Hoffman hammered to the Pitt two yard line on third down. Lewis replaced Murphy at quarterback with orders from Warner to throw a flat pass. Bobby Sims took the pass from Wilton and ran towards the Pitt right end but was smothered, and as he was hit the ball popped out of his hands.

Wilton had been hoping for a chance to redeem himself for his costly fumble, and here was the opportunity. He beat two Pitt defenders to the ball, grabbed it, and dashed over the goal line. Hoffman added the extra point to give the Cardinals a 7-6 lead which they protected for the remainder of the game.

After the Rose Bowl game Maxwell Stiles, who later collaborated with Joe Hendrickson in the writing of *The Tournament of Roses, A Pictorial History*, wrote: "If Gibby Welch of the Pitt Panthers was an All American in 1927, what will they be saying about 'Biff' Hoffman of Stanford at the end of the 1928 season? Hoffman carried the ball 26 times, was a consistent ground gainer, and was a bearcat on defense."

Stanford authorities were unhappy with Pasadena and the Rose Bowl although the huge saucer in Arroyo Seco had been enlarged by some 15,000 seats to give it a capacity of 72,000 spectators. The players were unhappy because a majority of the fans rooted against them, even when they made a good play.

"Many of us did not look favorably upon this game, and it was only upon assurances that conditions had improved that we agreed to play," said Al Masters, Stanford's director of athletics.

Warner may have had some misgivings about his team following the loss to Santa Clara, but there were none after the game with Pittsburgh. Stanford gave an exhibition of championship football and clearly outplayed the Panthers. The Cards' versatility and the deception plus the sturdy defense were the main factors in a well earned victory.

"It's doubtful any team in the country could have defeated the Cardinals this day," said one writer covering the game.

Warner Wins The East

There's an old poem, sometimes attributed to Henry Wadsworth Longfellow, which goes like this: "There was a little girl, and she had a little curl right in the middle of her forehead. When she was good she was very, very good, and when she was bad she was horrid."

That was a pretty good description of the 1928 Stanford football team. It was one of the most unpredictable teams in Stanford history. On good days it was equal to any Cardinal team, but it lacked consistency. With Hyland and Hill gone, Warner restyled his attack and revealed his newest offensive creation, "Formation B" which featured two fullbacks, Hoffman and Smalling. A requirement of the B formation was that the back man, who was some six yards behind the center, be a good passer and kicker with good speed. The closer man, who was three yards back of the line and slightly to the right of the fullback, must be a good plunger and also handle the ball on reverses.

Stanford joined Washington and California in voting not to participate in the Rose Bowl game, but the Golden Bears, after finishing the season with a 6-1-2 record, relented and accepted an invitation to Pasadena and named Georgia Tech as their opponent.

Two of the standouts of the season for the Cardinals were Seraphim "Dynamite" Post and Don Robesky, who formed one of the strongest guard combinations of any college team that year. Both earned All America honors as Stanford compiled an 8-3-1 record. The season was to prove a big disappointment to Warner, however, as the Cardinals were beaten by Southern California, 10-0. It was the first time Warner had lost to Howard Jones in 20 years.

Stanford was favored over the Trojans and had a big edge in statistics. The Cardinals gained more than 100 yards more than USC, picked up 10 first downs to 0 on the ground, but could not get into the end zone. Stanford lost the ball five times inside the Trojan five yard line on fumbles or some other reason.

In the first quarter the Cardinals marched to the USC three yard line, but a fumble by Sims ended the threat. Stanford had another chance in the second period when it again advanced to the Trojan three, but this time Hoffman fumbled. Southern California took a 7-0 lead after Jesse Hibbs intercepted a Hoffman pass on the Cards' 35. Russ Saunders passed 20 yards to Larry McCaslin, and then Lloyd Thomas passed to Don Williams for a first down on the three. Williams was held three times on rushing attempts, but on fourth down he flicked a two-yard pass to Saunders for the touchdown.

Just before the half Stanford made another scoring bid when Hoffman passed to Smalling for a 42-yard gain. Smalling looked back after catching the ball to see how much of a lead he had on his pursuers and was caught by Thomas on the USC 10. The gun ended the first half before the Cardinals could take advantage of their position.

Williams returned a Stanford punt 39 yards to the Cardinal 26 late in the third quarter and passed to McCaslin to help the Trojans reach the Stanford nine early in the final period, but the Cards held, and Hibbs kicked a field goal from the 15.

Stanford had practiced only a week when it launched the 1928 season with a doubleheader against YMI and the West Coast Army. Warner played his reserves against the YMI eleven and lost 7-0 as Ed Storm, an ex-Santa Clara player, intercepted a pass by Harlow Rothert in the closing minutes and ran 86 yards for a touchdown. The Cardinals won the second game from the Army 21-8 as Hoffman scored two touchdowns and Wilton one. Hoffman passes to John Preston helped set up two Stanford scores in the second quarter.

The Cards also lost to the Olympic Club 12-6 as Mort Kaer, a former USC star, played a major role for the clubmen, passing for one touchdown and returning a Hoffman punt 68 yards for the other score. Stanford's lone score was by Hoffman after he had put the ball in scoring position with a 28-yard pass to Wilton which carried to the Olympic Club six. Stanford got to the two yard line in the second quarter, but a penalty set the Cards back and they lost the ball on downs at the three.

Hoffman enjoyed a big day as a passer as Stanford whipped Oregon 26-12 at Eugene. He passed for one touchdown and set up two others with his tosses. The Cardinals dominated the game after spotting the Ducks a touchdown on the first play when Wilton fumbled and Everett McCutcheon recovered for a score. Hoffman passed to Wilton for the first Card tally and scored the second after throwing to Herb Fleishhacker for 18 yards to advance to the Oregon 12. Muller intercepted a pass by Ira Woodie and returned it 30 yards for a touchdown. Smalling made the final score after a Hoffman pass had advanced the Cards deep into Webfoot territory.

UCLA returned to the Stanford schedule for the first time since its 82-0 loss in 1925 and played the Cardinals to a 7-7 tie in the first quarter. The Bruins' G. Forster returned a kickoff 97 yards for a touchdown, but Stanford scored two touchdowns in each of the last three periods for a 45-7 victory. A Simkins to Lewis pass produced one Card touchdown after Joe Bush had recovered a fumble by Bert LaBrucherie on the UCLA 12. Frentrup scored twice, and Smalling added the final touchdown on a 28-yard run.

Idaho held the Cardinals scoreless in the first quarter and trailed only 7-0 at the half in a game played on a foggy day at Kezar Stadium in San Francisco. But Smalling, Simkins, and Lewis tore up the Vandals' defense in the second half for a 47-0 victory. Stanford made 45 first downs to only three for Idaho. Warner played his reserves in a 47-0 romp over Fresno State as he rested his regulars for the upcoming game with Southern California. Harlow Rothert, who also starred in basketball and later broke the world shot put record, scored four touchdowns in the win over the Bulldogs.

President-elect Herbert Hoover was in the stands as Stanford raced to a 31-0 triumph over Santa Clara at Stanford Stadium. Warner had decided to abandon Formation B after the disappointing loss to USC and returned to Formation A. Smalling and Fleishhacker led the Cardinal attack which featured eight completions in sixteen passing attempts, three of them for touchdowns. Smalling scored twice, once on a 16-yard run after an earlier 30-yard dash to the Bronco 29. The second was on a 43-yard pass play from Hoffman. Smalling fumbled the ball after starting to run but picked it up and completed his 24-yard scamper to the end zone. Reserves took over for Stanford in the fourth quarter and scored three touchdowns. Simkins passed 18 yards to Muller for one, and Lewis returned a pass interception 30 yards for another.

Hoffman and Fleishhacker did not play the following week when the Cardinals hosted Washington, and Stanford had a hard time with the Huskies. After a scoreless first half, tackle "Tiny" Sellman recovered a fumble on the Stanford 42, and the Cardinals took advantage of this break to score. Sims passed 18 yards to Muller for the touchdown. Sims and Muller hooked up on another pass in the fourth quarter for a 35-yard gain, and the Cardinals had to call on the same combination for a one yard touchdown toss when the Huskies' defense braced. The final score favored Stanford 12-0.

California came into the Big Game with one of "Nibs" Price's better teams. The Bears had lost only to the Olympic Club, 12-0, and had played a 0-0 tie with Southern California. They had scored 121 points while allowing only 22, a touchdown by Santa Clara and a field goal by Washington State being the only scoring allowed by Cal besides the Olympic Club's 12 points.

Six pass interceptions helped California earn a 13-13 tie in a game which saw Stanford come from behind in the final two minutes to score the tying touchdown. Roy Riegels, California center, smothered the point after touchdown attempt which

Frosh bonfire is rebuilt November 21, 1928, after original was destroyed by a time bomb at 9:45 a.m. Tuesday, November 20.

would have given the Cardinals victory. Interceptions by the Bears kept Stanford in the hole in the early going. Harry Gill intercepted a Hoffman pass at the Cards' 37, and later Frank Fitz batted another toss and Russ Avery intercepted at the Stanford 10. Heinecke, Fleishhacker, and Sellman stopped the Bears cold on three straight plays, however, and on a fake kick on fourth down Stanley Barr's pass was knocked down by Sims.

Relying mostly on short ground gains, Stanford marched to the California 22 in the second quarter where another aerial attempt backfired. Steve Bancroft, a Bear tackle, picked off the throw and ran 76 yards for a touchdown. Late in the second quarter California made it 13-0 when Benny Lom passed to Avery for 38 yards and a touchdown. It was one of only four passes the Bears completed in nine attempts during the after-noon for a total of 58 yards. Stanford completed 10 of 22 passes for 124 yards.

Frentrup, a Berkeley boy, finally got Stanford untracked in the second half when he returned the opening kickoff in the third quarter 26 yards and then punted to the California 15. When Lom kicked back, Frentrup returned 19 yards to the Bears' 28. A Simkins to Frentrup pass gained 10, and Frentrup and Simkins pounded out a first down on the four. Two plays later Simkins scored.

Stanford threatened again in the fourth quarter but twice was stalled by interceptions. Simkins passed 27 yards to Lewis, but his next effort was intercepted by Irving Phillips, the California captain. Then with only three minutes left to play, the Cardinals made a final bid, marching from their own 34 to a fourth and 10 situation on the Bears' 23. Phillips had batted down a third down pass, but Frentrup got free in the corner of the end zone on the next play and Simkins was right on target with a throw that tied the score.

All of New York was waiting to see Warner's new double wing formation when "Pop" and his mighty Stanford team went east to meet Army on December 1 in Yankee Stadium. Warner had installed the double wing in 1924 explaining that by placing a halfback outside each end he opened the way for a new series of double reverses, passing possibilities, and blocking power on wide plays to either side. Stanford proved his point by befuddling an Army team which had established itself as one of the top Eastern teams, 26-0. The Cadets, whose offense was built around famed Christian "Red" Cagle, had won eight of nine games, losing only to Notre Dame.

Stanford proved Warner's point, dazzling Army with reverses, ends around, double reverses, delayed bucks, and passes to uncovered receivers. On the first offensive play of the game Hoffman passed to John Preston for a 29-yard gain, and Wilton followed with an 11-yard run around end. The Cards marched to the Army one but failed to score. The next time Stanford marched to the 10 but again was unable to crack the Cadet defense. A short Army punt gave the Cardinals a third chance at the West Pointers' 28, and this time there was no stopping the team from the West Coast. Hoffman, Wilton, Fleishhacker, and Sims moved the ball down to scoring range where Hoffman plunged over.

Army got to the Stanford 10 in the third quarter for its most serious threat of the game before Hoffman capped a 56-yard drive by Stanford for his second touchdown. Another drive by the Cardinals was temporarily interrupted in the fourth quarter when Cagle intercepted a Stanford pass, but Piper fumbled and Heinecke recovered on the Cadets 13. Frentrup gobbled up eight yards, and Sims scored from the five on the next play. The final Stanford score came when Frentrup fumbled a bad snap from center but then recovered to dash 65 yards for the touchdown.

Grantland Rice, who was among the 86,000 fans watching the game, called Stanford "the best football team the East has seen this season." The Cardinals ran up 372 yards to Army's 113, and made 26 first downs to eight. Cagle had been hailed as the greatest halfback in modern times, and compared to Willie Heston, Jim Thorpe, Walter Eckersall, and Benny Friedman, but Stanford completely smothered him.

Bob Sims, who never was substituted for because of injury during his three years at Stanford, was responsible in a large part for keeping Cagle under wraps. After the game the Army star came to the Stanford locker room looking for Sims. "You are one of the greatest defensive halfbacks I've ever played against," he told Sims.

Warner Changes
From B To A

One of the major rule changes prior to the start of the 1929 football season was one which prohibited a defensive player from running with a fumble. "Pop" Warner denied he had anything to do with the new rule but did approve of its adoption.

"The ball is enough reward," he declared. "A touchdown should be earned, and this rule will prevent a lot of fluke plays which give a weak team a chance to win over a much superior team."

Warner also made some changes in his Stanford team, shelving the B formation and returning to the A formation in which the fullback handled the ball. "Pop" also spent some anxious time awaiting a report from the doctors on the condition of little Walt Heinecke, the Cardinals' outstanding center who was in the Palo Alto Hospital for three weeks with a weak heart.

"I'll be in there the first game and finish up the season," Heinecke declared. He later was given permission to play.

Although the season had a couple of disappointments—a 7-0 loss to Southern California and a 13-7 setback from Santa Clara—it ended in impressive fashion with wins over California and Army.

The Big Game was played at Stanford and attracted a crowd of 89,000. Tickets were in such demand that one California player reportedly traded six tickets to the game for a 1925 Lincoln touring car.

California was undefeated and came into the game a 13-7 favorite, and Warner went along with the odds. "I think Stan-

Warner with 1929 Captain Don Muller.

ford's chances of winning the ball game are very slim," he said. "California has the stronger team, and the Bears are better organized. However, my men are fighting mad, and although I like the Bears to take the game I still have plenty of hope and won't give up until the final gun."

The Cardinals were worthy of Warner's faith as they registered a 21-6 upset for what was considered the greatest Stanford win since 1892. Captain Don Muller recovered a California fumble by Rusty Gill on the Bears' 45, after which Chuck Smallling handed the ball to Tom Driscoll who passed to Harlow Rothert for 14 yards, the Cards scoring in the first five minutes of play. Lud Frentrup punched over from the two to cap the drive. Later in the first quarter the Bears turned a Stanford fumble into a touchdown, getting the ball at the 30 on Frentrup's bobble and working down to the four. On fourth down everyone figured California would pass, but Stanford did not apply any pressure. Lom had plenty of time to pass to Ellis Thornton for the touchdown.

After that the Cardinals stopped the Bears' running game and soon put a stop to California's passing attack until late in the game. By then it was too late to matter.

Muller, who played the best game of his career, blocked a Lom punt, but the Bears halted Stanford on the one yard line. Then Muller blocked another kick and recovered for a touchdown to give the Cardinals a 14-6 lead at the half. Late in the

90

third quarter Stanford was penalized 37 yards, half the distance to the goal line, because Corwin "Chang" Artman, giant Cardinal tackle, took a swing at Ted Beckett of the Bears when he was tackled after intercepting a pass. Artman was ordered off the field because of the incident.

The preceding and the substitution of Phil Moffatt into the backfield fired up the Cards, and they stormed 65 yards to a touchdown with Moffatt and Guido Caglieri doing most of the work. Moffatt finally darted through left tackle from the seven yard line for the score.

"The boys played their best football of the year to win as I thought they would," Warner said. "We were handicapped by injuries all year but managed to get the boys in pretty good shape for today."

"Our team played its best football because it had more fight than ever," said Captain Muller. "The fight is what won for us." Accounts of the game credited Heinecke with outplaying Roy Riegels, California's great center, and Rothert with outpunting Benny Lom. Caglieri led Stanford ballcarriers with 58 yards in eight carries. Moffatt and Smalling each gained 48 yards and Frentrup 38.

Frentrup, who was a Berkeley boy, had fumbled twice in the first quarter, and Warner had pulled him out of the game. "I'm not nervous, but I don't know what's the matter with me," said Frentrup who had caught a pass the year before to give the Cards a 13-13 tie.

In the second half Moffatt, who was a sophomore and had replaced Frentrup, went to Captain Muller and said: "I think we ought to let Lud finish this game. He's a senior, and it's his last game." Muller went to the bench to talk to Warner, and Frentrup went back into the game and made good yardage on reverses and intercepted a pass to help check the Bears.

It was no happenstance that Stanford blocked California's conversion attempt or Lom's punts. Warner had planned an attack against Lom involving Muller, Heinecke, and James Thompson, and it paid off.

The Stanford win over California threw the conference race into a three-way tie for the title, since California had beaten Southern California 15-7 and USC had beaten Stanford 7-0.

Stanford Stadium had been jammed with 89,000 fans when the Cardinals and Trojans collided in what reporters called

91

"the outstanding game of the decade." The two teams were considered two of the greatest in the country. It was the first time the stadium had been sold out except for the Big Game.

Warner had decided to take to the air against USC. Later he admitted he was wrong in adopting these tactics. Three times the Cardinals had fourth down passes fall incomplete. Once on a tackle-out lateral, Simkins-Ray Tandy-Rothert, they went to the three, but the Trojans turned back attempts by Smalling, Simkins, and a reverse to Frentrup. Simkins' fourth down pass was incomplete. The Trojan line averaged 202 pounds and outweighed Stanford 16 pounds per man. That proved a little too much for the Cardinals.

Marshall Duffield was responsible for the only score of the game. Employing a new "short side slant" which Howard Jones had developed, Duffield cut to his left and dashed 28 yards before Smalling caught him. Minutes later USC had a fourth down and two, but Duffield skirted end for four yards. The

Walt Heinecke, 1927-29, one of all-time centers.

next time Duffield went into a spin and when he came out of it dropped back and floated a pass to Francis Tappan for 25 yards and a touchdown. That was early in the second quarter, and it ended the scoring.

Late in the game Duffield ran a punt back 65 yards, but the score was nullified and the Trojans penalized for roughing the Cardinals' kicker, Phil Moffatt. Statistics for the game were very even with the Trojans gaining 228 yards rushing to Stanford's 211, and 45 yards passing to the Cards' 42. The difference was that USC threw only 11 passes and completed 3 while Stanford tried 21 passes and also completed only 3.

Stanford wound up its season with a 34-13 victory over Army before 75,000 spectators at Stanford Stadium, as the Cardinals again bottled up Chris Cagle. The Cadet All America back was limited to 48 yards in 11 carries while Stanford's Smalling proved the outstanding player of the game by gaining 163 yards on 26 carries and scoring three touchdowns.

Coach "Biff" Jones of Army held secret practice before the game, but the Cardinals practiced in the open, running a lot. of wide plays and throwing laterals, maneuvers they did not employ in the game.

During the game Warner wanted to try out a couple of new plays which he had numbered 31 and 32. "Pop" sent in word with a substitute for Muller to try the plays, but Muller did not call them. Finally Warner wrote the numbers on a slip of paper and stuck it in the shoe of a sub who was sent in. Still Muller did not call them. Between halves "Pop" asked Muller why he had not called the plays? "I just forgot about them," Muller answered.

Army was so impressed by Stanford that the Cadets picked Muller, Tom Driscoll, Moffatt, and Smalling on their all opponent team.

Dick Hanley, Northwestern coach, also was impressed by Driscoll. "Did you watch that Driscoll stopping them in the middle and way outside of tackle besides?" Hanley asked. "That boy was the strongest guard I have seen, digging in and knocking down everything everywhere on defense. What he did to those Army lads was terrible. I never saw a better guard than Driscoll Saturday."

A New Name,
And Axe Comes Home

Several things stand out about the year of 1930 in relation to Stanford football. One of the foremost was the changing of the Stanford nickname from Cardinals to Indians. The name Cardinals had been used since 1892 mainly because of the red uniforms worn by the football team. On November 26, 1930, the student executive committee adopted "Indians" as the official symbol of the university and the nickname for its athletic teams. Cartoonists and writers had been referring to the "Red Indians" of Stanford since about 1928 and using the figure of an Indian in their drawings, thus the change did not come as a complete surprise.

Other outstanding things about the year were the recovery of the axe by Stanford students, a smashing 41-0 victory over California, and an equally disastrous 41-12 loss to Southern California. The win over the Golden Bears was the most decisive margin ever recorded in the series, while the defeat by the Trojans was one of the most crushing setbacks in Stanford history.

Warner had warned against over-enthusiasm before the start of the season although he was not worried about his backfield with a wealth of talent that included Harlow Rothert, Bill Simkins, Phil Moffatt, Guido Caglieri, Harry Hillman, Bill Clark, Rudy Rintala, and a promising sophomore, Ernie Caddel.

"I know it looks pretty rosy to a lot of Stanford fellows," Warner said. "But they must think I can pull rabbits out of a hat if they expect me to fill such vacancies as left by Muller, Heinecke, Fleishhacker, and Smalling, to say nothing of Driscoll, Frentrup, and Preston, all of whom were in my first string lineup last year.

94

"I've about made up my mind that Phil Moffatt is our best bet as signal caller. The Los Angeles boy has a good football head and is fairly certain to be in the game much of the time as he is probably the fastest and shiftiest man on the team."

Moffatt earned a starting berth, which was a bit unusual since Warner seldom played sophomores, but Phil already had spent a year on the grays or "goof" squad and had impressed everyone with his speed and football knowledge. At 161 pounds he was the smallest member of the Stanford backfield, the other three weighing close to 200 pounds apiece. Warner had moved Rothert from right half to fullback and had installed Caglieri at right half. Hillman was at quarterback.

Rothert, Moffatt, and Hillman all were from Los Angeles, and the first two had played together at Los Angeles High School. "One of the reasons I wanted to go to Stanford was because I liked the way they went about things," Moffatt said. "Phil Wilson, a Stanford graduate, brought his son and me up to see Stanford play Washington, and that sold me. There were no scholarships then, but the tuition wasn't too steep. We had won the city championship at Los Angeles High, and all of us were given a strong rush by USC. But quite a few came to Stanford, in fact, Los Angeles High had the biggest single contingent on the Stanford squad, followed by Lowell High of San Francisco.

"A lot of the Los Angeles players went to Southern California, of course, and I remember that during my sophomore year I got into the game with the Trojans in the second quarter, and Don Muller was calling signals. He called 49 reverse on which I carried the ball. Francis Tappan, who also had played with me at Los Angeles, tackled me, and as we were getting up he said: 'What are you doing here, you little SOB?' I said, 'You're not so big yourself you so and so.' Referee Herb Dana overheard us and said, 'Let's not have any fighting.' We told him we had gone to high school together and were only kidding each other. 'Well, there'll be no swearing, or I'll throw you out of the game,' he said. USC always was the cleanest game we played. Howard Jones wouldn't stand for anything of that kind, and 'Pop' didn't like dirty football either."

The USC game of 1930 was a major disaster, however. Stanford had won its first five games and had shut out the first four opponents. The only points allowed by the Indians were by Oregon State in a 13-7 win the week before the game with the Trojans.

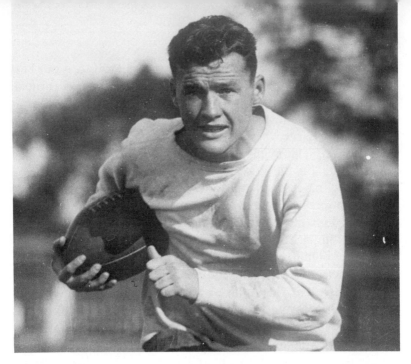

Phil Moffatt, star halfback of 1929-31 teams and 1930 All America.

"We were a three point underdog to USC," Moffatt recalled. "Pop took us off campus the night before the game to a hotel in San Mateo. The campus was full of excitement, and he wanted us to get away from it. That night he gave us all a laxative. He said it would help us relax. It sure did. I was playing safety, and I made seven tackles in the first half. They were driving our line and linebackers right on back." Marshall Duffield, Jim Musick, Irv Mohler, and Ernie Pinckert all took a hand in the Trojan scoring. Duffield scored twice, Musick once, Mohler once and passed to Garrett Arbelbide for 23 yards for another. Pinckert scored the final touchdown when he caught the ball, after Mohler had fumbled, and ran 75 yards.

Moffatt scored both Stanford touchdowns against USC, taking a flat pass from Rothert for the first after Phil Neill had partially blocked Shaver's quick kick and recovered at the Trojan 25. An interception gave Stanford the ball on the USC 15 in the fourth quarter, and a 13-yard pass from Simkins to Moffatt produced the second score for the Indians.

Warner called his signal callers together before the November 22 Big Game with California at Berkeley and told them to pass on the first two downs of every series. They weren't allowed to call a running play until third down unless they were

96

inside the California 30 yard line. If they were inside the Stanford 30, they were to throw a long pass.

Stanford held only a 6-0 lead at the end of the first half, but Rothert scored three touchdowns and threw a pass to Moffatt for a 53-yard touchdown in the second half. Simkins passed to Bill Laird for 34 yards and the final score.

"'Pop' wasn't trying to run up the score," Moffatt explained. "He used every player we had. We scored two touchdowns in the first few minutes of the third quarter. We missed a couple of other touchdowns in the first half, one when I dropped a pass in the end zone because I turned around too late. The other one was a 36-yard run by Bill Clark on a reverse that was nullified when it was called back because of a holding penalty. California was having internal problems at the time with some fraternity squabbles among the players. Their game with USC was called with five minutes left to play, with the Trojans leading 74-0."

The loss to Southern California was the only blot on Stanford's 1930 record, but Minnesota held the Indians to a 0-0 tie in a game played at Minneapolis. Stanford was favored by two touchdowns, but the 97 degree temperature on the stadium floor, and a tough Minnesota defense, kept the West Coast eleven out of the end zone.

Stanford was deep in Gopher territory five times during the game but lacked the punch to put the ball across. On one occasion Rothert passed 25 yards to Phil Neill who lateraled to Moffatt. The Stanford halfback apparently was away for a touchdown only to be stopped by a desperate tackle by Walter Haas at the 8. Moffatt, who shared game honors with the Minnesota defense, was stopped on fourth down at the one foot line to end that threat. Other bids were stopped on the Minnesota one in the fourth quarter and at the 12, 17, and 18.

"We made 14 first downs to only 2 for Minnesota, but each time they would stop us Biggie Munn would kick out of danger. He could really boot the ball as well as play defense. I dropped from 161 pounds to 147 that day in the heat," Moffatt said.

"On the train ride from Minneapolis to Omaha, Nebraska, I had to listen to Warner tell me what a lousy signal caller I was. But after he had chewed me out for quite a spell 'Pop' took me down to the team physician and told him to give me a shot of medicinal bourbon.

"In the next game with Oregon State 'Pop' started the second string, and I was determined to try to show 'Pop' he was wrong about the previous week. We scored two touchdowns in three and a half minutes, in the second quarter when the regulars got in, with a forward pass-lateral play and a 37-yard pass and slant to the flag, and we won the game 13-7. Those were the first points scored against us that season. I remember that at one stage in the game Paul Schissler (Oregon State coach) got excited and came out on the field. The referee stepped off a 15-yard penalty against the Beavers. On the next play there was a flagrant holding by an Oregon State player out in the open. When it wasn't called, Warner got excited and rushed out on the field, and the referee stepped off 15 yards against Stanford."

Stanford played its first ever night game in its meeting with UCLA in Los Angeles, and the Indians had trouble with the damp football, all except Rothert, that is. The big fullback, performing before hometown fans, netted 118 yards and averaged 44 yards on his punts, kicking one out of bounds on the Bruin one yard line. Rothert scored two Stanford touchdowns in the third quarter on runs of 65 and 40 yards.

A pep talk by Moffatt fired up the Stanford team before its game with Washington, and the Indians registered a 25-7 win using a pass and lateral to fool the Huskies. "You look like you like it, and you act like you like it," Moffatt told the squad before going on the field. "Any outfit can come down here and push you around. You can make something out of this season yet, or you can be the worst bunch of Joe Doaks that ever lived, which is just what you are now. If you've got any stuff, you'll snap out of it. I'm sick of it. Let's go."

And go the Indians did, outplaying the Huskies all the way except for the opening minutes. A 42-yard punt return by Moffatt set up the first touchdown, which came on an 18-yard pass play from Simkins to Neill to Moffatt. The second score resulted from a Moffatt to Marcellus "Mar" Albertson to Caddel pass and lateral.

Stanford closed its season with a 14-7 win over Dartmouth in a game which saw the Indians play the entire contest without a fumble, only the second time they had accomplished this in the seven years Warner had been at Stanford. Dartmouth was undefeated and had scored five shutouts, but Stanford still was the pregame favorite. Moffatt was the leading ballcarrier for Stanford with 96 yards for 16 carries. Stanford had a first quarter touchdown called back after Moffatt had scored after taking a lateral from Don Colvin. On the play Rothert passed to Colvin who batted the ball to Moffatt. However, the officials called it back with the explanation that Colvin had to get possession of the ball before he lateraled.

The Stanford Axe had been a symbol of tradition since 1899 when a Stanford student displayed the broad bladed weapon at a Stanford-California baseball game April 15, 1899, and chopped blue and gold ribbons into small pieces. But he made a mistake of not having enough companions along when he left the game, and a group of California students captured the prize and kept it for 31 years, locking it in a bank vault except for pre-Big Game pep rallies when it was put on display.

On April 3, 1930, a group of 21 Stanford students headed for Berkeley with a plan to bring the axe back to Stanford. Bob Loobourow posed as a reporter and Warren Gage, Ray Walsh, and Eric Hill as photographers. The axe had been taken from the vault of the American Trust Company in Berkeley to a rally at the Greek Theater on the California campus. While it was being returned to the bank, the raiding party asked to take pictures. Loobourow grabbed the axe, someone set off a smoke bomb, and the raiders jumped into their three waiting cars and sped off in the direction of Palo Alto. In the fracas that followed the seizure of the axe, however, four of the Stanford men were captured and held prisoners. Included were Hill, Henry Powell, Howard Avery, and Art Miller. Other members of the raiding party were Don Kroop, Gerald Bettman, Ed Soares, Loobourow, Gage, Walsh, Jim Trimingham, Robson Taylor, Bob Snodgrass, Albert Jensen, Glenn Brunson, Matt Lehmann, Bill Eberwine, Louis Ferrino, George Likens, Robert Gordon, and John Coons.

Robert G. Sproul, new president of the University of California, expressed belief that the theft of the axe would start a new university tradition and expressed the hope that Stanford would put the axe up as a football trophy. Sy Steinbeck, president of the Associated Students at Stanford, also proposed that the axe be made a symbol of victory in the Big Game, an idea which later was adopted and is now in effect, although there have been occasional forays by over-zealous students of both universities to pirate the trophy without waiting for a football victory.

Trojans Foil Warner

Warner worked behind barred practice gates for three weeks perfecting a special defense which he figured would stop the Southern California running attack in the 1931 game with the Trojans. "Pop's" idea was to split his two ends about 15 yards out from the tackles and have them running parallel to the line of scrimmage just before the ball was snapped. Warner figured that with this momentum they could crash in and break up the play before it got under way. "Pop" liked crashing ends anyway, but he was running short of ends in practice before the USC game rolled around.

The maneuver did not work out the way Warner planned it. The Trojans were using a shift in which the center came up to the ball while the rest of the line was a yard back with hands on knees. From this stance the line moved forward into either a balanced or unbalanced formation. Warner planned to have his ends start in motion once the USC line was set. Howard Jones crossed him up, however, by having the Trojan quarterback hold the snap signal occasionally, and the Indians were caught offsides.

Southern California won the game 19-0, handing Stanford its first loss since the Trojans had won the previous year's game, a string of 12 games. It was the third time in four years that Warner, one of the greatest offensive coaches in American football, had failed to score against Jones. It was a bitter pill for "Pop."

Stanford completed only two of sixteen passes for 11 yards as a passing attack, which many football followers thought would dent the USC defense, was stopped completely.

Ernie Pinckert turned in a great all-around performance for USC and broke a 32-yard run to the Stanford 16 to set up USC's first score. Gus Shaver tallied from the four. Southern California scored again in the second quarter when Irv Mohler circled left end for seven yards for a touchdown after Shaver had followed Mohler's blocking for a 34-yard gain to the Indians' 10.

Stanford was handicapped by poor punting and the loss of star running back Phil Moffatt on the opening kickoff. Moffatt was a doubtful performer after aggravating a back injury in the Washington game, but he was determined to play since it was his final chance to perform in his home town. Moffatt took the opening kickoff and returned it to the Stanford 34 but, in trying to get out of bounds when he was tackled by Ernie Smith, tore ligaments in his knee and was through for the game.

"A great thing happened after the game," said Moffatt. "Howard Jones came into our dressing room looking for me. He asked if I thought Smith had tried to injure me on the tackle? 'If he did, he'll never play another game for me,' Jones said. I told him I was sure Ernie hadn't made an effort to hurt me, that it happened because I had twisted while trying to get out of bounds."

California had not won a Big Game since 1923, but that streak came to an end in 1931 as the Bears scored a 6-0 victory. Hank Schaldach starred for California, scoring the only touchdown. He also broke loose for a 44-yard run to the Stanford 15 late in the game. Only a great effort by Jack Hillman, who overhauled Schaldach to make the tackle, prevented the California star from going all the way. Schaldach also got off a 56-yard quick kick which rolled dead on the Stanford two to put the Indians in a hole.

Stanford's biggest threat came in the fourth quarter when Jack Hillman picked up 22 yards on an off-tackle play to reach the California 22. Caddel got 15 yards on a lateral, but a bad snap from the center cost the Indians 11 yards back to the 24. Caddel made eight yards to the 16, and the threat ended there as Stanford lost the ball on downs. Stanford fans felt Moffatt was a vital spark which Stanford needed, but he spent the game on the bench with his bad knee.

Warner took his first loss to California hard, but a week later everyone in the East was raving about the Warner system as the Indians romped to a 32-6 victory over Dartmouth in a game played in Harvard Stadium. Moffatt was back in action for this game, which wound up his career, and completed eight of eleven passes, including a pair of touchdown tosses to Caddel for 27 and 57 yards. Dartmouth was no match as Stanford pulled out all the stops.

On the first scrimmage play after the opening kickoff Caddel took a reverse around the right side and behind great blocking romped 72 yards for a touchdown. A few minutes later, on the same play, Caddel went 62 yards for another score. Dartmouth threw 31 passes and completed only 4 for 63 yards. Stanford intercepted seven of the throws. Dartmouth was limited to 71 yards rushing while Stanford gained 364 and added 111 yards on passing. Stanford lost another four possible scores on fumbles and penalties.

"'Pop' devised a brace for my leg so I could play," Moffatt said. "I couldn't move from side to side, but I could run all right. We knew they had this pass play, so I was prepared for it and ran over and intercepted it. All of a sudden I felt my knee pop, and it quit hurting. After that I was able to throw better. There was one play, though, where the end was wide open, but he had to come back to get the ball. When he came back to the huddle, he asked me why I hadn't gotten the ball to him when he was in the open? I told him 'Heck, I can't throw the ball that far.'

"We had gotten into Boston on Wednesday, and Thursday was Thanksgiving," Moffatt recalled. "We all bought black derbies and pearl gray spats. We were a very fancy outfit. The Stanford bench at the game was the first row of the grandstand, so there were fans right alongside the players on the end of the bench. Some of the spectators had hip flasks and as the game progressed began offering some of the players on the end a sip. Some of them didn't figure to get in the game so they decided 'why not?' But as the score mounted Warner began using substitutes, and in the final minutes of the game he sent in one player who spent about 30 seconds trying to find someone to give his card to. We had substitution cards in those days, and if you went in on offense you handed it to the referee and if it was defense to the umpire.

"After the game many of the restaurants and places around town offered everything free to the Stanford players. We were in a restaurant and, after we had eaten, the waiter brought a bill. There was a discussion about whether we had to pay. Finally one of the big guards from Stanford jumped up and grabbed a chair and took a stance in front of a big glass aquarium in the room. 'Is this on Dartmouth, or isn't it?' he demanded as he raised the chair. We got things straightened out in a hurry."

Stanford played scoreless ties with the Olympic Club and Washington, and also had close games with Santa Clara and UCLA in 1931. As was his habit in games which he did not take too seriously, Warner started his reserves against UCLA, and the Bruins took a 6-0 lead in the first half as the result of a 25-yard run around right end by Bobby Decker. Stanford's regulars started the third quarter and tied the score as a result of Robert Milligan's recovery of a Bruin fumble on the 18. Charles Ehrhorn took a handoff from Harold "Dusty" Allen and passed to sophomore Jack Afflerbaugh for the touchdown.

The Indians had another opportunity when Art Hardy returned a punt 37 yards to help Stanford reach the Bruins' eight where the drive stalled. With less than two minutes remaining in the game Stanford was on its own 29 yard line. Afflerbaugh gained a first down on the 40, but the Indians gained only eight yards on their next three plays.

On fourth down Allen faded back and threw the ball as far as he could. Don Colvin, the Indians' left end, was taller than L. Bergdahl and F. Haslam of the Bruins and made the catch on the UCLA 25. Only seven seconds remained in the game when Allen passed to Colvin for a touchdown and a 12-6 win for Stanford.

Stanford was a three touchdown favorite over Washington, but a Seattle downpour washed out those odds, and the two teams played a scoreless deadlock. The only time Stanford got into Washington territory was in the third quarter when Allen intercepted a Husky pass on the Stanford 37 and the Indians staged a march with Moffatt and Hillman leading the way. The drive reached the Washington eight before John Cherberg intercepted a pass by Allen. Afflerbaugh had punts of 50 and 70 yards to stave off Washington threats.

The punting of "Diamond Jim" Paglia of Santa Clara kept Stanford bottled up in its own territory in the first half, and it was not until the last five minutes of the game that the Indians were able to score for a 6-0 win over the Broncos. Paglia twice kicked out of bounds inside the Stanford seven, and Les Powers, who filled in for Paglia, kicked out on the five and nine.

Stanford threatened early in the third quarter when a pass

play from Allen to Moffatt was good for 40 yards to the Santa Clara 19. Hillman and Rudy Rintala smacked to a first down on the nine, but the Indians gave up the ball on the seven when George Grey missed a field goal. On two other occasions Stanford advanced to the Bronco 10 without scoring. But it was not until the final five minutes that the Indians were able to stage a 54-yard march when Tom Lambert, Moffatt, and Hillman settled down to the business of knocking out gains of four to seven yards on reverses for four first downs to reach the Santa Clara four. Hillman burst through center on the first play to score.

Hillman was in the hospital with a temperature of 102 when Stanford met Minnesota so Warner moved Caddel to right half and inserted Rintala at fullback. The Gophers stalled the Indians' first drive when Pete Somers intercepted a pass on the Minnesota one in the second quarter, but in the second half Somers fumbled one of Moffatt's punts and Milton "Red" Hand recovered on the Gophers' 21. An Allen to Caddel pass was good for 16 yards and Caddel scored from the three.

A tackle by Moffatt kept "Pug" Manders from going all the way for Minnesota. Later Moffatt added the second Stanford touchdown when he outran the Gopher defense on a nine-yard dash around left end. Two penalties appeared to have stalled the Indians' drive, but Moffatt passed to Afflerbaugh for 18 yards to keep the march moving and set up the scoring run. Stanford outgained Minnesota 252 yards to 73 rushing and 130 to 16 passing.

In February of 1932 the Stanford Board of Trustees discarded the proposal of absentee president Ray Lyman Wilbur, who had taken a leave to serve as Secretary of the Interior, to gradually eliminate the freshman and sophomore classes and make Stanford a graduate university. Dr. Wilbur surrendered to the protests of alumni and faculty members and agreed to retain the policy of having all four classes of undergraduates. Warner also was given a new five-year contract to coach the Indians.

No one knew what to expect when the football season got under way. A squad of 101 players reported, but the newspaper writers labelled it a "mystery team" and the term stuck. The Pacific Coast Conference had become a tough league, and it was felt no one could survive without a defeat. Warner abandoned the double fullback and reverted to his A formation, but the season was to be "Pop's" worst at Stanford. It also was to be his last.

The Indians won their first five games in impressive fashion, allowing only a single touchdown in a 20-7 victory over USF. But Stanford lost four of its last six games and tied another to finish with a 6-4-1 record. Three of the defeats came on successive weekends to USC, UCLA, and Washington. The loss to USC was the fifth straight, and the defeat by Washington was the first in seven years. The UCLA victory was the first ever by the Bruins over Stanford.

No one could explain why such a highly geared team should suddenly flounder in three straight conference games. The situation was such that the Board of Athletic Control banned all future radio broadcasts.

Southern California was reported to be weaker than the Trojans' 1931 national champions, while Stanford was considered stronger than the previous year. Warner rated the game a toss-up, but the Trojans registered a 13-0 victory, the fourth shutout in five years for Howard Jones.

"USC had no great offense, but it had two forward passes, great kicking, and a punch at the goal line," wrote Curley Grieve of the *San Francisco Examiner*.

A 21-yard run by Bill Sim and a 15-yard holding penalty on the Trojans helped Stanford advance to a first down on the USC 15 in the first quarter. But with fourth down and one Caddel was held to a half yard and the Indians gave up the ball on the Trojans 5½ yard line, and the Stanford attack was through for the afternoon.

Homer Griffith's kick was downed at the Stanford three to put the Tribe in a hole in the second period, and when Sim punted out Mohler ran the kick back 24 yards to the Stanford 21. On second down Bob McNeish took a reverse and passed 17 yards to Ford Palmer for a touchdown. The Trojans added their other score in the third quarter when Gordon Clark passed 35 yards to Palmer who ran another six before he was tackled by Afflerbaugh on the Stanford nine. Mohler gained four yards and then five for the score. It was no consolation to Warner that Stanford out-downed USC 13 to nine.

Two blocked punts by Verdi Boyer, a sophomore guard, were responsible for UCLA's 13-6 win over the Indians. Stanford marched to a touchdown at the start of the game and was stopped on the Bruins' eight at the end, but otherwise it was a big afternoon for Coach Bill Spaulding's team from Westwood.

There were only 15 seconds left in the first half when

Boyer broke through to block Stan Anderson's punt. Bob McChesney of the Bruins recovered on the eight and ran it in for the touchdown. In the third quarter Stanford held the Bruins at the three, and Mike Frankovich's field goal was wide. However, a holding penalty put Stanford back to the seven, and Boyer again blocked Anderson's kick with D. McGue recovering for UCLA on the Indians' seven. W. Clark scored on second down from the one.

Stanford and California battled to a 0-0 tie before 77,000 fans at Berkeley in the Big Game. Despite the lack of scoring the game had plenty of excitement. A first quarter drive by Stanford was stopped on the California two, while a fourth quarter march by the Bears was halted by the final gun at the Indians' five. California did not make a first down during the first three quarters but collected six in the final period.

A holding penalty helped stall Stanford's bid for a score in the first quarter, and later in the game Sim broke loose for a 21-yard run deep into California territory. He was hit by Arleigh Williams at the Bears' six and slid across the goal. A year earlier it would have been a touchdown, but under the new dead ball rule put into effect in 1932 the ball was put back on the two and Stanford failed to score.

In early December Dr. Thomas A. Storey, head of the Stanford physcial education department, and Al Masters, graduate manager, denied rumors Warner was going to quit as Stanford coach.

"We are wholly satisfied with Mr. Warner's season. It is one of the best he has had at Stanford. He has done a whale of a job," Storey said.

The statement followed remarks attributed to Warner while he was in Pittsburgh where Stanford had dropped its final game of the season to the Panthers, 7-0. Warner was reported to have said that certain Stanford alumni had become too bothersome, and that they would not be satisfied until he was supplanted by Ernie Nevers.

On December 5 Warner resigned to accept the head coaching position at Temple University. He blamed Los Angeles alumni for clamoring for a change but said he had no fault to find with the administration or the student body. The salary offered by Temple was believed to range between $15,000 and $18,000. He was supposed to be getting about $12,000 at Stanford.

106

Claude (Tiny) Thornhill, named to replace Warner January 6, 1933.

One of the things that annoyed "Pop" was Stanford's high scholarship requirements which deprived him of the opportunity of getting good football players. Warner felt that it was difficult to get good players to stay in Stanford because of the educational achievements required.

Andy Kerr, coach of the undefeated, untied, unscored-upon, and uninvited Colgate team, was considered the leading candidate to succeed Warner. Also mentioned for the job were Dick Hanley of Northwestern, Maurice "Clipper" Smith of Santa Clara, Ernie Nevers, Dud DeGroot, and Fred Swan. Kerr was said to have been willing two years earlier but apparently was not interested in 1932.

Dink Templeton, writing in one of the Bay area papers, pointed out that one of the finest crops of freshman athletes in history had entered Stanford that year. Included in the group were Bobby Grayson, a Portland, Oregon, prep star who was everything Dick Hyland had been and more, Jim Moscrip, who was to become one of Stanford's greatest ends, Bob Hamilton, Alf Brandin, and Wes Muller.

Stanford officials received 60 written applications for the coaching position, but on January 6, 1933, the job was given to Thornhill with a three year contract.

Charles Prelsnik remembers Warner as a coach who did not hesitate to change his offense if he thought it gave him an advantage in a game. Prelsnik, who served Santa Clara County as sheriff for many years, came to Stanford on a scholarship as a mile runner. He had played end in high school at Butte, Montana, and went out for that position on the freshman squad at Stanford. "There wasn't much room to play, however, with Phil Neill, Jay Tod, Don Colvin, Bill Doub, and Carl Wittenau around so I moved to tackle," Prelsnik said.

"Warner had his single-wing A formation, the double wing B formation, and the C formation which split the ends. We ran so many different offenses I ran out of adhesive tape." It was a practice for players to stick strips of adhesive on their pants on which they wrote their blocking assignments.

"'Pop' even changed his offense just before the Big Game," Prelsnik said. "Another thing was that we used the 'butterfly' tackle, on defense. The left tackle would drop back a yard or two from the usual seven man line, from there he either jumped back in the line or stayed back to help out on a pass or end run. It was one of the first changes in the normal defense."

"Vow Boys" Take Over

Much of the brilliance of the 1933 season was attributed to the startling and consistent performances of a bunch of sophomores who had acquired the name of the "Vow Boys" because of a pledge they had made the previous year as freshmen that they would never lose to Southern California. Of even greater value was the playing of guard Bill Corbus, who had earned All America honors in 1932 and repeated in his senior year. Greatest of the individual backfield stars was Bobby Grayson, a sophomore fullback from Portland, Oregon.

"The 'Vow Boys' pledge was made by Frank Alustiza," Grayson said. "It was made very simply as we were dressing for practice on Monday following a humiliating varsity defeat from USC the prior Saturday (13-0). The freshman team was discussing the humiliation of the varsity, and Frank simply said, 'We will never lose to USC.' Bones Hamilton said, 'Let's make that a vow,' and it apparently was forgotten. However, the following year we were preparing for the USC game knowing we would be starting eight sophomores. Harry Borba (of the *San Francisco Examiner*) wrote a story about the 'Vow Boys.' From then on we had to live with it."

In their three years at Stanford the "Vow Boys" lived up to their name. They beat Southern California 13-7 in 1933, handing the Trojans their first loss in 27 games going back to the first contest of the 1931 season. California had not been included in the original vow, but with a Rose Bowl bid at stake some of the writers made the Bears a part of it, and the Indians went along and also beat California each of the three years.

During their career the "Vow Boys" never did enjoy an

undefeated season, but they went to the Rose Bowl three straight years, the first team to achieve this distinction. They also won 25 games while losing 4 and tying 2. Two of the losses were to Columbia and Alabama in their first two Rose Bowl appearances. In the three years they rolled up 20 shutouts including 8 in 11 games in 1934 and 7 in 9 games in 1935. Only twice in the three seasons did opponents score more than a single touchdown against Stanford. One of those was Alabama in its 29-13 victory in the 1935 Rose Bowl game.

Thornhill had a pessimistic outlook going into the 1933 season, giving Stanford little chance to finish better than fifth in the conference. "USC is on top again, and then we have to place California, Washington, and Washington State ahead of us," Thornhill said. "We're about on a par with UCLA. I don't know anything about Oregon and Oregon State."

"Tiny," who had been Warner's chief lieutenant since 1922, inherited a team which included 12 lettermen, 5 of them regulars. He also had the bright but untested sophomore prospects headed by Grayson. Other top talent from the freshman squad included Monk Moscrip, Al Norgard, Dave Packard, Larry Rouble, and Woody Adams. The fate of the Stanford team appeared to hang on the tackle positions, but Thornhill had been an All America tackle under Warner at Pitt in 1918 so the feeling was that he could develop someone to fill the bill. "Tiny" had some big men, for those days, in Ed Lettinich, 230; Jack Holwerds, 230; Bob Reynolds, 232; Gordon Dunn, 250; and Bennett Palamountain, 210. Corbus weighed in at 197.

"Playing football under 'Tiny' Thornhill was fun," said Bobby Grayson. "During our three years, when we had the horses to knock heads with anyone and fight our way through with the Warner double wing with emphasis on power, it was downright exhilarating. Later on the tide turned in the late '30s, but it was still a great experience for the players, but everyone likes to win. We didn't realize it at the time, but the game was changing radically right under our noses. At Stanford we didn't do much passing because we could move the ball well on the ground. But the pass was on its way to prominence before we got bombarded by Dixie Howell and Don Hutson of Alabama in the 1935 Rose Bowl game.

"Until then teams hesitated to throw a second pass after missing the first one because the second miss called for a five yard penalty and five yards could be pretty hard to make

One of Stanford's all-time greats, Bobby Grayson, starred with the Vow Boys in 1933-34-35. A two-time All America, he ranks third on Stanford's career rushing list.

against a stacked defense. All of that changed during 'Tiny's' tenure. We elected to keep plugging away on the ground, and we didn't do too badly. The only trouble was that the forward pass had so opened up the attack that you had to score more points to win. Also the lack of versatility allowed the defense to stack men on the line of scrimmage, and it took an effective passing attack to spread them out. As for me, I think I prefer it the old way. But the old tactics could work only under the old rules, and they are gone forever."

Grayson rates Stanford's 13-7 victory over Southern California in 1933 the "most exciting game" of his career. "They were the national champions the previous year, and were undefeated through seven games when we met them," he said. "We started eight sophomores against the Trojans and defeated them 13-7."

There were 90,000 fans on hand at the Los Angeles Coliseum that November 11 afternoon, but the Stanford team almost did not make it to the game. The Indians had left Palo Alto early Friday evening on the overnight train trip to Los Angeles, expecting to arrive about 8 o'clock Saturday morning. Just north of Salinas, however, the train was halted because of a washout that had done considerable damage to the roadbed causing the tracks to sink and making it unsafe for the train to continue. There was a five hour delay as railroad workers dumped crushed rock along the roadbed.

With all this commotion going on there was little chance for the players to sleep as officials pondered what to do about the situation. Al Masters, Stanford graduate manager, solved the dilemma by asking Southern Pacific officials if the track would hold the weight of the engine and three passenger cars? When assured it would, Masters proposed that the team's three special cars be hooked onto the engine for the rest of the trip, leaving the remainder of the train, plus a couple of special rooters' trains behind.

After a wild ride in a bid to make up lost time, the Stanford team arrived in Los Angeles only an hour before game time, and rushed to the Coliseum with a police escort. With little sleep, and a team made up largely of sophomores, who never had played before a crowd of this size, Stanford took the

Thornhill, assistant coach Jim Lawson, and graduate manager Al Masters prepare for train trip to Los Angeles.

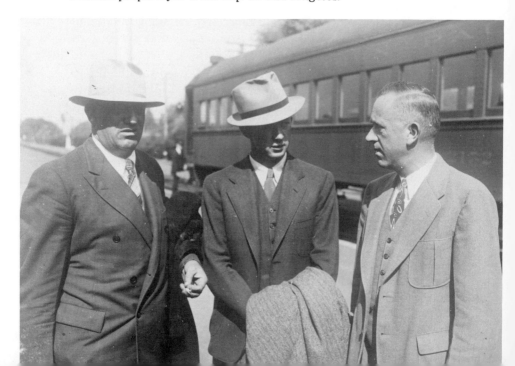

field against a USC team which was unbeaten in 27 straight games and had allowed only 10 points while rolling over seven opponents that season. Because of Stanford's delayed arrival the odds favoring the Trojans had lengthened to 5-1.

Stanford repulsed the first two USC thrusts at the Indians' 29 and later the 19, but the next time the Trojans got the ball Irving "Cotton" Warburton dashed 43 yards through the Stanford defense for a touchdown. The Indians retaliated in the second quarter with one of their great offensive efforts of the season. Taking the ball on their own 33 after Cal Clemens had punted out of bounds, the Indians moved the 67 yards in 10 plays.

Grayson faded back to pass but could not find an open receiver so he ran for 16. The next time he dropped back Grayson hit "Buck" Van Dellen, who had replaced Bob Maentz at left half, with a 20-yard pass to the USC 26. Grayson lost a yard to Aaron Rosenberg but on a reverse passed again to Van Dellen who made a leaping catch at the 15 and ran to the 12 before being pulled down.

Grayson made six yards, and "Bones" Hamilton added 3½ for a third down and two feet on the 2½. Grayson made a yard and a half for a first down on the one and then ploughed over on the next play to tie the score. It was the first power play touchdown to be scored against USC in two years.

Stanford's power got stronger in the second half. The Indians threatened twice in the third quarter but failed to score as Corbus missed two field goal attempts, but Alustiza's kicking kept the Trojans in a hole. Once the Stanford quarterback kicked out of bounds on the USC one yard line.

After a fumble recovery had stopped one USC march, Van Dellen halted another when he intercepted a Homer Griffith pass and returned 22 yards to the Trojans' 35. Grayson made 12 yards at end but then lost 3 to Bob McNeish. A shovel pass to Hamilton picked up a yard, and then Grayson passed to Al Norgard who almost got away but was caught by Rosenberg at the 15 after a gain of 10 yards. Southern California's defense held at this point, and Corbus, who earlier had missed from the 25, kicked a field goal from the 22 to put Stanford in front 10-7 with four and a half minutes left to play.

Minutes later Bob Reynolds smeared Griffith for an eight-yard loss, forcing USC to pass. Clemens juggled the throw from Bill Howard, and Bill Bates, Stanford senior, scooped the ball out of Howard's hands and raced to midfield. Moscrip got away for 30 yards on an end around reverse, and the Indians advanced to the Trojans' eight before they stalled again. From an angle at the 14 Corbus kicked his second field goal for the final 13-7 margin. It was almost unbelievable that this team of sophomores, using straight football with no laterals and very few reverses, could defeat the mighty Southern California Trojans.

The Stanford axe was put up as a Big Game trophy for the first time for the November 26 game at Stanford, and 88,000 people turned out to watch the Indians bid for the Pacific Coast Conference title. California was out of the running, having lost to USC and having tied UCLA and Washington State, but Stanford needed the win to finish ahead of Southern California.

The Bears took a 3-0 lead in the second quarter when Arleigh Williams passed to Harry Jones for a first down on the Stanford 20. But the Indians held, and Williams kicked a field goal from the 25. Corbus had missed a field goal for Stanford from the Bears' 26 in the first quarter.

Stanford threatened in the third period, advancing to the California 16. But James Keefer batted down Grayson's third down pass, and a fourth down pass just missed. Moscrip had the ball for a second but in bringing it down dropped it, and the touchdown was lost. Late in the quarter Van Dellen intercepted a Williams pass and returned 16 yards to the California 39. On the next play Grayson cut in towards left tackle, swerved out, and swept around end for 26 yards before George Relles and Chuck Stewart pushed him out of bounds. Stanford failed to score, however, as Milo Quisling and Relles smothered Grayson on third down for an eight-yard loss, ending any field goal possibilities. Grayson's fourth down pass, intended for Hamilton, was flicked away by Williams.

Late in the fourth quarter Stanford found itself on its own 45 and still trailing 3-0. Frank Alustiza had been kicking well all day, blocking, carrying the ball when asked, and averaging almost four yards per play. Now they asked him to pass. Alustiza exchanged positions with Grayson, faded back, and cut loose with all he had. Norgard, who had slipped behind Williams, caught the ball on the California 30, eight yards ahead of the nearest California man. There was no chance to stop him.

The Indians, who had been unable to go through the tough Bear defense, had stolen the game. There were less than four minutes left to play, but California did not quit. The Bears stormed back with a 73-yard drive to the Stanford four yard line but got no farther. Stewart tried center but was stopped by Wes Muller for no gain. Stewart next probed left guard but was met by Moscrip and Muller for a gain of half a yard. The Bears tried Jack Brittingham on an end around play which had gained good yardage earlier, but Norgard, who had been blocked down, got a hand on Brittingham's leg and tripped him for a three-yard loss.

On fourth down Floyd Blower rifled a pass in the left flat intended for Stewart. The throw looked good, but Hamilton, the "perfect Stanford right halfback," snatched the ball off Stewart's fingertips and raced upfield, threading his way through players for 60 yards before Blower pulled him down on the California 40. Stanford had a 7-3 victory and an invitation to the Rose Bowl.

"That Thornhill, there's the boy," said Grayson after the game. "You know what he said to me after the game? He said just what my father would have said. 'Boy,' Tiny said, 'You can call plays for this ball club all the time, you've got guts.' Did I feel good when he said that. Boy, that Tiny, he's all right."

Stanford had some other close calls that season. The Indians edged UCLA 3-0 on a first quarter field goal by Corbus,

All America guard Bill Corbus, the "Baby-Faced Assassin" 1931-33.

who barely missed another in the fourth quarter when his kick hit one of the uprights. Stanford beat San Jose State 27-0 in the season opener, but the Indians fumbled 12 times so their fans were not too jubilant.

Northwestern held the Indians to a 0-0 tie in a game played at Soldiers Field in Chicago. Stanford was on the Wildcats' two yard line as the first half ended. The only loss of the regular season was a 6-0 defeat by Washington at Seattle in the rain. Bill Smith kicked two field goals for the Huskies, the first coming after Stanford held for downs on its six inch line. Grayson had a pulled knee muscle and played only briefly in the fourth quarter.

Corbus, the "Baby-Faced Assassin" from Vallejo, was selected to the Walter Camp, Grantland Rice, Associated Press, and International News Service All America teams, which amounted to unanimous choice in those days. Corbus was considered one of the most outstanding linemen ever produced on the Coast.

Lion By The Tail

Only 35,000 spectators showed up for the 1934 Rose Bowl game between Stanford and Columbia University of New York. There were two reasons for the small turnout. The most torrential rain in 50 years hit the Los Angeles area 48 hours before the game, flooding the floor of the Rose Bowl with a foot of water. Fire trucks were called in to help pump water off the field and managed to get the playing surface reasonably free of water although there were a few puddles visible at the opening kickoff.

The other reason fans failed to show much interest was the selection of Lou Little's Columbia team to oppose Stanford. Harry Grayson, *New York World Telegram* writer, had written to his nephew, Bobby Grayson, urging him to convey to Stanford graduate manager Al Masters that Columbia was the very best team on the Atlantic seaboard.

The Lions had a 7-1 record, losing only to Princeton, while defeating Penn State, Syracuse, Navy, Cornell, and Virginia, among others. Damon Runyon, an authority among eastern sportswriters, also had boosted Columbia, but Henry McLemore, United Press writer, had poked fun at the selection of Columbia.

"The limping Lions, picked from all the outfits in the country to do battle with one of those super, man-killers of the mighty West, and in the biggest game of them all," McLemore wrote. "No pardner, it can't be true. It's a joke. The fellows who thought it up just jumped the gun on repeal and got a little too ossified." His reference was to the fact that prohibition had just been voted out.

Stanford had resumed practice on December 4 after taking a week's break following its victory over California, but the Indians were unable to engage in any drills the final two days in Pasadena while waiting for the rain to stop. Meanwhile, Little had refused to bring his team into Pasadena early and stayed in Tucson, Arizona, where he was able to hold workouts. Columbia arrived in town on Sunday for the Monday game.

Stanford was a 2½ to 1 favorite before the game, and the odds were even that the Indians would win by 12 points. But the Cardinals' cutback style of attack was of no avail on the muddy field. Early in the game Bob Maentz, Stanford left halfback from Allegan, Michigan, broke loose on a reverse and with good deception and blocking appeared headed for a touchdown. But just when it looked as though he would go all the way he slipped in one of the puddles on the field and fell, without a Columbia player laying a hand on him.

Columbia won the game 7-0 as the result of a perfectly executed hidden-ball play, known as KF79 in the Columbia play book. The maneuver was a naked reverse with all of the Columbia players, except the ballcarrier, going one way.

"It all started from a blocked kick," said an account of the game. "Alustiza got a bad pass from center, was hurried, and a trio of Columbians sifted through to smother the kick. It was only third down, however, so when young Bob Reynolds, Stanford tackle, fell on the ball it was still in Indian possession. Alustiza, of course, kicked again, and Cliff Montgomery returned to the Indians' 45 yard line. Stanford was penalized five yards, and then Montgomery hurled a pass to Tony Matal. The Columbia end made a leaping catch and came down sliding. He skidded along three yards more before he was stopped on the 17 yard stripe.

"In his first try Al Barabas fumbled, but he recovered for a half-yard loss. On the next effort Montgomery took the ball from center, wheeled in a deceptive reverse, and handed it to Barabas. A Columbia back sifted through between right tackle and right end, drawing the secondary away. So Barabas, using the hidden ball ruse, took off around Stanford's right end. There was no Stanford man in the way and Barabas loped the 17 yards to the goal line."

There were a couple of humorous incidents in the game. Once Grayson broke into the clear, but ran into umpire Tom Thorpe, and by the time he managed to get clear of the official

118

Robert (Bones) Hamilton, Vow Boy halfback, 1933-35.

Montgomery had time to tackle him. Ed Brominski, the Columbia right half, tried to steal the ball from Grayson several times after making the tackle. Each time he would look at Grayson and ask, "Have you got that football?" Grayson replied,

*Quarterback Frank Alustiza, outstanding punter, who is cred-
ited with "Vow Boy" pledge.*

"You're damn right I've got it." After Grayson had rattled off
four first downs Brominski asked, "Have you still got that football?" Grayson answered, "Certainly." Brominski grinned and
said, "Okay."

Stanford helped nullify its offensive efforts by fumbling
eight times, with four of the bobbles coming inside the Columbia 10 yard line. Grayson fumbled near the goal line in the third
quarter, but tried to throw the ball into the flat, hoping one of

120

his teammates would fall on it. But Columbia recovered on the two yard line to end that threat. Grayson received a couple of broken ribs on the play.

Grayson carried the ball 27 times for a net 152 yards compared to 174 for the entire Columbia team. Stanford finished with 296 yards rushing, but the soggy ball made passing almost impossible, and the Indians completed only two of 12 attempts for 23 yards. Columbia tried only two passes and completed one, the toss from Montgomery to Matal which set up the Lions' second quarter touchdown.

One of the standouts in the line for Stanford was Bob "Horse" Reynolds, who played every minute of the game at tackle. Reynolds also played 60 minutes of the 1935 and 1936 Rose Bowl games to set a record which never will be equalled or broken unless the colleges return to single platoon football. Bill Corbus, a two-time All America guard, and quarterback Frank Alustiza, who Grayson called "the heart and brains of the 'Vow Boys,'" were other top performers.

Eight Shutouts

The year's experience made the "Vow Boys" more confident, more flexible, and more vicious in 1934 than the previous season. They scored 211 points while allowing only 14 during the regular season and shut out 8 of their 10 opponents while chalking up a 9-0-1 record. A 7-7 tie with Santa Clara kept the Indians from a perfect season. The only other team to score was California which gave the Tribe a battle before losing 9-7.

Considering the crippled condition of the Stanford squad, the victory over the Bears had to be rated an outstanding achievement. Moscrip was sidelined with an injured leg suffered the day before the game, and Grayson was hurt in the first quarter and forced to leave the game. The first half was scoreless although Stanford had marched to the California 17 in the opening period, and the Bears had made two deep penetrations into Indian territory.

Shortly after the start of the second half Carl Schott, a sophomore end, blocked a California punt and the Indians recovered on the Bears' 22. Hamilton broke the tie by scoring on a double reverse around right end with the help of some good blocking. But Schott missed the important extra point. Later Schott gave Stanford a 9-0 lead when he kicked a field goal from the 15 early in the fourth quarter.

California reached the Stanford three late in the game but, after being denied that time, took advantage of a short punt to get on the scoreboard. Arleigh Williams, the Bears' All America halfback, passed to Jack Brittingham for a 30-yard touchdown with less than three minutes remaining.

Stanford had romped over San Jose State 40-0 in its season

opener with Grayson scoring three touchdowns and having another 75-yard scoring dash called back. Moscrip proved himself a satisfactory replacement for Corbus in the kicking department as he booted a field goal and three extra points. Grayson gained 161 yards for a 9.5 average, and when he went out of the game Hamilton moved to fullback and accounted for 103 yards.

It was a hot day on September 29 when the Indians tackled Santa Clara and the Broncos put the heat on the "Vow Boys" as Coach "Clipper" Smith shuttled his Bronco players to keep fresh troops in action. Grayson put Stanford in front with a second quarter touchdown, but the Cardinals were hard pressed to hold off Santa Clara in the closing stages of the game. The Broncos tied the score on an 18-yard pass from Don De Rosa to Hall, and Santa Clara threatened again when De Rosa intercepted a pass by Alustiza and galloped 30 yards to the Stanford 41. The Broncos picked up a pair of first downs to reach the Indians' 16 before Moscrip deflected a field goal attempt to save a tie for Stanford.

The Indians missed an earlier scoring opportunity after Reynolds had intercepted a Frank Sobrero pass at the 50 and returned to the Bronco 30. Grayson and Hamilton hammered out a first down on the nine, but Sobrero stopped the threat when he intercepted Moscrip's pass from a fake field goal formation.

Grayson carried the ball 25 times and gained 119 yards, almost twice as much as the entire Southern California backfield, as the Indians beat the Trojans 16-0 to hand USC its first ever loss in Stanford Stadium. Grayson scored two touchdowns, the first coming a minute and a half before the end of the first half, while Moscrip added a third quarter field goal from the 20.

Stanford's great line power and great backfield blocking were too much for the Trojans, who got past midfield only once, advancing to the Stanford 47 in the first quarter. Grayson carried the ball nine times in a fourteen-play march as Stanford drove 64 yards in 24 plays without a pass to score.

John Reisner intercepted a Warburton pass and with blocking from Bob Black and Aly Trompas returned 39 yards to the USC nine to set up Stanford's second touchdown. Grayson scored from the three on third down. Muller and Rouble were outstanding for the Indians. Topping, Van Dellen, Grayson, Calloway, and Muller all played the entire 60 minutes for Stanford.

Bob Reynolds, tackle, played three 60-minute games in Rose Bowl, 1934-35-36.

Grayson was supposed to be weak on pass defense so Washington tried to take advantage of him when the unbeaten Huskies invaded Stanford Stadium. The strategy proved a big mistake, however, as Grayson intercepted four passes. The fleet Stanford back grabbed one pass in the second quarter and dodged 34 yards through the Washington team for a touchdown. On the final play of the game he picked off another and ran 40 yards to score as Stanford rolled to a 24-0 victory. Grayson wound up with 104 yards on 27 carries.

After the 7-7 tie with Santa Clara, Stanford started a string of seven straight shutouts, beating Oregon State 17-0, Northwestern 20-0, USF 3-0, USC 16-0, UCLA 27-0, Washington 24-0, and the Olympic Club 40-0. Grayson missed the Northwestern game with a bruised hip, so Hamilton took his place and gained 99 yards in 25 carries. Alustiza ran 47 yards with a pass interception for one of Stanford's scores and Hamilton made the other two on runs of 16 and 6 yards.

Grayson and Reynolds were consensus All Americas, Grayson being named on the Associated Press, United Press, International News Service, All America Board, and the Collier's

(Grantland Rice) teams. Reynolds was honored by the AP, INS, and Collier's. Moscrip also earned All America recognition on the All America Board and UP first teams.

It was during this time that the Stanford Buck Club, a group interested in raising funds to support the athletic program, was formed. The instigators of the plan were Murray Draper, now a Superior Court judge, J.C. "Jake" Irwin, former Stanford ticket manager and equipment manager, the late Bill Leiser, and the late Harry Borba. All were Stanford graduates. Leiser became sports editor of the *San Francisco Chronicle*, and Borba was an outstanding sportswriter for the *San Francisco Examiner*.

"Borba came up with the idea of calling it the Buck Club," said Irwin. "The idea was to have something that anybody could afford, even in depression times, which those were. It also was an arrangement where nobody could take any credit for the amount he had donated, or expect any favors. The first year after we started we had some 144 fellows signed up to pay their buck each month.

"There was a story they used to circulate that when we first started the Buck Club the first collection included $3 and an IOU," Irwin said. "They used to kid me and ask if I ever had made good on that IOU. We didn't know how the president would accept the idea, but he appreciated it."

No Match For Tide

Stanford had been scored on only twice during the 1934 season, but the Indians' defense was not prepared to handle Alabama and one of the great passing combinations in college football history in the 1935 Rose Bowl game.

Alabama was supposed to be a running team, but Millard "Dixie" Howell and Don Hutson put on a dazzling display of passing that led Mark Kelly to write that the Crimson Tide duo should top the list of two-man combinations in football history ahead of the likes of Gus Dorais to Knute Rockne, Wyman to Bert Baston, and Benny Friedman to Bennie Oosterbaan.

Grantland Rice wrote: "Dixie Howell, the human howitzer from Hartford, Alabama, blasted the Rose Bowl dreams of Stanford with one of the greatest all-around exhibitions that football has ever known. The slender stripling, weighing 161 pounds, led a passing, kicking and running attack that beat a big, game Stanford team, 29-13, as 85,000 sat beneath a blue California sky and saw the sunny atmosphere full of flying footballs thrown from Howell's rifle-shot hand into Don Hutson's waiting arms."

Howell threw only 12 passes, not a great sum compared to the modern use of the aerial routes, but he completed nine of those tosses for 160 yards, and Joe Riley, who relieved Howell, added a 54-yard touchdown pass to Hutson to lift Alabama's total passing yardage to 214 for the afternoon. Howell also scored two touchdowns, one on a 67-yard kickoff return, and punted six times for a 44.8 yard average. Hutson caught six of eight passes thrown to him for a total of 164 yards and two touchdowns.

Stanford got the jump on the Crimson Tide when Keith Topping pounced on an Alabama fumble on the Tide's 29 yard line. Grayson tallied from the one foot line after teaming with "Bones" Hamilton and "Buck" Van Dellen to move the ball to that point. Alabama exploded for 22 points in the second quarter, however, to take command. Howell scored from the five after setting up the score with three pass completions. Riley Smith put Alabama ahead with a 22-yard field goal, and then when Stanford elected to kick off, Howell ran the kick back 67 yards for another score. A pass interception gave the Tide another chance to score just before the end of the half, and with eight seconds left Riley hit Hutson with a 34-yard pass and the Alabama All America end ran another 20 for a third touchdown of the period.

Stanford tallied in the third quarter with Van Dellen scoring from the 12 and threatened again late in the period but was stopped by an interception. The Indians appeared to have Alabama stopped on the 41 as the third quarter ended. The Tide had second and 23, but Howell threw a strike to Hutson on the Stanford 20 and he rambled the rest of the way for a final score. A closing threat by the Indians died when they lost the ball on downs at the Alabama 10.

Playing opposite Hutson on the other end of the Alabama line that day was Paul Bryant, who later coached at Maryland, Kentucky, and Texas A&M, before returning to coach at Alabama in 1958.

One Point Shy

Defense was the trademark of the Stanford football team in 1935 as the Indians blanked six of their regular season opponents and allowed the other two a total of 13 points. But injuries were a constant source of trouble for Coach Thornhill, and the Tribe had problems scoring points of its own in several games.

UCLA spoiled an undefeated season for Stanford with an upset 7-6 win that also cost the Indians the services of little Frank Alustiza whose pass interception and 25-yard return in the first quarter led to the Stanford touchdown. Alustiza left the game in the third period with an eye injury. An examination the next day showed it was a detached retina, putting an end to Alustiza's career.

Stanford had missed the conversion attempt after its score, and five minutes later the Bruins recovered a fumble on the Indians' 40 yard line. A penalty moved the ball to the 35 and then Chuck Cheshire broke through left tackle for 27 yards to the eight. Ted Key scored from there and kicked the extra point to put UCLA ahead and the Bruin defense checked Stanford threats the rest of the game.

Hamilton also was hurt in the UCLA game and missed the next three contests as Stanford barely scraped through with a 6-0 win over Washington, 9-6 over Santa Clara, and a 3-0 decision over Southern California. Washington was undefeated when the Indians invaded Seattle and had a potent offense, but was unable to score against the tough Stanford line. By Haines broke loose once, but was pulled down by Jim Coffis, the Stanford safetyman, and the Huskies were stopped on the 16.

Twice Stanford mounted drives into Washington territory, with Grayson leading the way. Both threats fell short, however, and each time Moscrip kicked field goals, thus reversing the Huskies' victory two years earlier when Washington won on two field goals.

Thornhill used only 14 men and 7 of the starters played 60 minutes as Stanford had to come from behind to beat a fired-up Santa Clara team the following week, 9-6. The Broncos grabbed an early lead when Hal Sherman intercepted a Grayson pass on the 15 and ran 85 yards for a touchdown. A poor kick by the Broncos gave Stanford the ball on the Santa Clara 24 in the second quarter, and a 21-yard pass from Ray Todd to Coffis and Bill Paulman's plunge gave the Indians the tying score. Todd had replaced Grayson early in the second quarter when the Stanford star had reinjured his ankle.

A Nello Falaschi pass to Tom Dutton for 30 yards put the Broncos deep in Stanford territory, but the Indians finally held on the two yard line and from there marched to the Santa Clara 12 where Moscrip kicked a field goal for a 9-6 win.

Stanford never was in much danger of losing to USC, but the Indians also came close to not winning. The Cardinals made a lot of yardage at midfield, but lacked the punch when they got in scoring position. Late in the fourth quarter Grayson hooked up on a couple of passes to Keith Topping. On the second one Topping lateraled to Bill "Doc" Luckett who fell on the USC 25.

Monk Moscrip, star end and field goal kicker, 1933-35.

Grayson faded back to pass again, but saw a hole and ran to the 14. There were two minutes left to play. Grayson made eight yards in two plays, but the ball was out of position for a field goal attempt. Vigna circled right end to put the ball at midfield and, with less than a minute remaining, Moscrip stood on the 13 yard line and put the ball squarely through the uprights for the winning three points.

Despite their record, both this season and the previous two years, the "Vow Boys" were underdogs to California going into the Big Game. The Bears, in their first season under Leonard B. "Stud" Allison, had rolled to nine straight victories and had allowed only nine points while blanking seven opponents. Cal had beaten USC 21-7 and UCLA 14-2, while Stanford had trouble with both teams and had suffered its only loss to UCLA.

California had an early opportunity to score when Bob Brittingham recovered a Stanford fumble, but Hank Sparks was wide on a field goal attempt. From its own 20 Stanford marched to a score in 12 plays with Grayson capping the drive from the one yard line.

Stanford got another score when Wes Muller recovered a Perry Schwartz fumble at the California 29. Grayson passed to Hamilton, who lateraled to Paulman for a first down on the 12. Two plays later Coffis took a reverse and scored from the nine to make the final score 13-0.

Mustangs Hobbled

Southern Methodist University was a popular choice to oppose Stanford in the 1936 Rose Bowl. Coach Matty Bell's Mustangs, led by All America halfback Bobby Wilson, had made a big hit with the Los Angeles fans and press earlier in the season when they defeated UCLA 21-0. They were undefeated in 12 games and had wrapped up the bid by defeating TCU 20-14 in their final game. Wilson had outplayed Sammy Baugh and capped his outstanding afternoon with a sensational catch of a pass from Bob Finley for the winning touchdown.

Fans had expected an offensive show from the free-wheeling Texans, but the game turned out to be a defensive battle as Stanford registered a 6-0 victory. The only score of the game came in the first quarter after Paulman had put the Mustangs in a hole with a 62-yard quick kick which Moscrip and Topping downed on the SMU 10.

The Mustangs were unable to move and were forced to kick out, and Coffis returned the punt 29 yards to the SMU 41. The Cardinals strayed from their usual pattern by taking to the air on the first play as Hamilton took a reverse from Grayson and passed to Coffis who made a great catch of the ball and ran to the 19. Grayson made six yards at end, and Hamilton ploughed through the Mustang defense for 12 more. With the ball on the one, SMU figured Grayson would carry the ball on the next play and bunched its defense for such a thrust. Hamilton and Coffis led Grayson into the right side of the line, but Paulman had taken the ball and, with no interference, slipped around the opposite end of the line in much the same fashion that Al Barabas had done for Columbia against Stanford two

Keith Topping, star of 1936 Rose Bowl.

years before.

Led by Wilson's passing the Texans bounced back to march from their own 25 to the Stanford 39 where they uncorked a bit of their razzle-dazzle. Wilson passed to right end Maco Stewart, who lateraled to fullback Harry Shuford, who in turn lateraled to right halfback R. Finley, who ran to the Cardinals' five. The play had been a spectacular one, and the Mustangs decided to try it again instead of using straight ahead power to get into the end zone. This time the Stanford line smashed through to break up the play before SMU could complete its deft ball-handling maneuvers. Topping and Muller both had a hand in wrecking the play, and Muller recovered for Stanford. That was the only threat of the afternoon for the Mustangs.

Topping and Moscrip, along with Muller and Reynolds, played outstanding defensive games for Stanford. Pete Bruneau, writing in the *Los Angeles Daily News*, nominated Topping as "an honorary member of the SMU backfield" because he spent so much time in it.

"I doubt if anybody ever saw greater end play than Keith Topping and Monk Moscrip revealed," Braven Dyer wrote in the *Los Angeles Times*. "It is questionable if there is a better tackle in the country than Bob Reynolds was this day. And if any center ever hit harder and more consistently than Wes Muller, he must have been arrested for mayhem."

Stanford's defense limited Wilson to 21 yards in 13 carries. Southern Methodist did an equally effective job by holding Grayson to 27 yards in 18 carries and Hamilton to 21 yards in 15 attempts.

The "Vow Boys" must go down as one of the all-time great collegiate football teams. Grayson, Moscrip, and Reynolds were consensus All Americas in 1934, and Moscrip and Grayson repeated in 1935. Corbus was a consensus All America in 1933, and Hamilton was picked on numerous All America teams. Also outstanding were Muller, guards Woody Adams and Larry Rouble, and quarterback Paulman.

Thornhill Under Fire

It was quite a comedown for Stanford in 1936 as the Indians won only two games while losing five and tying two. Thornhill faced the tremendous job of rebuilding a team which had lost nine superstars. Stanford had been a winner for three straight years, but now some of those who had been praising Thornhill became critics who claimed he lacked leadership.

There were a number of reasons put forth for the Indians' slide from the top. Foremost, of course, was that a team could not expect to have the kind of talent the "Vow Boys" had boasted. Others felt the Stanford alumni had become too complacent and were not pushing as hard with their recruiting.

The Stanford record really was not as bad as it looks on paper. The year before, the Indians possessed the talent and the skill to win the close games. This season they lacked it. Southern California registered a 14-7 victory when the Trojans intercepted a Jack Brigham pass and returned it for a touchdown. Washington State claimed a 14-13 win at Pullman, but had to hold off a Stanford rally in the second half after taking a 14-0 lead in the first two periods.

Santa Clara, with an experienced squad which was headed for the Sugar Bowl where it defeated LSU, handed the Indians a 13-0 setback. The other losses were to Columbia 7-0 and California 20-0. Stanford had sought a rematch with Columbia after the 7-0 loss in the 1934 Rose Bowl, but the Lions could not find a spot on their schedule for the Indians until 1936, the year after the "Vow Boys" had graduated. This game turned out the same way as the first meeting except that this time the game was played in a snow storm in New York City. The field

134

was treacherous because of snow and ice, but it did not bother George Furey of Columbia who took the opening kickoff and returned it 75 yards for a touchdown, the only scoring of the day. Pete Zager, a sophomore tackle who played the entire 60 minutes, blocked or partially blocked seven punts during the afternoon, but Stanford never was able to capitalize on any of them.

Center Louis Tsoutsovas was the iron-man of the Stanford squad. The rugged pivot man played 42 minutes of the season opener against Santa Clara and then played every minute of the eight remaining games. Left end Jack Clark played 60 minutes in six games.

There was not much cause for Stanford rooters to cheer in the Big Game. Grant Stone recovered a California fumble in the first quarter but Tony Calvelli's field goal attempt was short, and the Indians never threatened again. California scored in the second period on a 35-yard pass, and later added two more touchdowns for a 20-0 win. Among the few bright spots for Stanford were the punt returns of Coffis.

Stanford came from behind to defeat Oregon State 20-14 at Portland as Calvelli scored with only seconds remaining in the game. A 50-yard pass from Calvelli to Stone set up the winning

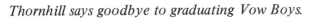

Thornhill says goodbye to graduating Vow Boys.

135

touchdown. The Indians scored twice in the second quarter for a 13-7 half-time lead with the go-ahead touchdown coming as a result of Bob Matthews' pass interception. Matthews lateraled to Tsoutsovas, who lateraled to Coffis, who scored.

Coffis also had a big hand in the Indians' 19-6 win over UCLA. Coffis ran a pass interception back 58 yards for Stanford's final touchdown after Sam Brigham had led the Indians on a 73-yard drive to take the lead.

A twisting 42-yard run by Vigna accounted for Stanford's score in a 7-7 tie with Oregon, but the Indians probably came up with their best performance of the season when they battled the conference champion Washington Huskies to a 14-14 tie. After twice turning back Husky threats Stanford yielded a touchdown, but came back with a march of its own to reach the Washington 12. Here quarterback Earl Hoos eliminated the shift and sent Fred Williams inside end for the touchdown.

Stanford grabbed the lead in the third quarter when Brigham plunged over from the one after moving the ball into scoring position on a pass to Coffis. Washington rallied to tie the score on a five-yard pass to Jim Cain.

The 1937 team did not do much scoring, but it also did not allow its opponents to do much either. The Indians tallied only 68 points and yielded 53 while posting a 4-3-2 record. Two of the victories came against Washington and Southern California and were a bit unusual. The Indians virtually "stole" a 13-7 win over Washington at Seattle, managing only 32 yards from scrimmage and three first downs while the Huskies rolled up 224 yards and 15 first downs. Grant Stone recovered a Washington fumble in the end zone for the first Stanford touchdown, and Jim Groves smashed through tackle for the winning score following another Husky bobble.

The USC game in Los Angeles followed a similar pattern. Ambrose Schindler and the Trojans ran all over Stanford in the first half, but managed to score only a single touchdown, and that was the result of a blocked kick which gave USC the ball deep in Stanford territory. The tide turned in the second half, and the Indians got a touchdown on a 41-yard pass from Groves to Pete Fay. "Doc" Luckett kicked the extra point to give Stanford a 7-6 victory.

The underdog Indians surprised UCLA and the 15,000 fans who turned out with a 12-7 win over the Bruins as Fay and Fred Ledeboer came to the front as ballcarriers with averages of

5.0 and 5.8 yards respectively. Groves scored in the first quarter on a 10-yard run around right end, and Fay tallied the winning touchdown in the second period with a 19-yard sweep around left end.

Stanford had a big edge in statistics over Oregon, rolling up 376 yards to 200 and 19 first downs to 8, but Bill Foskett blocked Groves' conversion attempt to give the Ducks a 7-6 win. A 40-yard pass from Bob Smith to Jay Graybeal produced the Oregon score in the second period. Groves tallied for Stanford on a four-yard blast in the fourth quarter.

California's conference champions whipped Stanford 13-0, but the underdog Indians battled the Bears on even terms except for an eight minute stretch in the second quarter. Cal marched 83 and 65 yards for touchdowns as 86,000 fans turned out despite a drenching rain. Stanford advanced to the California 18 yard line late in the game for its most serious threat. Thornhill acclaimed Calvelli the best man on the field.

Stanford invaded Baker Field in New York and was a 3-1 favorite for its third meeting with Columbia. But for the third time the Indians could not score a point against the Lions. However, they managed to also hold Columbia scoreless to claim a 0-0 tie. Fay had a long touchdown run called back when an official ruled he had stepped out of bounds. Luckett failed on a field goal attempt in the closing minute. Although he failed to produce any scoring, Columbia's Sid Luckman lived up to his All America reputation.

Stanford had its biggest day of the season in a 23-0 victory over Washington State. Thornhill adopted one of Warner's tricks and started his second team, and the reserves outplayed the Cougars. Fay romped 13 yards around end for a second quarter score to get the Indians on the board after Neil Rasmussen had recovered a Washington State fumble. Zager blocked a Cougar punt, and Stone picked up the ball at the five and scored in the third period. Paulman, who had been moved from quarterback to fullback, kicked a 41-yard field goal, and Coffis ran 67 yards for a touchdown to complete the Stanford scoring.

The Indians won two of their first three games in 1938, but then a series of injuries and ailments hit the squad and Stanford did not win another game until the final contest of the season when the Indians beat Dartmouth 23-13. Pete Fay's speed in pulling away from the Washington State secondary produced the only touchdown as Stanford beat the Cougars 8-0. Zager blocked a punt and the ball rolled through the end zone for a safety for the other points.

Fay was in the hospital with a throat infection the following week as the Indians beat Oregon 27-16. Zager blocked another punt, and Bill Willard recovered and ran for a touchdown. Two passes produced touchdowns before the end of the first half.

Paulman joined Fay in the hospital, and Norm Standlee and Calvelli were below par as Stanford dropped a 13-2 game to USC. The next week Thornhill found himself without a backfield reserve on the bench as Glenn South, a promising ball-carrier and receiver, suffered a broken collar bone. Stanford outgained and outpassed the Bruins, but UCLA took a 6-0 win.

Ledeboer passed to Billy Kirsch for a touchdown, but Hugh Gallarneau's 65-yard sprint for another score was called back on a holding penalty as the Indians dropped a 10-7 decision to Washington. Stanford turned in its finest running and passing exhibition of the season in the win over Dartmouth.

The 1939 season was one of the darkest in Stanford history. The Indians lost seven games and tied one before beating Dartmouth in the season windup. Stanford scored only 54 points, an all-time low since American football was resumed in 1919.

The Indians turned in an outstanding effort, to gain a 14-14 tie with heavily favored UCLA. Stanford was robbed of victory in the closing minutes when UCLA scored following a pass interception which was returned to the Indians' 22. Standlee was a one-man offense as he carried 32 times for 115 yards.

The strangest game of the year was an 8-5 loss to Washington in Seattle. A first quarter safety gave the Huskies a 2-0 lead, but Groves put Stanford ahead with a 20-yard field goal in the second period, 3-2. Washington regained the lead 8-3 with the only touchdown of the game in the third quarter, but the Indians came back to threaten with a Jack Mullin to Gallarneau passing attack. The Huskies halted the drive, however, and eliminated the possibility of a Stanford victory by giving the Indians a safety just before the game ended.

Alternating at tailback on this squad were sophomores Frank Albert and Pete Kmetovic, who were to star the next season on Clark Shaughnessy's "Cinderella" team.

"Thornhill was a hang loose, old time coach who didn't utilize his material," Kmetovic said. "Shaughnessy was all business and was well liked."

Kmetovic had been a star back at nearby San Jose High School and a 9.9 sprinter on the track team. As a schoolboy he had attended Stanford games with a friend of the family, and "naturally wanted to come to Stanford."

Albert was out of Glendale High School, and also "always wanted to go to Stanford. Jim Reynolds, a prominent Stanford alumnus, was instrumental in my getting to Stanford," Albert said. "He helped a lot of Southern California boys get up there."

Shaughnessy's Magic Touch

Stanford had had its "Vow Boys" in the 1930s, now the Indians came up with the "Wow Boys" as Clark Shaughnessy took a 1-7-1 team and transformed it into a "Cinderella Team" in 1940.

"When the chance came to coach at Stanford I grabbed it," said Shaughnessy. "Although I had a lifetime job at the University of Chicago with the rank of professor, I considered myself first of all a football coach, and Chicago no longer had a team. Once spring practice began and I got a look at my material, I had no doubts as to whether I'd made the right choice. With George Halas and Ralph Jones of the Bears I had been working for some time on the renovation of the old T formation, where the quarterback took a position under the center and the three other backs line up abreast behind him. The traditional T had been principally an inside running formation, but it was weak when going wide and on passing.

"Our version of the T used men in motion and spread ends to make the wide attack effective and to get receivers open for passes. I'd wanted to give this formation a test, and when I saw the personnel at Stanford I was convinced that this was the place. The modern T called for the quarterback to be the key man. Major requirements for the position were leadership and ability to select plays effectively. Also needed were finesse in ball handling, and faking, and ability to pass accurately. Running ability was not an important requirement.

"I found Frankie Albert, a little left hander, who would never be outstanding as a wingback because he wasn't fast enough, but who was ideal for the T quarterback spot. He was a

Clark Shaughnessy, 1940 "Cinderella Man."

magician with the ball, a gifted field general, wonderfully observing, and courageous to the point of almost foolhardiness.

"The fullback had to be more than the traditional line plunger. He had to have speed to go to the outside and the strength to be the backfield workhorse since he would carry the ball twice as often as either halfback. Imagine my pleasure at discovering a Norm Standlee backed up by Milt Vucinich. The halfbacks had to be fast starters for quick opening plays and have speed to run wide and get deep as pass receivers. Pete Kmetovic and Hugh Gallarneau were just the ticket. Pete set

141

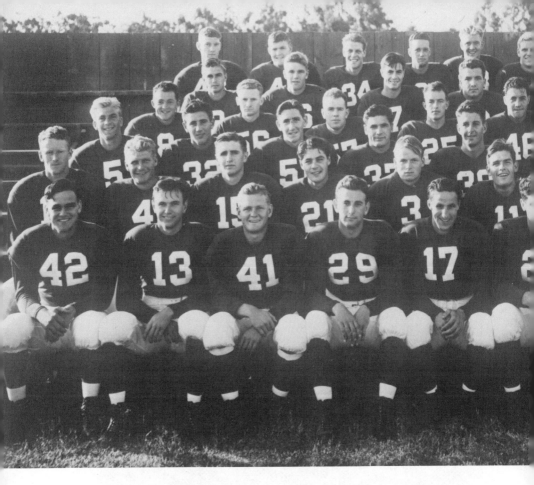

tongues wagging immediately, and Hugh proved many times that he was the most underrated member of the backfield. Pete was an excellent runner, but was miscast in a wing formation because he couldn't pass.

"Ends had to be good one on one blockers and able to hang onto a pass. I stumbled onto three very fine ends in Stan Graff, Fred Meyer, and Clem Tomerlin. Tackles had to be effective in one on one situations and have the lateral mobility to pull and cross block and have the speed to get downfield. Finding Bruno Banducci, John Warnecke, and Ed Stamm waiting for me didn't hurt a bit.

"Guards had to be fast enough to pull out and lead the backs on both off-tackle and wide plays. Dick Palmer was a peach, and for the other spot I converted a sophomore blocking back, Chuck Taylor. He developed fairly fast. In the modern T the center becomes a full blocker since he keeps his head up on a blind snap to the quarterback, a big advantage over the forma-

1940 Stanford varsity, 10-0 Wow Boys. Left to right, front row, Ken Robesky (42), Frank Albert (13), Stan Graff (41), Hugh Gallarneau (29), Pete Kmetovic (17), Norm Standlee (22), Jack Warnecke (31), Art Meiners (27), and Bill Willard (23).

tions requiring a long pass with the center looking between his legs. He had to be quick enough to block left, right, and straight ahead. Vic Lindskog was a great one and with Doug Stahle to back him up we had few worries. A hot first string alone is not enough. There must be a minimum number of talented reserves to spell them."

No one had seen the T formation so there was a lot of skepticism about it at the start of the 1940 season. Shaughnessy, himself, had some doubts during spring practice when the varsity failed to show much against the freshmen.

"I remember a short scrimmage with the freshman team a week before we were going to open the 1940 season when we didn't do much against them. We about got a standoff," Frankie Albert recalled. "Starting with USF we didn't know what we had, nor did they. The first six games our opponents were favored to win. The writers thought any moment we were going to collapse. USF was heavily favored, but from there we went

143

on to an undefeated season."

"It was a lot of fun coming off a losing year," Albert said. "The T seemed to suit our talents at that time. Pete Kmetovic and I had been playing the same position in 1939, bouncing from first to third string. Pete could run, but couldn't handle the passing too well. I could handle the passing a little bit, but couldn't run. The best tailback of the bunch was Jack 'Moon' Mullin. He could both run and pass. When Shaughnessy arrived the T seemed to suit both Pete and me, and Hugh Gallarneau and Norm Standlee. In fairness to 'Tiny' Thornhill though, we had a good nucleus of a line coming up from the frosh in 1940.

"Clark Shaughnessy was such an innovator, and kept bringing new wrinkles into the formation like the man in motion, this and that. Teams just weren't equipped to defense us. You could call Shaughnessy a strict disciplinarian. He was a man that commanded a lot of respect from you. Some of the sportswriters had come up with some nicknames for him, and I remember his opening talk to the team. He gathered us together and introduced his assistants and then he said 'I'm Coach or Mr. Shaughnessy, not "Soup,"' one of the names the writers had used. Shaughnessy was a most refreshing person. He was a very positive thinker and had a job to do. After all, we were a bunch of losers, more or less."

Shaughnessy also was considered a loser, his Chicago team having finished the 1939 season with a 2-6 record that included losses to Michigan 85-0, Ohio State 61-0, and Harvard 61-0. He had lined up one of the finest staffs of assistants ever assembled at Stanford with Marchie Schwartz, former Notre Dame All America halfback who had coached at Creighton, and Phil Bengston, ex-Minnesota All America tackle, joining Jim Lawson who was retained from the Thornhill staff, and "Husky" Hunt. He also had Bernie Masterson, quarterback from the Chicago Bears, to teach the quarterbacks the fine points of the T formation during spring drills.

Stanford opened its season against the University of San Francisco in the second half of a doubleheader at Kezar Stadium in San Francisco. Utah played Santa Clara in the first game and Mac Speedie, later to become a star end in professional football with the Cleveland Browns, was a member of the Utah team. Speedie was in the showers when one of his teammates who had dressed in a hurry came rushing into the locker room and said: "Hey, get out here. There's the dangdest forma-

144

Frank Albert, 1940-41 All America quarterback. Suited to T.

tion going on out there you've ever seen.''

Stanford was a 10-7 underdog to USF on that September 28 afternoon when the Indians unveiled their new T formation and launched their undefeated season with a 28-0 win over the Dons. "We put Kmetovic in motion and no one on the USF defense would move," Albert recalled. "I took the ball from center and we had a little quick pass that was almost a lateral to Kmetovic. He would take it over his shoulder and had quick speed so he faked to cut in and would go outside. With his speed he'd make what today would be no gain or a loser into a first down or a 30-40 yard run just on his ability. And Gallarneau the same way. It's hard to believe teams didn't defense better."

Gallarneau gained 17 yards on a man in motion pass play and Standlee added 20 yards to set up Stanford's first score. Other touchdowns were scored by Eric Armstrong, a substitute for Kmetovic, on a 37-yard sprint through left guard, Kmetovic on a 60-yard punt return, and Standlee.

Southern California was undefeated in 17 straight games and had won the Pacific Coast championship the past two years when it ran into Stanford in the fifth game of the year. Three of the Trojan backs were ranked in the top nine in the conference in average gains, Bob People, Bobby Robertson, and Jack Banta all averaging five yards per carry. Kmetovic of Stanford was fourth with a 6.7 average and Gallarneau sixth.

Warnecke injured his shoulder in practice on Monday and was replaced by Ed Stamm, a sophomore. But the Stanford defense proved most impregnable as the Indians registered a 21-7 victory. The only Trojan score came in the second quarter when field judge George Hicks called interference against Gallarneau on a pass from Ray Woods intended for Joe Davis, giving USC a first down on the one yard line.

Other Trojan threats were stalled on the Stanford 28, 23, and 15 in the first half, but USC did not have possession of the ball in Stanford territory in the second half.

"Shaughnessy was a great man and a great coach," said Albert. "We won several games because he devised a new play which caught the defense flat-footed. One such occasion occurred in the 1940 USC game when he noticed Banta coming up to stop Standlee on end runs. So he sent in a pass play to take advantage of Banta the next time we had the ball."

Kmetovic took a pass from Albert for a 61-yard touchdown that gave Stanford a 7-0 lead in the first quarter. "We called a fake end run," Kmetovic said. "Gallarneau went in motion and blocked in the end, and I faked like I was going to block Banta, making it look like a developing end run. Then I got behind him and got six points." After moving past Banta, Kmetovic took the pass from Albert on the USC 35 and outran Peoples, Ed Dempsey, and Floyd Phillips to the end zone. USC's second quarter touchdown tied the score at 7-7, and it stayed that way until late in the fourth quarter.

Three pass interceptions by the Trojans cut short Stanford threats in the second half. Peoples intercepted an Albert pass on the goal line to stop one drive, picked off a throw by Armstrong on the 15 to halt another, and Banta grabbed another of Albert's throws on the 15. With four and a half minutes remaining, Stanford's passing game finally began to click, and the Indians started a march from their own 20.

Albert hit Al Cole for a 24-yard gain to midfield and then passed 25 yards to Tomerlin. Next, despite a strong rush by Al Krueger and Bob Jones, Albert got off a pass to Meyer for 21 yards to the Trojan four, and Standlee scored on the next play. Albert's conversion gave Stanford a 14-7 lead.

With time growing short Southern California took to the air in a bid to achieve a tying score. Woods faded into his own end zone to pass but was rushed by Al Norberg. Albert inter-

146

cepted the throw on the 13 and with a block from Gallarneau ambled for the final touchdown.

Stanford held only a 144 to 113 edge in rushing yardage, but the Indians completed 10 of 24 passes for an additional 208 yards while the Trojans had only one completion, and that was on the pass interference. Each side had three interceptions. Howard Jones, USC's coach, called Stanford "more versatile than the 'Vowing Sophomores,' and just as effective as either Duke or Tennessee," the two teams the Trojans had beaten in the Rose Bowl the two previous years.

"USC's defense that year had a very big line that would hit and slide," Albert said. "They wouldn't come across and commit where you could trap them, and it made our passing a little easier because those big devils weren't back in our backfield. But it really cut off our quick openers, probably more effectively than any other team. The quarterback always was pretty well instructed with a game plan going into the game, but Coach Shaughnessy was pretty quick to spot weaknesses in a defense and he sent in a lot of help."

Standlee had his greatest game of the year as the Indians defeated UCLA 20-14, and Stanford went into its game with Washington with the conference championship at stake. Both

Norm Standlee, 1938-39-40 fullback. No. 1 offensive threat.

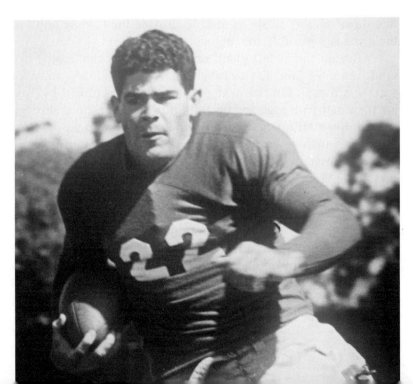

teams were undefeated in league play and the Huskies had lost only to Minnesota in its opener, 19-14. Washington boasted the best defensive record, but Stanford was a 7-5 favorite in the pregame odds. Things went bad for the Indians right at the start, however, as Standlee went to the sidelines with an injured ankle.

"When Standlee came off the field our No. 1 offensive threat was gone," said Shaughnessy. "He took with him our bread-and-butter plays. But the boys got their heads together and Albert and Gallarneau decided that Gallarneau would carry all of Standlee's plays from his regular right half position. They ran off these plays successfully and we went on to win the game. That shows Gallarneau's natural versatility and adaptability."

Washington took a 7-0 lead in the second quarter when Jack Stackpool romped 55 yards before Kmetovic caught him at the Stanford 36. On third down Dean McAdams passed to Earl Younglove on the 15 and he ran the rest of the way for a touchdown. The Huskies increased their lead to 10-0 in the third quarter when John Mizen kicked a field goal from the 16. Washington got the opportunity when Lindskog, playing with a bandaged hand, centered the ball over Albert's head on a fourth down kicking situation, and Albert was smeared on the 19.

A few minutes later the Huskies again were in Stanford territory as the result of a short punt, but Chuck Taylor stopped this threat almost single handed to provide the turning point of the game and possibly the season.

Gleason ran at left guard on the same play that earlier had produced a big gain. Taylor caught him, but he slipped away for a nine-yard gain. On the next play Gleason was caught by Taylor for a half-yard loss, and on third down Taylor sliced through to pull down McAdams short of the first down. Stackpool tried again on fourth down, was spilled by Taylor, and Stanford took over on downs on its own 31.

"The story was developed more than it was worth," says Taylor. "But it just happened that I had just come off an ankle injury, and I really couldn't run. I had a pretty well wrapped ankle which kept me from doing much except for playing my position and protecting a territory of five or six yards. By virtue of being semi-crippled and confined to a small area that particular day, I got pretty lucky because I couldn't chase myself and make a lot of mistakes and run out of there. We were behind

Chuck Taylor, player, coach, athletic director.

10-0 and they were on another march when they ran three straight plays right at me. Of course I wasn't about to get out of there, because I couldn't, and we were lucky enough to stop them and that sort of was a turning point. I don't think it was the turning point, but at least it stimulated the team and from then on Frank and the other guys did a helluva job scoring three touchdowns to win it."

After stopping the Huskies, Stanford scored in three plays. There were three and a half minutes left in the third quarter when Kmetovic went in motion to the left and took a pass from Albert on the Washington 47. The fleet Indian halfback cut

149

inside Rudy Mucha and Bill Means and then outran Bill Sloan and McAdams to complete the 56-yard scoring play.

Late in the period Gleason, pursued by Stamm and Taylor, threw a pass intended for Younglove. But Albert intercepted on the Washington 46. Albert's passing and Gallarneau's running produced a touchdown to put Stanford ahead 14-10. Kmetovic added the final score when he intercepted a McAdams pass on the 43 and outran five Huskies down the left sideline. Gallarneau carried the ball 25 times and averaged 4 yards per carry while Kmetovic averaged 3.9 yards for 15 carries.

The Indians completed their first undefeated season since 1926 with a 13-7 victory over California as Taylor's outstanding defensive play helped blank the Bears until the final 16 seconds. Taylor's steady pounding on Harlan Gough, the California center, finally resulted in a bad snap over the head of Orv Hatcher and helped Stanford gain field position. Gallarneau, with blocks by Taylor and Standlee, ran for 22 yards and several plays later Kmetovic took a pitch from Albert at left end and, with blocks from Stamm and Taylor, scooted 20 yards to the California one before he was caught by Morley Mathewson. Kmetovic scored on the first play of the second quarter.

Another bad snap by Gough gave Stanford the ball on the Bears' 35 and led to the Indians' second score. Gallarneau accounted for 11 yards and Albert added 12 on a play on which he appeared to fake to Vucinich, but kept the ball and circled right end. Shaughnessy said later Vucinich was supposed to get the ball, but was overanxious and missed the handoff. Gallarneau got the touchdown from the two yard line.

Carl Hoberg intercepted an Albert pass on the California 43 and appeared headed for a touchdown, but was caught by Albert and Jack Francis at the five and stopped on the one after a 56-yard return. Taylor stopped Stan Donohue for no gain on the first play, and Stamm crashed through to drop Jack McQuary for a one-yard loss on second down with help from Meyer and Banducci. McQuary failed to gain again on third down, and on fourth down Hatcher was knocked down at the one on an attempt at right end.

Albert was a unanimous All America choice at quarterback, being named by the All America Board, Associated Press, United Press, International News Service, and *Collier's*. While Albert collected the top honors, the rest of the cast was worthy of recognition. Kmetovic, Gallarneau, and Standlee were outstanding in the backfield. Vic Lindskog anchored the center of the line and his vicious blocking helped clear the way for the backs, along with Taylor and Dick Palmer at guards. Bruno Banducci and Ed Stamm were outstanding at tackle and Stan Graff and Fred Meyer were a pair of top ends.

"Clark Shaughnessy had a diametrically opposite personality to 'Tiny' Thornhill, under whom I had played the previous year," said Hugh Gallarneau. "Thornhill, a hail-fellow, well-met type of an individual, exerted no discipline nor provided any constructive leadership for his squad. Shaughnessy, on the other hand, was a self disciplined, highly intelligent leader who, by his own example, made players and assistant coaches alike follow his leadership willingly and gratefully. An example of his ability: he took the 1939 squad almost to a man, who had lost every conference game and had beaten only Dartmouth in a non-conference game, and in 1940 molded them into an undefeated team which culminated the season by defeating Nebraska in the 1941 Rose Bowl game 21-13."

Indians Sell T Formation

Shaughnessy and his T formation had attracted a lot of attention on the Pacific Coast, but Stanford's appearance in the 1941 Rose Bowl sold the system to the entire nation and revolutionized college football. "The nationwide trend was toward fast, precision football, and this game, probably more than any other, dramatized the new system and the ushering in of a new era with great forcefulness to the country at large," "Cyclone" Covey stated in his book *The Wow Boys.*

Stanford wound up No. 2 in the national rankings behind Minnesota, and since the Big Ten had a ruling which prohibited members from playing in post season bowl games at that time, Al Masters selected Nebraska to oppose the Indians. The Cornhuskers were ranked seventh, and had lost only to Minnesota in their opening game, 13-7.

Shaughnessy later called Stanford's 21-13 victory over Nebraska one of the 12 greatest games in football history to that time. "The 1941 Rose Bowl game was an important one in the course of football," he said, "because that was the game that sold the T formation—the modern T style of offense to school and college football. Prior to this game the system had been regarded as too intricate and too complicated for use by school and college teams. The performance by the Stanford boys in their first year with this system proved it could be worked. Then everybody accepted it. That's why I contend this was an important game—one of the most important games of modern football."

Stanford didn't know too much about Nebraska, but Shaughnessy was worried about Butch Luther, who had made a

Hugh Gallarneau, underrated in Wow Boy backfield.

lot of yardage and scored a lot of points for the Huskers while playing at wingback, usually on reverses that produced long gains. Accordingly, Shaughnessy altered his defense to protect the outside against the reverses, moving the weak side tackle out and splitting the guards a little wider. In the excitement of the early moments of the game, however, the guards reverted to their season-long habits and played in closer, leaving big holes which Col. "Biff" Jones of Nebraska quickly spotted and effectively took advantage of, and the Huskers marched downfield for a touchdown in the first three minutes of the game.

"As a sophomore, it was an exciting period of time for me," said Chuck Taylor, who later returned to the Rose Bowl as coach of the 1951 Stanford team, and as athletic director when the Indians played in 1971 and 1972. "It looked like we were in trouble at the beginning. I can remember playing in the middle of the line, and my technique was that I was always kind of an aggressive guard and always got across the line of scrimmage. Under certain circumstances this can be good, but under others it can be a little dangerous with all the traps the single wing used in those days, and boy, they really wiped me out on a number of occasions on traps. I think I probably caused the first touchdown they made, but it turned out all right as time went on."

Hugh Gallarneau, now associated with Hart Shaffner and Marx Clothes in Chicago, also remembers a humorous incident following the Nebraska touchdown. "As we walked by the bench, preparatory to receiving Nebraska's kickoff, Frank Albert noted Shaughnessy's extremely agitated condition. Frank quickly spoke up and said: 'Shake it off, coach, we haven't had the ball yet.'"

Stanford changed its defense to stop Vike Francis and late in the first quarter Kmetovic, who had produced 35 yards in two plays in an earlier series, ran a punt back 24 yards to the Nebraska 47. From here Stanford scored in four plays. Kmetovic dashed 29 yards behind the blocking of Standlee and Ban-

Stanford prepares for 1941 Rose Bowl Game with Nebraska. Left to right in the line are Fred Meyer, Bruno Banducci, Dick Palmer, Vic Lindskog, Chuck Taylor, Ed Stamm, and Stan Graff. The back-field: Hugh Gallarneau, Norm Standlee, Frank Albert, and Pete Kmetovic.

ducci to the 18. A pass to Gallarneau lost two, but Kmetovic picked up nine on the same play he had run earlier, and then on a well executed quick-opener at center, Gallarneau covered the remaining 11 yards. Good fakes by Albert, Kmetovic, and Standlee helped make the play work, along with blocks by Palmer, Lindskog, and Taylor.

Early in the second quarter Herman Rohrig tried a quick kick on third down, but Lindskog broke through to block it. However, Nebraska recovered on the 15 and safely punted out. Stanford marched to the Nebraska nine before being halted, and Albert's field goal attempt from a difficult angle on the 16 yard line was wide.

Nebraska regained the lead after recovering a fumbled punt when Kmetovic lost Rohrig's kick in the sun, and Allen Zikmund recovered for the Cornhuskers on the Stanford 33. Rohrig faded back and passed to Zikmund, who caught the ball on the nine behind Gallarneau and beat the Indian defender to the goal line. Taylor blocked the conversion attempt.

Stanford took the lead before the half on a 40-yard pass play from Albert to Gallarneau. Assistant coach Jim Lawson had spotted a weakness in the Nebraska defense and relayed the information to Shaughnessy with instruction to call 63 flare pass 26. Gallarneau went in motion to the left as a wingback and both ends raced downfield, fanning out to the sidelines. Gallarneau moved slowly in an arc towards the middle and took a wobbly 30-yard pass from Albert on the 19, eluded Rohrig and Zikmund, and picked up the touchdown. Albert's PAT put the Indians in front 14-13.

Zikmund took the second half kickoff on his own 15 and returned 46 yards to the Stanford 39 before finally being pulled down by Kmetovic. Graff smeared Zikmund for a 14-yard loss, but pass interference on Kmetovic gave Nebraska a first down on the 34. The Huskers got another first down on the 23, but could advance no farther, and a fourth down field goal attempt fell short on the Stanford seven.

Stanford's depth was becoming a serious problem. Shaughnessy had played everyone more liberally than in any previous close game, but Nebraska had two full teams of almost equal ability, and Jones had rested his first team through most of the second quarter. But Stanford had Kmetovic and Nebraska didn't have a defense to stop him. The Indians had a third down

Bruno Banducci, 1940-42 tackle.

and 19 situation on their own 27 in the third quarter when Kmetovic took a lateral from Albert, evaded Francis and Luther, and rambled 43 yards to the Nebraska 30. Standlee was out of the game with his head and ear bandaged and would not return, and Gallarneau also was on the sidelines. At the 15 Albert underhanded a pass to Kmetovic who was flanked near the sideline, and Pete went to the one before he was tackled by Luther. Without Standlee, however, Stanford was unable to punch the ball over the goal.

Hopp punted out from deep in his end zone, but Tomerlin and Meyer applied a hard rush along with Stamm and Banducci. Taylor and Lindskog piled up the left side to keep several of the Huskers' linemen from following the kick. As a result of the pressure, Hopp's punt carried only to the Nebraska 39 where Kmetovic took the kick near the left sidelines.

Pete ran four or five steps to his left as Armstrong blocked out Preston and then abruptly reversed his field at the 36 and started to his right, picking up speed and blockers. Kmetovic circled back to the 45 to get running room and enable his team-mates to get in position to block and then set sail for the goal line. Stanford players did a fantastic job. At one time there wasn't a red-shirted Nebraskan on his feet. Dick Palmer belted Francis with such force that the big fullback did a complete somersault. Luther was the last defender between Kmetovic and the goal, and Meyer took him out at the five.

"Biff" Jones, the Nebraska coach, said later, "I don't think I saw a Nebraska man on his feet on that run." Glenn Presnell, Nebraska backfield coach, called it "the greatest play I've ever seen." Shaughnessy called the punt return the greatest he had seen from the standpoint of complete team response.

As far as scoring was concerned that was the ball game, although Stanford had a couple of other opportunities. Lindskog blocked a punt on the Nebraska 16 but the Indians were unable to capitalize on this chance. Later they had another opportunity on a pass interception at the Husker 31 but again had no success.

Stanford wound up with 347 net yards to Nebraska's 128 and completed seven of 14 passes while Nebraska completed only three of 14 and had four intercepted. Kmetovic accounted for 141 yards on 14 carries with Gallarneau adding 89 on 17.

Shaughnessy was named Coach of the Year, and Albert was selected unanimous All America, and Gallarneau made the

NEA All America squad. Albert, Kmetovic, Standlee, and Meyer made the All Coast team with Banducci, Taylor, Lindskog, and Gallarneau on the second team.

Following the Rose Bowl game Jones remarked: "Tell Clark Shaughnessy I'll buy him 120 acres of fine corn land if he'll tell me where we can get a Frankie Albert. That kid had too much kick and too much noodle for us."

Kmetovic, who was named "player of the game," described his punt return for a touchdown more of a "run from fright" than anything else. "I had no place to go," he said. "We didn't have set punt return plays in those days and didn't set up well. Because we were going both ways we didn't have time to spend working on special return plays. I just happened to pick up everyone on the way back across the field. Albert blocked in both directions on that play."

Albert, however, takes little credit. "They said I got two great blocks on the play," he said. "Actually I got blind-sided both times. Boy, that Kmetovic could go. He was a player. That Standlee was a great one too. He maybe played his best football, if not with us, the first year he was with the Bears. At 230 he could run the ends, was a good blocker and faker, and backed up the line. Gallarneau got us some super yards. You know he didn't play any football in high school. He came to Stanford as a boxer.

"Chuck Taylor said that when he coached he got out the films of our games and checked the statistics. We were supposed to be a wide open club. Heck, we only threw the ball nine or 10 times a game. Our game plan was that if we had the ball inside the 20 at the start of the game we might punt on first down. Inside the 30, punt on second down, and always punted on third down until the game developed and you either had a lead or were behind in the score."

Albert was a consensus All America, being named on the All America Board, Associated Press, United Press, International News Service, and Collier's teams. Standlee was a second team choice on the AP.

Pete Kmetovic, "Player of Game" in 1941 Rose Bowl

159

Too Many Cogs Missing

Despite his personnel losses Shaughnessy expected to come up with another undefeated team in 1941, but his hopes were dashed by losses to Oregon State, Washington State, and California. His 1940 team had been lucky to escape serious injuries to key men, with Standlee and Warnecke the only two to miss appreciable time. The 1941 team was good, but unlucky, particularly with regard to injuries. This, plus the loss of Standlee, Gallarneau, and Graff through graduation played a big role in the three defeats.

"Kmetovic was injured and Lindskog was hurt, and neither came back to their 1940 performance," said Albert. "But the loss of Standlee and Gallarneau was the big thing. Shaughnessy put in some new wrinkles, putting Kmetovic at fullback, and using big backs for quick poppers. But Pete got hurt in the Oregon State game, which we lost, and then we lost our last two games."

The loss to Oregon State at Corvallis was the first defeat for Stanford in 14 games under Shaughnessy, and also marked the first time the Indians had been held scoreless since he had taken over as head coach and installed the T. The game was played in the rain on a muddy field and that slowed down the swift flanker movement of Stanford's man-in-motion.

The Beavers chalked up a 10-0 victory after a late tackle put Kmetovic out of the game with a leg injury. Oregon State drove to the Stanford eight, and Warren Simas kicked a 26-yard field goal in the first seven minutes of the game to give the Beavers a 3-0 lead. Quentin Greenough, OSU center, pounced on a Bobby Mitchell fumble on the Stanford 14 in the third period, and eight plays later Bob Dethman scored from the one foot line to make the final score 10-0 as Lon Stiner became the first coach to stop Stanford. Chuck Taylor was outstanding on defense for Stanford, repeatedly stopping Oregon State plays to his side.

Shaughnessy gave full credit to Oregon State. "It was definitely the better team today," he said. Stanford had three good scoring chances smeared by the Beaver defense and penalties.

Stanford beat Washington 13-7 at Seattle in one of its top performances of the season despite having two touchdowns called back in the fourth quarter because of penalties. Albert went back to pass in the second quarter, but could not find an open receiver. So he took off on a zig-zag 47-yard run to the Huskies' seven yard line with the help of a block by Ed Stamm. Milt Vucinich accounted for the Indians' first touchdown from the three.

Later in the quarter Taylor broke through to recover Bob Barrett's fumble on the Washington three, and Willard Sheller inched across on third down for the touchdown that proved to be the winning score. In the fourth period Kmetovic got loose on a 58-yard punt return but the score was nullified by a clipping penalty. Later Albert threw a 39-yard pass to Fred Meyer but this touchdown was wiped out by an offsides penalty. Ernie Steele's running kept Washington in contention.

"I'll always remember that game," mused Albert. "The points on the game were about even. We never did any betting in those days, but most of the players had sold the comp tickets they received and decided to bet the money with a fellow at a malt shop near the hotel where we were staying downtown.

"Coach Shaughnessy never could figure out how he had such great team spirit for that game. He probably thought he must have given a terrific fight talk. We'd make a first down and when I'd look over at the bench everyone would be jumping up and down and cheering. Freddie Meyer, our end, caught a couple of passes that day that were called back so the game remained pretty tight, and pretty much in question right up to the gun. We did win the ball game, but it was a typical Washington game.

"So, we're on the bus and on our way back to the hotel, and everyone is happy, but nervous about the money. We wanted to get it before we left town. The malt shop was a couple of blocks from the hotel so somebody asked if we could get off and get a malt. Coach Shaughnessy said: 'Sure, the walk will be good for you, but don't spoil your appetite with milk shakes and all that stuff.'

"So, the whole ball club piles out of the bus, and went in to get their envelopes. That made me think a bit. I know betting's no good, but that enthusiasm we had that day was really something."

One of the highlights of the season was a 13-0 victory over Southern California before 87,000 in the Los Angeles Coliseum. All of the scoring was crowded into the first quarter and came after Stanford had missed its first opportunity on a fumble after Kmetovic, Vucinich, and Eric Armstrong had advanced the ball to the USC nine.

On the next series Armstrong, a 165-pound speedster from Portland, Oregon, swung around left end and raced 69 yards for a touchdown. Later in the period Loren La Prade recovered a fumble by the Trojans' Bob Robertson on the USC 38. Albert passed to Arnold Meiners to set up the score by Sheller from the one. Stanford gained 400 yards from rushing alone that afternoon, and USC got past the Indians' 45 only once, advancing to the 18 where a fumble stopped the threat.

Santa Clara always gave Stanford trouble and the Indians had problems with the Broncos this season, too. Kmetovic was back in action and turned in some sensational running to spark Stanford to a 27-7 win. Al Santucci of the Broncos kept the Indians pretty well bottled up with his kicking until Albert faked a punt and Kmetovic ran 32 yards to the 40 to get the Cardinals out of a hole. A few plays later, from the Santa Clara 45, Kmetovic swept around end and with a block from La Prade went all the way for Stanford's first touchdown.

Santa Clara tied it 7-7 on a second quarter pass from Ken Casanega to Alyn Beals. Center Eddie Forrest recovered a fumble on the Stanford 39 to put the Broncos in business. A 32-yard pass to Beals helped advance the ball to the three, and it took another Casanega to Beals toss to get the ball over the goal line.

Buck Fawcett accounted for the second Stanford touchdown, intercepting a Bronco pass to give Stanford the ball on its own 16. On the next play Fawcett went off the weak side on the same play on which Kmetovic had scored, and romped 84 yards for a touchdown. Although the Broncos had the ball a big share of the time and piled up a lot of yardage, Santa Clara was unable to do any more scoring. However, Stanford added a pair of second half touchdowns. Kmetovic intercepted a pass and ran 45 yards to the Santa Clara 25 to set up the first. Albert ran for 10 yards, and then after a play lost a yard, passed to Meyer for 16 yards and the score. Later Albert passed to Bob Mastin for 43 yards to the 14 to set the stage for a final score.

Shaughnessy was "scared to death" of Coach Tex Oliver's University of Oregon team in the season opener, and it turned out he had good reason. Albert ran and passed the Indians to a 19-15 win, but it took a short punt that carried only to the Oregon 19 to help produce the victory. Stanford looked like the same team as in 1940. It had good passing and a good defense, but it lacked the scoring punch. Oregon led 7-6 at the half, and 13-12 in the third quarter before the Indians got the ball at the Ducks' 19 as the result of a bad punt.

Albert faded back to pass, but was trapped as he ran to his left. Reversing his field he picked up a block by Meyer, who took out two men, and ran to the Oregon one. Frank lost three yards on a fumble, but then scored on the next play. Oregon scored on a 50-yard pass from Curtis Mecham to Tom Roblin. Stanford failed to take advantage of a 63-yard run by Kmetovic, but later scored when Albert whipped a 15-yard pass to Meyer and Vucinich punched over from the four.

Stanford was listless and lacked its usual snap and precision for its game with Washington State. Kmetovic had been sick all week and also had an injured leg. It all added up to a 14-13 loss to the Cougars, a defeat which put Oregon State in the driver's seat as far as the conference race was concerned. Dale Gentry and Nick Suseoff, Washington State's two great ends, gave Albert a battering all afternoon, giving him little time to get off his passes.

Washington State drove to the Stanford one early in the game, but the Indians knocked the Cougars back to the three and took the ball on downs. When Stanford was forced to punt, however, Billy Sewell ran the ball back to the 25 to present another threat to the Cardinals' defense. Taylor threw Sewell for a 10-yard loss, but Stanford was offsides on the play, and after the penalty, Bill Holmes ran 14 yards on a reverse around right end for a touchdown. The try for the extra point was blocked, but Sewell scooped up the ball and ran for the extra point which was to prove so important later on.

A 37-yard run by Kmetovic to the Washington State 33, with a block from Taylor, gave Stanford an opportunity which looked even brighter when Albert's fourth down pass to Meyer gained 15 yards to the Cougar 11. But Stanford lost the ball on downs on the two. Sewell got off a short punt, but the Indians also failed to score on this occasion.

A 32-yard pass from Albert to Kmetovic produced a Stanford score in the third quarter and the Indians spent the rest of the period fighting off Washington State threats. Earl Brennel returned the kickoff following Stanford's score 66 yards to the Indians' 29, but Stanford halted this drive at the eight. The Cougars had other drives stopped at the 7 and 10 before Bechman recovered a fumble on the Stanford 22. The Cougars capitalized on this chance for the winning touchdown.

Albert was shaken up as he completed a 33-yard pass to Al Cole to the WSU 21. Cole took over at quarterback and got the touchdown as Bob Mitchell punched in from the three.

California handed Stanford its second shutout of the campaign in the Big Game, winning 16-0 as the Bears, led by All America tackle Bob Reinhard, repeatedly outcharged the Stanford line. Reinhard turned in a great defensive game and accounted for California's second touchdown when he recovered the ball in the end zone after Glen Whalen had blocked Cole's kick in the fourth quarter.

The Bears got two points on a safety earlier in the period when Jean Whitter blocked another punt. This time the ball rolled through the end zone and out of play.

Stanford's deepest penetration into California territory was to the Bears' 18 late in the game after Jack Francis had intercepted a pass at midfield. Albert passed 26 yards to Meyer to reach the 24, but the Indians were able to add only another six yards. Earlier Fawcett had broken a 30-yard run to the Stanford 48 in a bid to ignite a spark in the Stanford offense, but the Indians were stopped before they could advance much farther.

The Bears scored on their first offensive play in the opening minutes of the game when Al Derian, behind great blocking, swept around left end, reversed his field, and ran 46 yards for a touchdown with only 1:38 of the game played. That was the knockout punch as far as Stanford was concerned, although Reinhard also had something to say about it. The California defense held Stanford to a net 80 yards rushing and 45 by passing as Albert had his only off day in two years, and Kmetovic, who was used sparingly, was ineffective because of an injured leg. The Indians gained 177 yards on the ground, but were thrown for losses totaling 97 yards.

Shaughnessy informed Stanford officials the day after Pearl Harbor that he was leaving to accept a position as coach and athletic director at the University of Maryland. He was interested only in coaching and felt that Stanford, like many other schools, would be abandoning athletics for the duration of the war. As had been the case at Chicago, he did not want to stay around to fill a position in the physical education department.

Cards Finish Strong

Marchie Schwartz, the former Notre Dame All America halfback who had come to Stanford as an assistant under Shaughnessy, inherited the head coaching job in 1942 and held it during two of the most difficult periods in Stanford football history—the prewar and postwar eras.

"We had a great line in 1942 with players like Chuck Taylor, Bruno Banucci, Hank Norberg, and Jim Cox, but we were a little weak in the backfield," said Schwartz as he looked back on his coaching days while seated in his office on the 28th floor of the Trans-America building in San Francisco. "Ray Hammett had played only a little bit behind Frank Albert the year before, and we lost our first three games. Then we went right down the line after he got some experience and wound up beating St. Mary's Navy Pre-Flight, a team of experienced college players, at the end of the season. Once Hammett found himself he was great. We also had Buck Fawcett, who was a great and hard runner and was responsible for a big role in our win over California.

"I had learned the T formation pretty well under Shaughnessy. He spent a lot of time with the staff teaching us about it. The T was so new that when the war was over I conducted a three-day clinic at Stanford for high school and junior college coaches, and also went to Utah and put on a clinic. Jack Curtice was there at the time.

"We opened the 1942 season against Washington State and lost 6-0," Schwartz said. "Babe Hollingbery was coaching then and had a great back by the name of Bob Kennedy. We just couldn't do much with him."

Stanford was a 10-7 favorite over the Cougars, but only four pass interceptions helped the Indians escape a worse defeat. The only scoring of the day came in the first quarter when Jay Stoves, who had just been reinstated by conference czar Edwin Atherton, flipped a five-yard pass to Earl Brennels who ran another 20 yards for a touchdown. Suseoff again was a defensive standout for the Cougars, while Kennedy ran for 109 yards to lead the offense. Fawcett accounted for 45 yards for Stanford.

Stanford took on Santa Clara in its second game in Kezar Stadium and dropped a 14-6 decision as Jess Freitas hit Alyn Beals on a 59-yard touchdown pass in the first quarter and hooked up with the same receiver in the fourth period on a 16-yard scoring toss. The Indians got their touchdown on a 35-yard screen pass to Fawcett after earlier failing to score when they lost the ball on downs at the Bronco two yard line. Schwartz moved his backs around in a bid to find a combination that could move the ball consistently, but without much success.

Notre Dame overpowered the Indians 27-0 the next week at South Bend. "Pat O'Brien was on the bench with me that day," Schwartz recalled. "He had followed Notre Dame a lot after playing the role of Knute Rockne in the movie, *Spirit Of Notre Dame*. The score was 14-0 at the half and as we walked to the dressing room, Pat said to me: 'Now's the time to tell them about the Gipper.' Angelo Bertelli had a great passing day that day, completing 14 of 20 passes and throwing for four touchdowns. We outgained them on the ground as Buck Fawcett had a great day for us and made most of our rushing yardage."

Bertelli threw a 36-yard scoring pass to Bob Dove and a 16-yard pass to Joe Limont for second quarter touchdowns and connected with George Murphy for 26 yards, and Bob Livingston for 15, for scores in the second half. At one stretch he completed nine straight passes and wound up gaining 233 yards through the air during the afternoon. A Hammett to Norberg pass and Fawcett's running carried Stanford to the Notre Dame 30 for the Indians' most serious threat, but the drive was halted by an interception.

Stanford won six of its last seven games and got started on the winning trail with a 54-7 victory over Idaho. Fawcett scored three touchdowns for the Cardinals, one coming on a 19-yard run. Ben Morrison tallied twice, once on a 32-yard run and the

Marchamont (Marchie) Schwartz, difficult period.

other time on a 39-yard pass from Bob Andrews. Hammett set up another score with a 52-yard return of a pass interception to the Vandals' 18.

Because of war-time restrictions on travel Stanford played its game with Southern California in Kezar Stadium and pulled off a 14-6 triumph over the Trojans. The highlight of the game came in the third quarter when Taylor, who wound up as a consensus All America, broke through and stole the ball from a surprised Mickey McCardle and ran 35 yards for what proved to be the winning touchdown.

The Indians collected their other score on the final play of the first quarter after Vucinich had recovered a Jim Hardy fumble on the USC 35. Fawcett contributed a big lift as he followed Taylor's blocking for a 15-yard gain to the five. After a penalty set Stanford back five yards, Fawcett scored on fourth down from the one.

Southern California did not score until the last 35 seconds of the game when Paul Taylor passed 13 yards to Walt Jacobsmeyer.

Taylor, Norberg, and Roger Laverty outcharged the USC line all afternoon to bottle up the Trojan offense.

Only a 21-7 loss to UCLA kept the Indians out of the Rose Bowl game. The Bruins, who lost to Oregon, earned the bid on the basis of their win over Stanford. Bob Waterfield, who had suffered through a 33-0 defeat the year before as a sophomore quarterback, unlimbered a sharp passing attack to direct the Bruins to a win that could have been even more decisive except for penalties which stopped several other UCLA drives.

Stanford turned a fumble recovery into a touchdown seven plays after the opening kickoff as Laverty recovered on the Bruin 26 when Ev Riddle bobbled the kickoff. Fawcett and Rock Sheller alternated carrying the ball, with Sheller getting the touchdown. UCLA tied the score in the second quarter as Waterfield hit Al Solari on a 40-yard pass. Later he intercepted a pass and returned to the Stanford 30 to provide another scoring opportunity. Solari caught a pass to reach the eight and Snelling scored. Waterfield passed 24 yards to Vic Smith for a fourth quarter touchdown.

Vucinich stalled another Bruin threat in the third quarter when he intercepted a pass on the Stanford nine. Fawcett was hurt early in the game and the Indians felt his loss. Late in the contest Schwartz sent in a new backfield combination of Art Shipkey, a nephew of Harry Shipkey, former Stanford player, and a member of the Cardinals' coaching staff, Don Zappettini, Ben Morrison, and Bob Andrews. This group moved to the UCLA 13 before a penalty took some of the steam out of the march, which was halted completely when Burr Baldwin recovered a fumble.

Shipkey proved to be a new running threat as Stanford whipped Washington 20-7 in another game played at Kezar. The Huskies scored in the first five minutes of the game, but the

169

Indians came on with touchdowns in each of the last three quarters. Ross Dana intercepted a pass to stop a Washington threat in the fourth quarter and save the game. The score was 13-7 at the time and the Huskies had third down on the three yard line. Bob Erickson shot a pass into the left flat, but Dana picked it off and ran out to the 44 to get Stanford out of a hole. That changed an even-steven game.

Hammett's passing produced a Stanford touchdown in the second quarter. First Bob Hall caught one for 13 yards and then Dave Brown accepted a toss for 26. The drive appeared stalled, however, as the Indians came up with a fourth down on the 26. Hammett gambled on a screen pass to Shipkey, and the play picked up 24 yards to the two, from where Shipkey scored.

A short kick by Erickson that went out of bounds on the Washington 32 led to a second score for the Indians in the third period. On the first play Hammett passed to Laverty, who made the catch at the six and had no trouble getting into the end zone.

Zappettini tallied three touchdowns and romped for 85 yards as the Indians breezed past Oregon State 49-13. Stanford scored three touchdowns in the span of 14 plays in the second quarter. Zappettini carried the ball only five times during the game, but got his touchdowns on runs of 43, 16, and 6 yards. Bob Frisbee added 71 yards and Shipkey 70 as Stanford came up with a well-balanced running attack. Hammett connected with Dave Brown on a 45-yard pass for another Stanford touchdown.

Stanford scored in every quarter in a 26-7 romp over California in what was to be the last Big Game for four years. The Indians abandoned football after the 1942 season and did not resume play until 1946. Zappettini scored Stanford's first touchdown in the opening quarter when he sliced inside right end on a fourth down and eight situation. Norberg gave the Cardinals another scoring opportunity in the second quarter when he outraced John Graves of the Bears to gain possession of the ball on the California 27. The Bears had a first and 10 at their own 45 when the bad snap from center got away from Graves. On the first play Fawcett bolted through tackle for the score.

Norberg put the pressure on Grover Klemmerin the third quarter and the Bear football and track star punted out of bounds on the Cal 48. On the second play Hammett passed to Laverty for 27 yards and he ran another 20 to complete the

47-yard hookup. Dana accounted for the fourth quarter score when he ran 35 yards with a pass interception. Vucinich, Taylor, Stamm, and Banducci played outstanding defensive ball for Stanford.

Merriman Provides Lift

Schwartz, who had returned to private business in the Midwest after the 1942 season, was lured back to Stanford after the war and was greeted by a squad composed of returning veterans and youngsters. Most of them had not played any football for two or three years. No one expected Schwartz to win more than a couple of games, but he came up with a swift backfield headed by Lloyd Merriman, a 197-pound fullback who was compared to Standlee, and wound up with a 6-3-1 record.

"It was difficult to coach after the war," Schwartz said. "We had a lot of veterans. When they wanted to play they played well, but if they didn't want to play it was something else. They had been through a lot. This was a good team. Some of them had played before the war, but they hadn't played for three years. The rest of the teams did well. California and USC had played during the war and both were strong, and UCLA came up with a good team that included a couple of players who had been at Stanford before the war."

Schwartz had acquired a good staff of assistants. Phil Bengston was the line coach while Mal Elward handled the ends. Ray Hammett returned to coach the backs, assisted by Pete Kmetovic. "It was a good staff," said Schwartz. "Anyone good enough to go on and be Vince Lombardi's line coach had to be a good coach, and Bengston was."

Among the 130 players reporting to Schwartz for the start of practice were Fred Boensch, Jim Cox, Bill Hachten, and Dick Madigan, who had played for the Indians in 1942 but had performed for California in 1943 while studying military science at

Berkeley while in the service. Later Hachten had played with the El Toro Marines. Another candidate was a big, rangy center, Dick Flatland, from the Norman, Oklahoma, Navy team. But the key man was Merriman, around whom Schwartz was building his entire offense. Another returnee was Dave Brown, who had played at Stanford in 1942, but earned All-Coast honors at UCLA in 1943 while enrolled in the V-12 program. Although he had earned his A.B. degree under the Navy's accelerated program, the Pacific Coast Conference had ruled such players were entitled to another season of eligibility and Brown hastened to take advantage of the situation.

Stanford romped over Idaho 45-0 and USF 33-7 in its first two games and people began to reevaluate the Indians' prospects. Lynn "Buck" Brownson unlimbered two beautiful touchdown passes, one for 20 yards to Dave DeSwarte, and the other 44 yards to little Wayne Erickson, and Aubrey Devine hit Mike Titus on a 45-yard pass for a score in the easy win over Idaho.

Some of the Bay area writers started to compare Schwartz's team to Shaughnessy's 1940 squad after the easy win over USF. Merriman, who had piloted a Navy fighter plane during the war, was compared to Standlee after gaining 156 yards. Bob Anderson, a sprint swimming champion, was likened to Kmetovic as he contributed 94 yards as the Stanford speed and deception baffled the Dons. A 48-yard dash by Wayne Erickson and a 17-yard sprint around end by Merriman produced the first Stanford TD. Merriman threw a left-handed pass to DeSwarte for 29 yards, and Anderson's three-yard sweep at right end made it 14-0 early in the second quarter.

Forrest Hall, USF's speedy little back, provided the most dramatic moment of the game when he took the next kickoff and dashed 99 yards for a touchdown to put the Dons back in the running. But it took Stanford only three plays to get back the six points. Anderson outsnookered the USF defense with a 58-yard run to the Dons' four, after Merriman had carried the kickoff back 28 yards to the Stanford 38. Merriman tore through tackle to score from the four.

Al Hoisch, a former Stanford player, and Jerry Shipkey, nephew of ex-Cardinal stars Ted and Harry Shipkey, were on the opposite side of the field as the UCLA Bruins knocked off the Indians 26-6 before 90,803 fans at the Los Angeles Coliseum. The Bruins romped to a 20-0 lead in the first half before Stanford began to play football with some razzle-dazzle that produced big gains. On the first play after returning the opening kickoff to their own 30, the Bruins uncorked a lateral play that netted 36 yards.

Ernie Case whipped a short pass to Burr Baldwin, who pitched to Cal Rossi after a 10-yard gain. Rossi, after adding another 10, handed off to Tom Fears who carried for another 16 and a total gain of 36. In another six plays the Bruins were across the goal line.

Stanford stopped the Bruins at the 10, but the next time UCLA rang up a quickie score. Case passed over the middle to Baldwin, who lateraled to Roy Kurrasch, who outran Anderson to the end zone, completing a 36-yard play. Hoisch contributed 27 yards, and Shipkey made 16 to give the Bruins another score before the end of the first half.

Merriman, who had taken a first half mauling from UCLA ends Baldwin, Fears, Kurrasch, and Tinsley, put some muscle into the Stanford offense in the second half, but the best the Indians could get out of it was one touchdown. A pass interception by Rossi stopped the first threat after a Merriman pass to Brown had moved the ball to the Bruin 27.

Merriman reeled off a 42-yard run to the UCLA eight late in the third quarter, but this threat stalled on the four. The third time proved successful, however, as Merriman scored from the five after Johnny Higgins had caught a pass from Brownson for a 24-yard gain to the UCLA eight.

Stanford was an overwhelming favorite over Santa Clara, but had to fight off a fourth quarter threat by the Broncos to gain a 33-26 win. A pass interception and a fumble recovery gave the Broncos two fourth quarter touchdowns and left them trailing only 27-26. But a 32-yard dash by Anderson and a pair of eight-yard runs by Merriman gave the Indians breathing room at the finish.

Merriman raced 55 yards through the Broncos for a touchdown in the first six minutes of play and it appeared the Indians might be off to the races, but it turned out to be a nip-and-tuck affair.

The annual meeting with USC also was a sizzler with the Indians losing 28-20 when a pair of fourth quarter gambles backfired. Stanford had a 20-14 lead with a little more than a quarter remaining in the game after the Trojans had driven 57 yards in three plays to pull to within a touchdown of the Indians. Stanford had fourth down and one on its own 29 when

Lloyd Merriman, hub of the 1946 offense.

Bob Anderson, 63 yards against Trojans.

Brownson gambled on a running play and failed.

Southern California took possession of the ball on the Cardinals' 28 and in four plays had a touchdown and a 21-20 lead. From the eight Bobby Musick hit the middle for seven yards. But he fumbled at the one when hit by a couple of Stanford players. However, Doug Essick, who was leading the interference, was there to recover the ball in the end zone for a Trojan touchdown.

Stanford did not throw in the towel. Merriman took a pass for a 33-yard gain to the USC 43, but the play was nullified by a clipping penalty. The Indians came up with another crucial fourth down needing two yards to keep possession of the ball and the march alive. Brownson gambled again and gave the ball to Merriman who made all but three inches of the necessary yardage. The Trojans took over again and pushed to another touchdown to gain some extra breathing room, which they needed because Stanford was on the USC four at the final gun.

Anderson and Merriman turned in outstanding performances for Stanford. Anderson scampered 63 yards for Stanford's first touchdown. Merriman was the leading ballcarrier of the game with 132 yards on 27 carries. He scored a touchdown on a 45-yard screen pass and ran 37 yards from punt formation on another occasion.

Washington could not stop Merriman, but the Huskies did

manage to contain Stanford to register a 21-15 upset. The Cardinals were 5-2 favorites, although Ralph "Pest" Welch, the Washington coach, was inclined to rate the game a toss-up. Stanford might have won except that a 44-yard scoring dash by Merriman on the first play of the fourth quarter was erased by an offside penalty.

Stanford had taken a 15-14 lead on a fourth down, 14-yard screen pass from Brownson to Merriman, but a few minutes later Anderson fumbled a Husky punt while trying to execute a handoff to Merriman, and Washington acquired the ball on the Indians' 38 as Gail Bruce recovered. A Dick Ottele to Dick Hagen pass netted 18 yards, and Brooks Biddle scored from the three for the winning points.

Brown gave the Indians a final chance when he intercepted a Fred Provo pass and ran 10 yards to the Husky six. A clipping penalty stalled the threat, however, and Stanford finally had to yield the ball on the eight.

Schwartz had been optimistic that his Indians would win every week earlier in the season, but the Cardinal mentor did not agree with the 4-1 odds favoring Stanford before the Washington State game. "As I see it, it's an even game, a toss-up," said Schwartz. And that is just about the way it turned out. Stanford scored a 27-26 win, but it took a 23-yard pass from Ainslie Bell to Bob Anderson for a touchdown in the final 3:20 to whip the Cougars.

Don Paul scored three touchdowns for Washington State, plunging over from the two for one, and catching a pass for 75 yards and running right end for 27 yards for the others.

Bell replaced Brownson at quarterback as Schwartz decided to experiment and see if Bell might add some punch to the Stanford passing attack. Although he completed only 5 of 19 passes for 73 yards, Bell managed to come up with a clutch completion when it was most needed.

Bell passed for only 72 yards, but two of his throws were for touchdowns as Stanford rolled to a 25-6 triumph over California in the Big Game at Berkeley. The Bears were completely surprised by Bell's performance since they figured the Indians did not have a strong passing game. Stanford also had expected to run into problems with the California line, which was rated one of the best defensive units on the Coast. However, the Indians rushed for a net 149 yards and Bell completed 8 of 16 passes as Stanford dominated the game. Golden Bear rooters were so disappointed in the showing of their team they tore up planks in the rooting section, causing $1,500 damages.

Merriman, who had been the Indians' leading ballcarrier all season, was of little help in the Big Game. Merriman hobbled off the field in the second quarter after reinjuring his leg.

Stanford rushed over the first of its four touchdowns in the first six minutes after Bob Hall intercepted a California lateral on the Bears' 24. Hard-working George Quist ate up 22 yards in one play, but it took the Indians four plays to cover the last two yards. Anderson swept wide to the left for the final foot and the six points.

A Bell to Erickson pass for 13 yards moved the Cardinals to the Bears' 14 and then ran the same pattern for the final six yards and a touchdown. Stanford bagged another quick score when Marty Anderson picked off a Boots Erb pass at the California 16 and returned to the seven. On the first play Bell hit Dave Brown in the end zone.

Jack Swaner, who carried 11 times for 79 yards, finally got the Bears on the scoreboard in the fourth quarter. He picked up 42 of the 60 yards in a drive that ended with Swaner plunging over from the three.

In the Stanford dressing room, Marchie Schwartz pulled a rabbit's foot out of his pocket. "See that rabbit's foot," he said. "Well, Sam McDonald gave that to me before the game. He told me to carry it. He said it had been lucky for him for 20 years. I knew we couldn't lose when I had it."

Almost a month after the Big Game, Stanford wound up its season with an 18-7 victory over the University of Hawaii in Honolulu. The game was postponed from Saturday night until Monday night, December 22, because of near gale winds and drenching rain. Merriman started the Indians on their way to a first quarter touchdown when he intercepted a pass and returned 11 yards. Anderson scored from the one. Bell flipped a 14-yard pass to DeSwarte for the final score.

Disaster Strikes

After the success of the 1946 season, Stanford followers were looking forward to the 1947 season with some optimism, but disaster hit the team even before the start of practice and continued through the year as the Cardinals wound up with an 0-9 record. Dave DeSwarte, a top end who had caught a pass for the final touchdown of the year against Hawaii the year before, was killed when he was hit by a train in Evanston, Illinois. Jack Eller, another letterman end, was getting on a bus when he was hit by a car and killed. George Quist, one of the Indians' top backs, broke an ankle. Lloyd Merriman, the best back on the squad, passed up his final year to sign a professional baseball contract with the Cincinnati Reds. Jim Cox, senior tackle who later played with the San Francisco 49ers, suffered an ankle injury and was lost for most of the season.

"We lost five regulars and had a lot of injuries," said Schwartz. "After we lost the first four games I was just trying to win one. I kept telling the press we were going to win a game, but of course I didn't specify which one. One of the few humorous things about such a season happened one Monday at practice. I was emphasizing the importance of line play, particularly on defense, and stressing that linemen could win a game, in fact, that most games were won or lost by the play of the linemen.

"The squad was sitting in some bleachers alongside the practice field and the freshman squad was working out on a field behind the stands. (Atherton) Phleger, one of our most important linemen, was sitting in one of the top rows, and I noticed he was watching the frosh squad. So I asked him where most games were won or lost. 'At Stanford, Coach,' he answered. That broke up the squad and ended the session."

Stanford went into the Big Game without a victory while California, playing its first season under Lynn "Pappy" Waldorf, had lost only to Southern California. The 1947 game turned out to be one of the all-time thrillers of the series. California was a prohibitive 10-1 favorite, the longest shot in the history of the rivalry, but the Bears had to come from behind in the final three minutes of the game to score a 21-18 victory.

"We had lost eight games, but the week of the Big Game Sam McDonald gave me a little vial of colored sands. Sam had served Stanford for 50 years as superintendent of buildings and grounds and the year before had given me a rabbit's foot before the Big Game," Schwartz said. "Sam said the vial was a secret charm that would mystify the California team so much it wouldn't know it was on a football field. Sam told me to keep it in my pocket, but to keep my hand on it at all times. If I took my hand out of my pocket I was to keep the vial in my hand."

The combination of McDonald's mystic spell and the fighting spirit of the Stanford team almost produced one of the biggest upsets in Big Game history. California scored a quick touchdown when Ted Kenfield bolted 29 yards to score, but the Stanford defense bottled up the Bears' offense for the next 25 minutes, and California managed to get over the midfield stripe only once. Meanwhile, Stanford began to move the ball and, putting one first down after another, arrived at the Bears' 17 yard line. Suddenly the 10-1 underdogs were trailing only 7-6 as Ainslie Bell lofted a pass into the corner of the end zone to Wayne Erickson.

California, after being put in a hole by Mike Durket's 74-yard punt, finally solved Stanford's 7-diamond defense, and with the help of a 44-yard pass from Bob Celeri to Frank Van Deren, pushed over a touchdown in the final 25 seconds of the half, taking a 14-6 lead to the locker room.

Stanford tied the Bears up again in the second half. Quist, who emerged as the outstanding player on the field, intercepted a Celeri pass and returned it 45 yards to the California 36. A 17-yard pass from Bell to Dan Mervin helped the Indians advance to the eight. After Bob Anderson made three yards, Erickson followed a block by Whit Budge to speed the remaining five yards to score standing up.

Suddenly it was a different ball game. Although Quist

missed his second extra point try, the winless Cardinals were trailing only 14-12. Billy Main intercepted one of Bell's passes to give California the ball at the Stanford 34, the first time the Bears had been past midfield in the second half, but the threat ended promptly as Joe Scott recovered Jack Swaner's fumble. Now the Indians were off again. Martin Anderson reeled off 10 yards, Quist collected 20 before he was hauled down, and Mervin added 11 on a quick toss from Don Campbell.

Martin Anderson got another seven and Quist made five, and now Campbell was throwing 11 yards over the center and over the California defense into the hands of Bob Anderson for a touchdown. The crowd of 85,000 found it hard to believe. Here was Stanford with an 18-14 lead over the California Bears, the sixth ranked team in the nation.

Stanford had still another chance when Quist intercepted another Celeri pass, but the Indians were halted as the Bears' defense braced, and Durket was forced to kick over the goal. There was 3:14 left to play as California lined up on its own 20. It was at this stage that Paul Keckley, injured California halfback, pleaded with Waldorf to let him go into the game. Keckley had an injured shoulder and Waldorf had not planned to use him, but he finally gave in. A couple of plays later Dick Erickson pitched a lateral to Jackie Jensen, the California fullback who was noted for his running ability but not his passing talent. Jensen, running to his right, threw a wobbly pass diagonally across the field. Keckley slowed down to make the catch and then took off on a 60-yard race to the end zone, aided by blocks from Bobby Dodds and Ken Peck, giving California a 21-18 victory in one of the greatest Big Games.

Dr. Donald Tressider, Stanford's fourth president and a sincere friend of the university's sports program, presented a bronze plaque to Schwartz and his team following the 1947 season. Inscribed on it were the words, "Nine times defeated, you never lost the will to win."

The season opener with Idaho probably should have been a hint of what was in store for Stanford. The Vandals always had been considered a "breather," but they failed to fall into that class this time. "Dixie" Howell, the former Alabama passing star who had plagued the Indians in the 1935 Rose Bowl game, was coaching at Idaho and had put some punch into the Vandals.

Stanford got away to what appeared to be a comfortable lead in the first quarter as Bell completed passes of 61 and 54

181

yards to Gene Martin for touchdowns for a 13-0 edge. Led by Billy Williams and Jerry and Bill Diehl, Idaho marched from its own 15 to the Stanford 10 where Jerry Diehl raced around end to score. Marty Feldman added a 27-yard field goal to give Stanford a 16-6 advantage at the intermission. But Idaho held the Indians scoreless in the second half and picked up a third quarter score when Williams passed to Orville Barnes for a touchdown after the Vandals had recovered a fumble on the Stanford 33. Ken McCormack recovered another Stanford fumble on the Cardinals' 20 in the fourth period and Williams passed to Bill Diehl for the score, giving Idaho a 19-16 win. All told, Stanford had seven fumbles and lost the ball five times. The Indians also lost a golden scoring opportunity in the opening minutes when a 23-yard run by Marty Anderson to the Idaho three yard line was nullified by a holding penalty.

It did not take long to discover Stanford was no match for Michigan when the Indians invaded Ann Arbor. The Wolverines scored on the second play of the game as Howard Yerges shoveled the ball to Bob Chappuis who passed to Len Ford for a 61-yard touchdown. Fullback Jack Weisenburger also scored on a 61-yard run through the middle, and Chappuis threw a 57-yard pass to Dick Rifenburg as Michigan piled up a 28-0 lead in the first quarter and a 42-0 advantage at the half. It ended 49-13.

Al Hoisch, who had played at Stanford before the war, ran 66 yards for a touchdown, and Carl Benton passed 44 yards to Bill Clements for another score as UCLA whipped Stanford 39-6, handing the Indians their worst defeat in the series. Stanford scored in the last 90 seconds after Gene Martin recovered a Bruin fumble on the UCLA 39 and wound up the afternoon with a net five yards from rushing.

Stanford could not stop Oregon State's short passes, and could not hit on its own passes although the receivers were open as the Beavers took a 13-7 win. The Indians lost an excellent opportunity to snap their losing streak when they lost the ball on downs on the Oregon State two yard line in the first half.

You could have named your own odds prior to the game with Southern California in Los Angeles. Some quarters were picking the Trojans to win by from 33 to 42 points. But Stanford surprised a lot of people by holding USC to touchdowns in the first and fourth quarters, thanks to outstanding defensive play by "Pinky" Phleger, Don Fix, Jack McKettrick, Bob Ghilotti, and George Quist, and lost only 14-0.

Norm Van Brocklin's passing proved too much as Oregon took a 21-6 victory. Van Brocklin, who became a star professional quarterback and coach, passed 21 yards to Jack Leicht for a first quarter touchdown, and to Larry Stoeven for 30 yards and a score in the second quarter. Stanford's touchdown came on a 26-yard pass from Ainslie Bell to Wayne Erickson, who took the ball away from Jim Newquist of the Ducks in the end zone.

Bears, Trojans Win By One

Schwartz had a number of newcomers on his roster as he prepared for the 1948 season. Among them were quarterback Tom Shaw from Portland, Oregon; Al Turrizianni, a swift halfback; and Emery Mitchell from Fresno State. Also, Bud Klein from the College of the Pacific, Bruce Van Alstyne from Menlo Junior College, Gordon White, and Al Laakso.

The opener with San Jose State was considered the key to what kind of season Stanford might expect. If they lost to the Spartans, the Indians could look forward to another dismal year. And for the major part of three quarters it appeared that Stanford might be headed for a continuation of its losing ways of 1947. The first-half performance by the Indians was pretty inept, producing only a net three yards by rushing and 29 by passing.

San Jose had capitalized on a fumble recovery by Joe Juliano on the Stanford 13 to score its first touchdown on a three-yard pass from Chuck Hughes to George Keene. The Spartans got a second score 40 seconds before the end of the first half when a center snap sailed over punter Mike Durket's head into the end zone. Durket managed to run the ball out to the four, but San Jose had another excellent opportunity and Hughes capitalized on it with a three-yard pass to Mel Stein for the score.

Pete Denevi got a third touchdown for San Jose from the one foot line after intercepting a flat pass by Shaw at the San Jose 40. Denevi returned to the Stanford one foot line before Gordon White managed to shoulder him out of bounds. There were only four minutes left in the third quarter when Don

Campbell finally got the Stanford offense moving with a 15-yard pass to Boyd Benson. The Indians appeared stalled, however, when they came up with a fourth down and 12 at the San Jose 26, but Campbell passed to Dan Mervin, who lateraled to Rupe Andrews, and Stanford was on the scoreboard.

The Indians really rolled in the fourth quarter to score three touchdowns. Stanford threatened on a 39-yard pass from Campbell to Andrews, but was halted by a fumble. Then San Jose's Fred Silva shook loose on a fake punt to run 60 yards for a score, only to have it nullified by an offsides penalty. Granted that reprieve the Indians capitalized on a pass interception by Campbell to get another touchdown, the score coming on an 18-yard pass from Campbell to Gene Martin.

Bob Ghilotti, who had been declared eligible just before the game on a telegraphic vote conducted by conference commissioner Vic Schmidt, blocked a Spartan punt and recovered the ball in the end zone for a Stanford touchdown to tie the score at 20-20. The defense also provided the winning points a few minutes later. There were only 3½ minutes left in the game when Atherton Phleger broke through to jostle quarterback Hughes as he pitched a lateral to one of his halfbacks. Jack McKettrick, big Stanford guard, picked the ball off in midair and lumbered 35 yards for the winning score, giving the Indians a 26-20 victory.

Only other wins for Stanford that season were over UCLA 34-14, Washington 20-0, and Montana 39-7. The Indians lost six games but, with the exception of a 43-0 trouncing at the hands of Army, the setbacks were close affairs.

Two of the defeats were by the margin of a missed extra point as Rose Bowl bound California and USC squeezed out 7-6 victories. "Actually, we should have beaten USC," said Jim Castagnoli, Stanford's rugged center. "They were heavily favored, but we pretty well dominated the game. We also should have beaten California. We were great from the 20 yard line to the other 20, but we couldn't punch the ball over. We always wanted to beat California, of course, but we sure hated to lose to Southern California. They always were a cocky bunch."

Castagnoli, Gordon White, Dick Abraham, Al Rau, and Bob White kept the USC offense pretty well within bounds most of the afternoon, but the Trojans scored on a 10-yard fourth down pass from Jim Powers to Bill Jessup 20 seconds before the end of the first half. Stanford held USC twice at the

185

five yard line, and Dean Dill missed on a field goal attempt from the 10 another time, after the Trojans had recovered a blocked punt on the Indians' 25.

A gamble midway in the third quarter almost paid off for Stanford. The Indians had a fourth down and two yards to go on their own 41 and Schwartz sent Durket in to kick. But the Stanford team waved him back to the bench and Mitchell rammed for three yards and a first down. The march finally was stopped on the USC 16.

In the fourth quarter Castagnoli recovered a fumble on the USC 40, and this time the Trojans did not stop the Indians. Mitchell passed 14 yards to Laakso and then to Andrews for five. On the next play Mitchell took a direct snap from center and passed to Andrews for the touchdown. Mitchell's conversion attempt was low and wide, leaving Stanford on the short end of a 7-6 score. The Indians made another threat in the closing minutes of the game, but Dill intercepted one of Mitchell's passes to save the Trojans.

A brilliant performance by Jackie Jensen, California's All America back who had beaten Stanford in the closing minutes the year before, featured the Bears' 7-6 win and produced California's first undefeated, untied season since 1922.

Jensen ran for 170 yards on 19 carries. On one occasion he was back to punt but saw his kick would be blocked, so he ran. Jensen needed 30 yards for a first down, and got 31. Another time Stanford had California stopped with a fourth down and 10 on the Indians' 23. Jensen could not find any pass receivers so he ran for 16 yards. Jack Swaner picked up the last seven yards in two plays for the Bears' score.

Stanford was without Don Campbell, the center of their offense after the loss of Mitchell two weeks before in the Army game. Campbell was hurt by a blow on the chin on the opening kickoff runback and was taken to the hospital with a concussion. California took the opening kickoff and marched for a touchdown following the lengthy delay while Dr. Frederick Reichert administered medical aid to Campbell. But after that the Stanford defense bottled up the Bears. Al Laakso, Gene Martin, Bob Ghilotti, and Ken Rose stopped the California end sweeps. Gordon White was a standout, and the Stanford team seemed to get stronger as the game went along.

Dave Field intercepted a Celeri pass and returned it 52 yards to the Bears' 28, but the Indians were unable to capitalize on it. Stanford blocked a Jensen kick, and twice recovered fumbles in California's end of the field. Stanford finally got a touchdown in the third quarter after Jack McKettrick recovered a Jensen fumble on the Bears' 22. White, Field, and De Young picked up a first down at the 11, and Shaw's quick jump pass over center to Ken Rose was good for a touchdown. Devine's try for the extra point, which would have tied the game, fizzled low.

California never threatened after that. Stanford had other chances but failed. Once, after Bob Rohrer had recovered for the Indians when a bouncing punt hit a California man, Stanford got to the Bears' four yard line before California braced and finally took the ball on an incomplete fourth down pass. The Indians staged other marches in the fourth quarter, but Paul Keckley intercepted a pass in the end zone to halt one, and Devine was checked on an attempted run from place-kick formation at the Bears' 23 to stop another.

Stanford was in an unusual role of 3½ point favorite over Washington and lived up to it with a 20-0 win over the Huskies. The game was the best one of the season for the Indians as Mitchell did just about everything but lead the band at half time. He caught a pass from Shaw for the Cardinals first touchdown in the second quarter, passed 13 yards to Rupe Andrews for the second, and hit Roland Kirkby of the Huskies so hard once that he caused a fumble, which Billy De Young recovered on the Washington 47.

De Young accounted for Stanford's other score with a 46-yard burst around end on a pitchout in the fourth quarter.

The Indians played another strong game in beating UCLA 34-14 in Los Angeles, as Bob White scored three touchdowns. White, a transfer from Glendale Junior College, had written Schwartz during the summer asking if he could report for football for a tryout. White ran 11 yards for his first score and wound up with 123 yards for the afternoon.

"We simply decided to play 60 minutes of football instead of one quarter," Devine said. "We just got together and played the way we should have been playing all this season. We pushed Oregon all around the lot. We should have beaten Washington State, and today, well, we clicked. We knew we had them when we were able to crash their ends."

A screen pass that backfired in the final five minutes of the game cost Stanford a possible upset over Oregon. Wayne Bartholemy intercepted a Shaw pass and ran it back 44 yards for a touchdown to give the Ducks a 20-12 win. John McKay, the current Southern California coach, scored the other two touchdowns for Oregon, one on a five-yard run and the other from 22 yards out. A pass interference call against Stanford allowed the Ducks to retain possession of the ball prior to the second score. The penalty gave Oregon a first down on its own 49, otherwise it would have been fourth down on the Ducks' 29.

Santa Clara recovered six of eight Stanford fumbles, and turned two of them into touchdowns in the first two minutes of the second half to score a 27-14 win over the Indians. Ellery Williams, a brother of former Oakland A's manager Dick Williams, recovered a fumble at the Stanford 25 on the first play after the second half kickoff. On the first play Billy Sheridan passed to Jerry Hennessey for a touchdown. Mitchell returned the next kickoff to the 42, but again the Indians fumbled on the first play and Williams recovered on the 36. This time Sheridan passed to Williams for the score.

Paul Conn darted 19 yards for the Broncos' first TD, and Al Martin passed to Williams on a 53-yard play for another to give Santa Clara a 13-0 lead at the half.

Sophomores Provide Boost

Schwartz came up with some outstanding sophomores for the 1949 season and enjoyed his most successful season, finishing with a 7-3-1 record. The losses were to Michigan, UCLA, and California. The victories included a 34-13 triumph over USC, one of the most lopsided Stanford wins in the series, and four shutouts. The young sophomores included Jesse Cone, a guard, Jack Rye, an end, and Bill McColl, who earned All America honors at end in 1950 and 1951.

In 1949, however, McColl had a chance to play a little bit of everything. "McColl was a great athlete," said Schwartz. "He was an end, but I played him at tackle, and then had him backing up the line. We were having trouble with our pass defense, so I put McColl at what they now call the free safety spot, and let him play the ball. He did a fine job no matter where you put him."

McColl, now an outstanding orthopedic surgeon in Southern California, had been a widely recruited prep star out of San Diego's Herbert Hoover High School. USC, UCLA, California, and a number of eastern schools had sought to lure him. "I came to Stanford because I wanted to get the best education possible and still play major football," he said. "Stanford impressed me as a school with a small college atmosphere with a top notch medical school.

"I had had a good freshman year and started the first couple of varsity games my sophomore year and did well as a receiver, but I was crappy as a blocker. I got so bad that I was benched, and my dauber was kind of down. I knew I wasn't going to play offense. We had lost several tackles due to injuries

189

and Phil Bengston came along and asked if I'd play defensive tackle. I wanted to play so I said yes. It was the first time I had played inside defensively. In the Santa Clara game I was opposite John Houck, who was a pretty good tackle, but I made such a good showing I was named 'Player of the Week.' Bengston coached me and I learned to enjoy the contact a lot better. I learned a different aspect of the game."

Stanford enjoyed one of its best performances of the season while whipping USC in Los Angeles 34-13. The Indians exploded for three touchdowns in the second quarter with a 77-yard run by Bobby White and a 69-yard punt return by Bill De Young accounting for two of the scores. Stanford added two more scores in the fourth quarter as Hugasian and Bob Andrews also took part in ball carrying.

"White had a field day in that game," Schwartz recalled. "He made a lot of yards running wide around the end with Emery Mitchell leading the interference. Mitchell was as fine a blocker as I've seen, and he had the USC end on the ground all day."

Guard Don Fix and tackle Al Rau were standouts in the Stanford line, especially on defense.

Schwartz had a chance to use everybody on the bench in the first two games of the season as Stanford thumped San Jose State 49-0 and Harvard 44-0. The Indians scored in every quarter against the Spartans as Hugasian, a sophomore halfback, contributed the longest run of the day on a 48-yard scamper. Gary Kerkorian, who developed into one of the Cardinals' top quarterbacks in the next two seasons, made his first start against Harvard. Again Stanford scored in every quarter as Schwartz made liberal use of his reserves in an effort to hold down the score. One of the eastern writers covering the game wrote that "Stanford found small holes in the Harvard tackles which extended to the sidelines." The Indians were scheduled to play a return game with Harvard in Boston the following year, but Crimson officials cancelled it following the one-sided loss, claiming Stanford was too strong.

Everyone played as Stanford whipped Idaho 63-0 in a game which merits mention only because Kerkorian kicked nine straight conversions in an unusual performance for the Indians, who in previous years had lost some games because of their inability to make good on extra point attempts. Stanford accepted a post-season invitation to play Hawaii in Honolulu,

Harry Hugasian, outstanding 1949-51 halfback.

and again Schwartz had little success in his attempt to hold down the score. The Indians romped to a 74-20 victory, scoring 42 points in the fourth quarter. One of the Stanford touchdowns came on a 59-yard pass from McColl to halfback Holbrook Boruck.

California was undefeated for the second straight year and had won 16 straight Pacific Coast Conference games, while Stanford had lost only to Michigan and UCLA going into the Big Game. The Indians gave the Bears a battle for the better part of three quarters and, in fact, held a 14-12 lead in the third period. But Jim Monachino, one of the outstanding backs for Waldorf's "Thunder Team," broke loose for an 84-yard run to the Stanford four. Jack Swaner bucked over for a touchdown to put California back in front and the Bears went on for a 33-14 win.

Russ Pomeroy recovered a fumble on the Bears' 16, and White raced over the goal line on the first play as Stanford grabbed a 7-6 lead in the second quarter. White, Kerkorian, halfback Eric Southwood, Bob Andrews, Mitchell, McColl, and Pomeroy all played outstanding ball for Stanford.

"We lost three linebackers in the second half, and that killed us," said Schwartz. "But Swaner had a great day for California. Pomeroy played a great game for us."

191

Hopes Run High

After the success of the 1949 season, a lot was expected of the 1950 Stanford team, possibly too much. There even was some talk of a possibility of it being a Rose Bowl year. These hopes were further expanded as Stanford ran up impressive scores in winning its first four games. However, there had been some problems with fumbles and penalties, and these all caught up with the Indians in their games with UCLA and Washington to produce identical 21-7 losses.

Although knocked out of the Rose Bowl race by the two defeats, Stanford salvaged something from the season by playing a 7-7 tie with California. The Bears had rolled over nine straight opponents and were seeking their third straight undefeated, untied regular season. "Pappy" Waldorf's Bears were headed for their third straight Rose Bowl appearance and their third consecutive loss to the Big 10 representative.

Stanford was at full strength for the first time since early in the season, but still California was established a 13½ point favorite. Waldorf rated Stanford the "toughest team California had met all season," and called the game a toss-up. A nine-day storm made the field gummy despite efforts to dry it out with the help of a helicopter and heat lamps.

Led by Gary Kerkorian, Bill McColl, Russ Pomeroy, and Bruce Van Alstyne, who returned to action for the first time in several weeks after being sidelined with a pinched shoulder nerve, Stanford battled California on even terms in one of the hardest fought contests in Big Game history. The Bears, with a great backfield of Johnny Olszewski, Jim Monachino, and Pete Schabarum, wound up with 292 yards net to Stanford's 272 and held a slim 14-13 edge in first downs. The Bears made 243 yards rushing to the Indians' 55, but Stanford had a 217 to 49 yard edge in passing. Kerkorian accounted for Stanford's passing yardage with 17 completions in 30 attempts to set a new Big Game record with McColl, Bob White, and Van Alstyne his favorite targets. The Stanford score, however, came on a six-yard pass to Boyd Benson after Leon King had jolted the ball out of Schabarum's grasp and John Bonetti had recovered for the Cardinals on the California 37.

Schabarum had given the Bears a lead at the start of the third quarter after Don Robinson recovered a fumble on the Stanford 31. On the first play Schabarum raced between left tackle and left end and, with blocks by Bob Bagley and Wally Laster, ran the 31 yards for a touchdown.

That stood up until the start of the final quarter. Schabarum's fumble late in the third period gave Stanford a good opportunity and Kerkorian capitalized on it. Two passes to McColl were good for 18 and 11 yards. Two running plays advanced the ball only to the six, and Stanford had third and six. Kerkorian crossed up the Cal defense with a flat pass to Benson who took the ball on the three and scored easily.

Stanford had another score nullified on a penalty. Kerkorian passed 28 yards to Bob White in the end zone, but referee Jim Cain ruled White had pushed Robinson before making the catch and called offensive pass interference. The Indians made another bid for an upset in the closing minute of the game on a surprise maneuver that saw McColl drop back from his end position to accept a lateral from Kerkorian. McColl then uncorked a 66-yard pass that appeared to be right on target, but just slid off the fingertips of speedster Bob Bryan on the California 10 yard line.

Stanford also played a 7-7 tie with Southern California, and missed besting the Trojans only because two first half scores were called back because of penalties. As things turned out, the Cardinals scored in the final three minutes, and then wound up on the USC 30 as the game ended after Jesse Cone had recovered a Trojan fumble.

Washington, runnerup to California for the conference title with a 6-1 record, ran wild in the fourth quarter to hand Stanford a 21-7 setback. The Indians played the Huskies to a scoreless deadlock in the first half, but Washington scored on a pass in the opening minutes of the third quarter. Stanford matched it with a score by Bob Meyers after Bryan had run 37 yards to the Husky seven, but then Washington dominated the final quarter. The Huskies completed 19 of 24 passes in a surprising show of aerial superiority and piled up 416 total yards to 226 for Stanford.

Bob Gambold, who later served as one of the top assistants on the staff of John Ralston when Stanford went to the Rose Bowl in 1970 and 1971, was the quarterback for Washington State and passed the Cougars to a pair of first quarter touchdowns before the Indians got the offense rolling. Kerkorian was more than a match for Gambold, however, and turned in a great exhibition to lead Stanford to a 28-18 win. Kerkorian passed for two touchdowns, recovered a fumble, intercepted a pass, and kicked two extra points in a show of all-around football ability as the Indians took a 14-12 lead at the half. In the third quarter Stanford added to its lead with a spectacular play that saw Kerkorian throw a 33-yard pass to McColl, who lateraled to Boyd Benson, who ran another 25 yards to score.

An undefeated Army team, rated second only to Oklahoma in the AP football ratings, invaded Stanford for the first time since 1929 and barely managed to eke out a 7-0 victory. Torrential rains had hit the Bay area early in the week and the downpour and high winds continued until after the game. Stanford Stadium's turf and the parking areas around the stadium were a quagmire, and some cars were bogged down in the mud for days. Despite the weather some 45,000 fans turned out for the game. Stanford's defense did a great job of checking the highly favored Cadets except for a 28-yard pass play in the third quarter which produced the only score of the day.

Schwartz had been under criticism from a small group of Stanford alumni, but President Wallace Sterling and the rest of the university officials were behind the coach and had offered Marchie a new five-year contract. Schwartz had been named to coach the West team in the annual Shrine game in Kezar Stadium. In the locker room after his West team had scored a 16-7 win over the East, Schwartz stunned sportswriters with a statement that he would not accept the five-year renewal of his contract at Stanford.

"There were a number of reasons for my retirement," Schwartz said. "The No. 1 reason was that I was 40 years old, and had a large family which I was unable to be with as much as I would have liked because of football. I had enjoyed coaching and the glamour which went with it. I had as fine a job as anyone could have in the country at Stanford. But you can get trapped into football, and I didn't want to do that.

"Another thing was that sometimes the alumni get mad because you don't win by a bigger score, even though you are winning. But the thing that really soured me on football was the proselyting of it. To have a good team you had to have good athletes, and the scholastic standards at Stanford made it tough to get top players. I disliked going out and begging a boy to come to Stanford where he could get a great education, and having the first question he asked be: 'What's in it for me?' That soured me completely.

"You have to want to coach to be a good coach. Injuries go against you, and there are so many things to contend with over which you have no control. I had finished school at Notre Dame in 1932, and had helped coach the backs while I was going to law school in 1933. I had been coaching for 16 years, and decided that was enough."

Taylor "Fills In"

There was a lot of pressure on Al Masters to land a "big name" coach when he went looking for a replacement for Schwartz following Marchie's surprise announcement. Bud Wilkinson of Oklahoma was the No. 1 choice. Second choice was Paul Brown, former Ohio State coach who then was with the Cleveland Browns of the All America Conference. Bob Voigts of Northwestern was the third choice, with Taylor fourth on the list. Chuck Taylor, who had returned to Stanford as freshman coach following his discharge from the Navy, had coached the first three post-war yearling squads to consecutive undefeated seasons, compiling a 14-0-1 record.

A tireless worker, Taylor had accepted the role of wrestling coach when the Indians discovered they did not have anyone to fill the role. He also took over as rugby coach and handled the intramural sports program. But in 1949 he accepted an offer from the San Francisco 49ers to serve as line coach under Lawrence T. "Buck" Shaw and was in that position when he was appointed Stanford coach on February 3, 1951, becoming the first Stanford alumnus to coach the Cardinals since Jim Lanagan in 1908.

"There was a big group behind Chuck, and we kept pushing until the Board of Athletic Control finally saw it our way," said Joe Payne, a long-time Stanford booster. "They figured they could get Chuck cheap, and that they would only keep him until the Korean War was over and then get another coach."

Taylor retained W. P. "Dutch" Fehring, Bob Ghilotti, Pete Kmetovic, and Mal Elward from Schwartz' staff. He added Joe

196

Ruetz, former Notre Dame All America and St. Mary's College coach, and George Lynn, ex-Ohio State quarterback, to his staff. In 1957 he added Herm Meister.

Taylor's material was good, but not outstanding, and most critics expected the Indians to wind up about in the middle of the conference race. Instead they won nine straight games and went to the Rose Bowl. Thus Taylor followed the path of Warner, Thornhill, and Shaughnessy, all of whom took Stanford teams to the Rose Bowl in their first years.

"There was no secret to going to the Rose Bowl my first year," Taylor stated. "I wasn't a very astute coach at that stage of the game. I don't think I ever was, for that matter. But I was a young coach, very naive, and was still learning. I did have some youngsters I knew and who had played for me as fresh-

Chuck Taylor, newly appointed Stanford football coach, discusses plans with athletic director Al Masters (left), and Don Liebendorfer, sports information director.

men and now were seniors—boys like Gary Kerkorian, Dick Horn, Bill McColl. These kids had some unique talents. We didn't have much to go with it in the form of outstanding backs or anything, but we had some good receivers and we had fine passers. I learned fast that we weren't going to run over anybody, so we went into a style of passing that was unique at the time and kind of did the job. We kept moving along, strangely enough, when we weren't really supposed to be on the field with most of the teams we were playing."

Taylor was unusual in that he kept predicting each week his team would win, and it became another Cinderella team, losing only to California in the regular season. Taylor was only 31 years old, but he wound up being voted "Coach of the Year."

"Our passing attack contributed the greatest amount to our success," Taylor said. "We had a very fine quarterback in Kerkorian. Besides being a very good passer he was an excellent team leader and the sparkplug of the team. Also, the offensive team had an outstanding end in McColl, a big boy who was very adept at going high and taking passes away from the defenders. It was probably Kerkorian's passing and McColl's sensational catches at crucial times that made the difference in many games.

"Even today I'm enthused about the passing game over the running game. I obviously know you have to have a certain

Gary Kerkorian led Cardinals to 1952 Rose Bowl.

amount of running too, but it's always been interesting to me the way coaches think in relation to run versus pass. I kind of think in terms of pass versus run and have always felt that if you can establish a strong passing game, it is going to force the opposition into a defensive setup you can run on. At least in my career, this seemed to be the pattern that was established pretty well. Although we never had great runners, we had some backs who could move, including Ron Cook, Harry Hugasian, Bob Mathias, Bill Tarr, Lou Valli, Chuck Shea, and Gordy Young. We were able to make pretty good yardage because of spreading the defenses so well with our passing offense."

Taylor disliked the dreariness of practice and the grimness of coaching, and as a result his practice sessions could be called "loose." But Chuck had a technique for handling men individually.

McColl, now an orthopedic surgeon in Southern California, recalled Taylor's method of handling him in his senior year in 1951. "I had a big game in which I had caught eight or nine passes, two or three for touchdowns," McColl said. "It was one of my better games and I was named player of the week. On Monday Chuck called me into his office to see the game films. 'Watch yourself in this movie,' he said. When I wasn't running for passes I was standing around. I either wasn't blocking or I was missing them. Chuck didn't criticize me, but my blocking improved from then on."

"I hated to walk on the practice field without some humorous things happening," Taylor said. "Practice can get awful dull, and I sort of tried to follow the pattern of having the players get out there and have some fun."

One of the things McColl remembers about the 1951 season was the pep talks Taylor gave before the games. "Every one was a gem," McColl said. "The first one was before the San Jose State game. We were in the locker room at the stadium, and Chuck was walking up and down. There was a big bag of ice there, and Chuck reached into the bag and pulled out a handful of ice. 'Anyone want some ice?' he asked. Another time he was trying to think of something to say to the team before the game. 'Anybody have to take a leak?' he asked.

"Midway in the season we were playing Washington in Seattle, and things were pretty tight. Chuck looked down the tunnel to the field and asked, 'Everybody got a date for tonight?' After the USC game he kicked the writers out of the

199

Bill McColl, All America end 1950-51.

locker room. We had come from behind to win the game 27-20. 'You did a hell of a job and I'm proud of you,' he said. 'All training rules are off tonight. If you get in any trouble give me a call at the Huntington.' The last one was before the Rose Bowl game: 'We've come a long way this year, won a lot of games and had fun,' he said. 'Go out and play as hard as you can. I hope we win, I really don't care if we win or lose, but I want you to have fun. Football isn't worth it if you don't have fun.'"

One of the games that stands out in Taylor's memory while he was coaching was the one with Southern California, which decided the 1951 Rose Bowl team.

"It was one of the greatest games," Taylor observed. "It didn't matter which side you were on because it had everything. It had great passing, great running, all kinds of sterling types of play. I remember that during the second half everyone was standing up. I don't think they sat down once. It was that type of game. We always seemed to have good games with USC. They're always tough. It's a tremendous rivalry."

Stanford and USC both were undefeated in seven games going into their game at the Los Angeles Coliseum, and 96,000 fans were on hand for the contest. The Indians held a 7-0 lead at the half, but the Trojans went 74 yards for a third-quarter score to tie the count at 7-7. Southern California grabbed a 14-7 edge in the fourth period on a 36-yard run by Al Carmichael. Then Bob Mathias, the 1948 Olympic decathlon champion, put Stanford back in the game with an electrifying 96-yard kickoff return. However, the Tribe missed the extra point and trailed 14-13.

Later USC added to its margin when Stanford fumbled and the Trojans recovered in the end zone for a touchdown to make it 20-13. But the Indians came back to tie it 20-20 when Kerkorian passed 30 yards to Sam Morley to put the ball in scoring position and Mathias rammed center for the touchdown.

Kerkorian, now a partner in a Fresno, California, law firm, accepted the blame for the fourth quarter fumble which put USC in front, 20-13.

"I fumbled when I was back to throw a screen pass," he said. "And the reason I fumbled was that I was hit because I held onto the ball too long and didn't throw it. The reason I didn't throw it was because the intended receiver, left end Bill Storum, never turned around to receive the ball, but continued to block.

"The reason he continued to block was because I called the play improperly in the huddle—I said something different than what I was thinking. In essence, I called the play in a manner, which under our blocking rules, made it impossible to execute. I called a screen pass with everyone blocking, and there was nobody to receive the pass.

"If there is any humor in that, it's in the fact that after the game Bill McColl told me he realized I had called the play wrong, but assumed that I knew what I was doing, and had a special reason for calling it that way. Harry Hugasian said the same thing.

"I could have killed them both for not having said something to me in the huddle. I guess I should take pride, however, in the fact that they assumed that I always knew what I was doing."

"Mathias was one of the best third down men around," McColl observed. "Harry Hugasian used to tell him it was third and five, and he'd get six yards. There were a lot of big plays in that USC game, a lot of ups and downs. One of the big plays, next to Mathias' kickoff return, came when Skip Crist intercepted a pass and ran it back 31 yards to the USC 11 to set up the winning touchdown. Joe Ruetz (an assistant coach) had warned Crist to stay back and watch for a Frank Gifford-to-Dean Schneider pass when USC ran a certain formation. As a result Crist was in position to pick off the pass."

Although they were set back five yards on a penalty, the Indians scored in four plays, with Hugasian getting the touchdown and Kerkorian adding the PAT for a 27-20 Stanford victory. The two teams had scored a total of 33 points in the fourth quarter. Kerkorian completed 18 of 32 passes for 218 yards for the Indians.

There was not much indication in the early games that Stanford would develop into a championship contender. "We were lucky in a lot of ways," McColl said. "We didn't really have the material. But Chuck did several things that made a difference. He went strictly platoon, and each unit developed great individual pride. Chuck also gave everyone a new look, a new start, and new enthusiasm. He made practices more enjoyable and less boring. He was totally punctual, never wasted time, but he also never was there ahead of time. Because of the platoons we could do things in half the time. And Mathias at fullback made a big difference in the offense, more than anything else. He was big and fast, could go around end, and also could get short yardage. He added speed to the backfield."

Mathias made his first appearance in a Stanford uniform in the Michigan game played at Ann Arbor when he went in to receive the kickoff. "That game was one of those we weren't supposed to be in, and yet we won 23-13," Taylor said. "That was the worst trip of my career. I had been taught as a young coach that travel arrangements had to be perfect, but on that trip everything went wrong. We got hung up in Chicago and couldn't get there. Then people couldn't get any sleep. It was just a bad deal, and yet we beat Michigan in a big upset. We played the best game of our lives. So since then I've never been too concerned about traveling and whether everyone is put to bed at the right time, is comfortable, or how much sleep they get or that type of thing."

McColl caught seven passes for 142 yards and Kerkorian completed six others for another 64 yards in the victory over the Wolverines. Kerkorian scored once and Bob Meyers twice as

Stanford took a 20-6 lead in the first half.

McColl was outstanding the following week as the Indians downed UCLA 21-7, and so was Mathias. Meyers was injured in practice during the week, and Mathias stepped in to fill the fullback spot. He had very little experience but carried the bulk of Stanford's running game. The Cardinals had trouble beating Santa Clara, and it was Mathias who took a handoff in the final two minutes and ran 17 yards for the winning touchdown in a 21-14 victory.

Then Stanford's defense, led by Ed Tanner, Chuck Essegian, John Rye, and Ron Eadie, checked dangerous Hugh McElhenny (with the exception of one 69-yard run) for a 14-7 win at Seattle. The Indians did not have as close a call as the score would indicate. Two touchdowns were called back on penalties in between a score after taking the opening kickoff 72 yards

Olympic decathlon champion Bob Mathias provided a big lift for 1951 Cardinals.

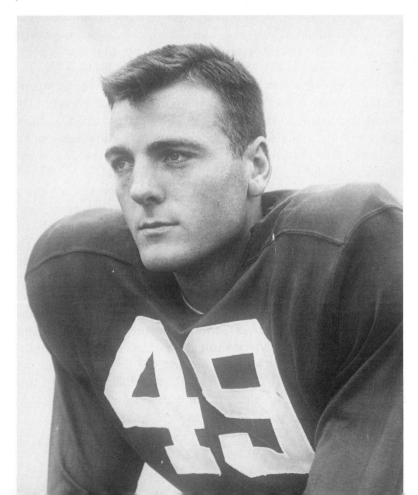

and a fourth quarter touchdown.

The Cardinals clinched the conference title and the Rose Bowl bid with a 35-14 victory over Oregon State. The Cardinals rolled to three touchdowns in the third quarter after being held to a 7-7 tie in the first half.

Stanford had been underdog in a number of its games, but it was favored in the Big Game with California. There were 90,634 fans on hand at Stanford to see the Bears hand the Cardinals their only loss of the regular season 20-7. California scored in the first, second, and fourth quarters to build up a 20 point lead before Stanford marched to a touchdown in the final period. The Indians were held to 28 yards rushing and 133 yards passing.

"I remember welling up with emotion when, with a couple of minutes to go, I realized that I was on the team that suffered the first defeat for Taylor," said Kerkorian. "I remember saying something to him to the effect of how sorry I was about our being beat by Cal, and the fact that we had broken his string of 23 straight victories (Chuck had three straight undefeated seasons as freshman coach and nine straight victories as varsity coach). I don't remember his response, except that it was made with a smile, and was to the effect 'don't worry about it.'

"Perhaps the best thing that can be said about Stanford football is that it was fun. I knew an awful lot of players that attended other universities that told me in later years that they didn't enjoy playing football at their respective universities. At Stanford, I recall talking to McColl about this one day as we were leaving the practice field—football was fun."

Taylor was named "Coach of the Year" and McColl was a unanimous choice for All America. Kerkorian, Dick Horn, and Norm Manoogian were named All Coast along with McColl. In the season McColl caught 42 passes, topping his previous year's total, but gained only 607 yards. Seven of his catches were for touchdowns.

Dick Hyland, the Stanford halfback of the mid-20s, visited the Indians' Rose Bowl training camp at Lake Arrowhead to do a story for the *Los Angeles Times* about the Pacific Coast Conference champions. Hyland noted the players drinking milkshakes at lunch and, after Stanford lost the Rose Bowl game to Illinois 40-7, wrote a story in jest, blaming their defeat on too many milkshakes. The story made papers all over the country and later took on a serious nature as time went on.

"We had milkshakes on our diet," said Taylor, "but that wasn't the cause of our losing. The cause was that we were up against a darn good Illinois team and the fact that we lost our quarterback (Gary Kerkorian) in the third quarter. We had to go with a young sophomore, Bobby Garrett, who later became very good, but at that stage of the game we didn't have much going for us, except for Kerkorian and our receivers group."

Illinois, which had posted an 8-0-1 record to win the Big Ten title, scored first by going 76 yards in six plays after taking the opening kickoff. Don Sanders blocked the extra point attempt. Then Stanford claimed a 7-6 edge by marching 84 yards with Kerkorian completing five straight passes, two each to McColl and Hugasian and one to Ron Cook. Hugasian scored from the four and Kerkorian added the seventh point.

Stanford missed a field goal attempt in the second period, and the collapse came in the third quarter following Kerkorian's injury. Illinois took a 14-7 lead midway in the period when Stan Wallace, an Illinois defensive halfback, intercepted a Kerkorian pass at midfield and returned to the Stanford 12. Illini Don Tate, who had contributed a 41-yard run during the Illinois scoring drive in the first period, scored on a pitchout, and from then on the Illini were in complete command.

Illinois blocked a punt and capitalized on other miscues to score four touchdowns in the final quarter. Illini coach Ray Eliot said a change in the Illinois pass defense was responsible for the Illini domination of the second half. The move, he said, called for the linebackers to drop back a couple of yards to stop Stanford's hook passes.

"Our offense got stopped by the way they held up our ends on the line," said Kerkorian. "They put two men on each of our ends, and often they couldn't get out of the line." Sam Morley, a Stanford end, had a slightly different version. "They kept grabbing our shirts," he said. "They used their elbows in the clinches, but they did it all very cleverly and got away with it."

So Close In '53

Looking back on his coaching career, Taylor could recall a number of outstanding games, but the two that topped his list were the 1951 victory over Southern California (27-20) and the 1953 upset over Rose Bowl-bound UCLA (21-20).

Taylor did not have very much reason to recall the 1952 season, however. Kerkorian and McColl were gone, and although Taylor had a new passing combination in Bobby Garrett and Sam Morley, they were a year away from greatness. Stanford won its first four games, including a 14-7 upset victory over Michigan, but then managed to beat only San Jose State in its last six starts.

Making the year a disappointing one was the fact that the Indians dropped all three games to their rivals in California, bowing to UCLA 24-14, USC 54-7, and California 26-0. Some of the problems in the final three games could be blamed on the fact that Garrett suffered a shoulder separation in the USC game.

The bright spot of the season came in the fourth game when Bill Rogers, a junior back, ran 96 yards down the right sideline for a touchdown against Oregon State. The mark still stands as the longest touchdown run from scrimmage in history by a Stanford player. The run helped the Indians down the Beavers 41-28.

It was a different story in 1953 as Stanford came within three points of the Rose Bowl. Garrett led the nation in passing and produced some of the finest thrills in the history of Stanford football. Among those thrills was the win over UCLA. UCLA was unbeaten and had given up only a touchdown to

206

Kansas in its first four games before coming into Stanford Stadium.

"We weren't really in the ball game with UCLA in the first half," Taylor recalled. "I made one of my errors by thinking we could run on a real outstanding UCLA team. We were behind 20-7 at the half. I took Garrett aside between halves and told him, 'Look, the next half, forget about the running. Every time you get the ball, wherever you are on the field, throw the damn thing. Let's see if we can't do something about it.' We won 21-20. It was one of those miraculous, interesting things."

Garrett completed 18 of 27 passes in that game and threw to Ron Cook and Al Napoleon for touchdowns and also kicked all three extra points. Henry "Red" Sanders, the UCLA coach, said after the game he never had seen a game dominated so much by one man.

"Over the years we have had a number of outstanding quarterbacks, and some great receivers," Taylor said. "Players like McColl, Morley, Chris Burford, Carl Isaacs, Gary Van Galder, Red Taylor—too many. I can't name all of them. But I'm a firm believer anyone can catch a ball if he concentrates on it. Of course, we were a passing team and our players could get so keyed up about never dropping a ball it became a matter of pride to develop that attitude. And it became effective. Whenever the ball is close enough for them they should be able to hang onto it. We had a lot of players who just sort of developed that attitude because it was the thing we were stressing."

The Indians had a tough time in Seattle the following week before downing Washington 13-7. Cook accounted for both Stanford touchdowns, returning a punt 52 yards for the first score with the help of blocks by Morley, Phil Wilson, and Ted Tanner. He took a 16-yard pass from Garrett for the winning score.

Through the years there have been some great battles between Stanford and USC, and the 1953 encounter was one of those which went right down to the final gun. USC's Sam Tsagalaksis kicked a 38-yard field goal in the final 14 seconds to give the Trojans a 23-20 win that stopped Taylor's pass-minded crew from going to the Rose Bowl.

Garrett had a great game against USC, completing 20 of 31 passes for 324 yards and three touchdowns, one of them a 76-yard pass-run play to Cook in the third quarter to tie the score at 13-13. Garrett hit 10 straight passes with Morley grab-

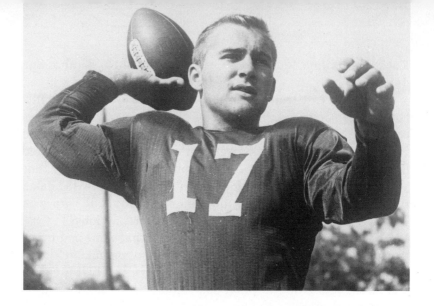

Bob Garrett, 1953 All America quarterback.

bing the last one for a touchdown that put Stanford in front 20-13. But USC bounced back to deadlock the game again. Then with a couple of minutes left to play Stanford recovered a fumble on the Trojan 20. Not willing to settle for a tie, Garrett gambled for a win with a pass and it backfired. USC intercepted the pass and ran it back deep into Stanford territory, giving Tsagalaksis a chance to kick the first of the USC field goals which were to prove to be heartbreaks for Stanford. In later years Ron Ayala and Chris Limahelu were to kick goals in the final seconds to lift the Trojans to victories over the Indians.

The loss to the Trojans spoiled Stanford's chance of going to the Rose Bowl, but the 21-21 tie with California completely wiped out any remaining hopes. UCLA defeated USC 13-0 in the final game of the season and gained the New Year's Day bid as California tied Stanford 21-21 that same day. The Bears scored twice in the fourth quarter to pull even with the Indians, who had taken a 21-7 lead in the third quarter when Garrett intercepted a pass by Paul Larson and returned 56 yards for a touchdown behind good blocking.

"I got enamored with the passing game, and I think the continuity of going into a passing style of attack primarily was something that has attracted passing quarterbacks to Stanford," Taylor said. "Most teams were still single wing and were run-conscious, but we by necessity were going the other direction and were able to get into school, players who tended in that direction. It sort of did its own thing as it went along."

Brodie's Type Of Man

"Chuck Taylor was the only college coach I could have played for at that time," said John Brodie. "He allowed me to see football the way I did. He wasn't a high pressure coach. But he also sort of forced my hand. He said my improvement between my freshman year and spring practice was so great that if I continued to develop at that rate, with my abilities, there was no telling how far I could go. 'The way we see it now we plan to start you at quarterback next fall,' he said. 'This is to prepare you for that and to give you a chance to begin getting ready.'

"Nobody recruited me. The only person that recruited me was my mother. My grades weren't good enough to get in when I was a junior in high school, but she went down and made a deal somehow that if I got straight A's my senior year and was able to pass the entrance exam that I would be accepted. I was a much better basketball and baseball player than I was football player in high school so I wasn't given a scholarship, and after I made first string I didn't qualify because I supposedly wasn't in need.

"Taylor was the reason I was able to play college football and, as a result, pro football. I never was enthusiastic enough about the game of football, and I just was not interested in all that rah-rah stuff. I was never a spartan. The spartan attitude always defeated the reason I was playing, which was to be more free. Many guys were playing the game who were more restricted. Well, Chuck realized I liked to play, but I didn't like all that stuff that was attached to it, so as long as I didn't have a scholarship he let me do things my way. He was such a straight-shooting guy that I always was in shape. I never missed a practice or a meeting. Contrary to what other people may say, I never was on the golf course when a football practice was in session. He knew what my interests were, and he thought those were the qualities that a quarterback should have, that were necessary for a quarterback to have, and so he let me develop myself. He kind of encouraged the way I was going. I wasn't insubordinate, but I just hated running up and down a football field in wind sprints to get into shape. I'd rather have a game where we'd have some reason for getting from here to there, and where we were getting in shape in the process. I got in shape playing basketball, handball, tennis, paddle ball, touch tackle—you name it. Then I'd throw the football.

"Chuck was great. You couldn't find a guy who was more instrumental in my career. If it hadn't been for him I wouldn't have continued playing football. I would have quit and gone out and played baseball. I could hit and I was a good fielder. I was second string All-City in Oakland behind Frank Robinson."

The first game Brodie played for Stanford was against the

Tackle Paul Wiggin and quarterback John Brodie, mainstays of 1954-56 Stanford teams.

University of Pacific in 1954, and the Indians barely squeezed past the Tigers 13-12. "I remember I hit my first 10 passes," Brodie said. "Three of them were dropped, but I still hit all of them. I didn't know if I could play at Stanford. At Oakland Tech I'm just another guy, and two years later I'm playing first string for a college team that I had held in awe all my life. I didn't know why I was playing, but that started giving me some confidence and it helped when we played Oregon up there and beat them 18-13. They were supposed to go to the Rose Bowl, but we beat them on a pass to John Stewart that bounced off George Shaw. After the game, which was played in Multnomah Stadium, the crowd was a bit ugly. Taylor got on the public address system and told the fans: 'Okay, I've held these guys back as long as I can. If you don't clear the area in two minutes I'm going to turn them loose.' We didn't have any problems after that.

"After that Oregon win I'm really sailing. But that was it for me. The roof fell in and I didn't play too well after that for the remainder of the season. We got beat 25-0 by Navy and 72-0 by UCLA. That's a lot. They played Jerry Gustafson the next week, and then we alternated the remaining games. At the end of the year I was a guy with a lot of promise, but it was unfulfilled."

Brodie completed 21 passes for 192 yards in the game with UCLA and yet the Indians were unable to score. The Bruins nullified much of Brodie's effectiveness with eight interceptions which they returned for 218 yards. Sam Brown scored three touchdowns for UCLA in that game, returning two punts for scores.

Stanford lost its last four games, bowing to Washington State 30-26, USC 21-7, San Jose State 19-14, and California 28-20. Fumbles played a big role in the loss to Southern California as bobbles halted two Stanford scoring drives, and the Trojans converted two others into scores. A 42-yard pass from Gustafson to John Neff produced the lone Stanford score in the third quarter. The loss to San Jose State was the Spartans' first ever in the series which dates back to 1900. In the loss to California, the Bears broke the Big Game open in the second quarter with three touchdowns and increased its lead to 28-0 before Stanford managed to rally at all. Gordy Young ran 34 yards for the first Cardinal score, and Bill Tarr intercepted a pass to set up another, but this was not enough to win.

Hopalong Halted

Stanford lost three games in 1955, and two of them were to the teams that played in the 1956 Rose Bowl game—Michigan State and UCLA. There were some bright spots to the season, however, as the Indians beat Southern California for the first time in four years, won their first Big Game since 1946, and whipped Ohio State 6-0.

"In the UCLA game I had a chance to put myself to the test," Brodie said. "For the first time in a year I was excited about getting into a game. We were behind 21-0 at the end of the first quarter, but in the third quarter I got in the game and we had the ball on the UCLA 35. It was third down and seven, and I called a pass play, intending to throw to the sidelines.

"The outside linebacker jumped into the hole in the line. I pictured the route Paul Camera was to run, which was behind the space vacated by the linebacker. I never had thrown to that receiver on that pass play, not even in practice. Suddenly things came into focus—why that route was part of the play pattern. I hit Camera for 25 yards, and he ran another 10 to set up a touchdown.

"I suddenly became aware of the other team's personnel and wound up completing something like 17 of 21 passes. The final score was 21-13, but we were on the UCLA one yard line at the final gun. That was the most fun I'd had in my life."

Brodie put on another spectacular passing exhibition to score a 28-20 upset over USC in the Coliseum in Los Angeles, hitting 14 of 26 pass attempts for 216 yards. "I was just winging it all over the place," said Brodie. "We weren't as good as those other guys, but obviously we wanted to beat them.

There's an awful lot of rivalry, but there never was the vicious-ness. There never was the feeling of 'we're going to get these guys.' Our junior year we got after them, but I think there's more rivalry between USC and Stanford than with California, especially in football. You don't hear anyone saying, 'Boy, we've got to beat Cal,' do you?"

In the USC game Brodie passed to Gary Van Galder and Mike Raferty for touchdowns, and Bill Tarr intercepted a pass and ran 55 yards for another score as Stanford capitalized on fumbles and pass interceptions to beat the Trojans.

There is something about being on television that seems to bring out the best in Stanford football teams, and that was the case as far back as 1955 when the Indians upset Ohio State 6-0. Stanford took the opening kickoff and marched 71 yards for the only score of the game, with Gustafson passing two yards to Paul Camera for the touchdown.

Paul Wiggin played a key role on defense for the Indians. Taylor gambled and keyed his defense to stop Howard "Hop-along" Cassady, and the strategy worked as the great Buckeye star was held to 26 yards rushing. And it was Wiggin who was responsible for a big share of the work. Meanwhile Tarr gained 102 for Stanford. Actually the score should have been bigger than 6-0.

Before the game Coach Woody Hayes of Ohio State sent a messenger to the Stanford locker room to ask Taylor if it would be permissible to change footballs when Ohio State had possession of the ball? Some teams had preferences as to the brand of football they used, and the rules had been liberalized to allow the teams to use their own ball.

"I don't care what kind of ball they use," declared Taylor, "They can use a basketball if they want." Then after a moment of thought he asked, "How are they going to change the ball when we kick it?"

Stanford beat California 19-0 in the Big Game, with the Indians dominating the game. Brodie's screen pass to Gordy Young on the second play of the game was good for a 62-yard gain as Young made excellent use of his interference to race to the Bears' eight yard line before being hauled down. Brodie got the touchdown from the one on fourth down.

Wiggin recovered a fumble on the Stanford 11 to halt a California threat late in the first quarter. The Bears reached the Indians' five in the third period, but lost the ball on downs.

213

That was the extent of the California offense for the day.

"Chuck Taylor was a great coach, one of the finest I've ever met. I really liked him," Brodie said. "He also was a fine man. I've heard you can separate the two, but I've never seen it done. You find a great coach and you'll find a helluva man too. Chuck knew where he was as a person. He was a tough 'bugger,' don't think he wasn't. He would call it just the way he saw it, but he also had a real good sense of humor, and he never put more importance on a football game than the health of your mother, or your own.

"He knew the purpose football held, and he wanted the guys to go out there and have fun because he knew that if they were enthusiastic about playing the game they were going to play a helluva lot better than if they weren't. With the talent we had we could lock up shop because we weren't going to win many games. His idea was to get the most out of what he had, and I can't think of a better way to go.

"Don't think Chuck wasn't tough. He was damn tough. But I don't mean unfair. He was fair and that's what made him such a great guy. You could respect him as a person. Nobody fooled him. I remember one guy who thought he would get away with something. Some people think they can run over you because you treat them square. It was getting hot during the two-a-day drills, and this guy asked Chuck if he could take off his shoulder pads because it was getting hot and he had been running all day.

"Chuck said okay. So when we lined up for contact work this guy wasn't going to take part because he didn't have on his shoulder pads. 'I didn't say you could get out of contact,' Taylor said. 'I just said you could take off your shoulder pads.'

"A couple of days later the guy took off his hip pads, saying it was too hot for him. Chuck walked over and said, 'Well, Jerry, you know we're trying to make it as easy as we can for you around here. We let you take off your shoulder pads, we let you take off your hip pads. Now is there anything else we can do for you? We've got 54 guys right here. If the defensive linebacker is hitting you alongside the head and it's hurting too much, you let us know and we'll get you some aspirin.' It was perfect. Everybody started laughing and carrying on, and there was no more fooling around."

Taylor liked to have players on his squad who could supply humor and keep up the morale. Sometimes he kept marginal

214

players on the roster or took injured players along on trips for just that purpose. One such occasion occurred in 1956 when Stanford traveled to Columbus, Ohio, to play Ohio State. Don Manoukian, one of the standouts in the line, was injured, but Taylor decided to take him along to keep up the morale.

"Manoukian and one of the other players were a little depressed after we lost to Ohio State and decided Columbus was overrated as a town," Brodie said. "They went out after the game and had a couple of beers, and when they came back to the hotel they noticed these trash cans located on each floor. They decided to throw them out the window and were working their way upstairs. They thought they were throwing the cans on an old building, but actually it was a theater. The police caught them and called Taylor to tell him they had a couple of his players at the jail and asked what they should do with them.

"'Let them stay there,' Taylor said. 'I'm not coming down there to get them.' So when we got ready to leave for home the next morning we drove the bus past the jail, picked them up and came home."

Another Near Miss

Stanford slipped back to another 4-6 season in 1956, but a couple of points might have made a big difference in the outlook for the Indians.

"We had won four in a row at the end of the 1955 season so when we came to our senior year we figured, 'Man, oh man, we've got something going,'" Brodie said. "Then all our guys went down like flies. We were always thin at Stanford. We always had the top quality athletes, but we never had enough of them. We had five or six who could play for any team in the country, play first string for anybody, and then we'd have 30 who couldn't make the squad for a lot of universities. They made up for it in knowing the game, or in the purpose that they had. So that's the way it worked at Stanford until more recent years.

"We played Oregon State, and if we had beaten them we'd have gone to the Rose Bowl. But we lost 20-19. We were ahead 19-7 with six minutes to play, and they ran two balls in on us. We didn't care after that. I can remember throwing Camera a pass and he had a step or two on his defender, and I just underthrew it and the guy picked it off. Then they ran it in, and then they ran another one in. You know they shouldn't do that, but they did, and that just shot us down. They had Joe Francis, and they went to the Rose Bowl. That really burned me."

Brodie earned All America quarterback honors his senior year, and he credits a lot of it to Stanford's performance in a 32-20 loss to Ohio State in Columbus, Ohio. "The most meaningful game, as far as my exposure was concerned, was in that losing game to Ohio State," Brodie said. "It was 26-20, but we had the ball and we were driving again in the fourth quarter. But a fumble kept us out, and they went down at the end of the game and scored. But we were a crappy team. We had 20 guys hurt at the time, and the only two guys playing were Wiggin and myself. It was like the last of the Mohicans. They were so much better. We had a third string guard, John McKenna, starting. It was the first game he had played and he was up against Jim Parker, an All America tackle. Well, that's a pretty tough go, but he did a hell of a job, and we almost should have beaten them.

"It was so easily exposed how much better they were than we were, and how we could have won the game. All the writers in the East were there, and it seemed like they said, 'Hey man, maybe he really can play.' If you're from the West coast you've got to do something outstanding. I was the guy Stanford was pushing for All America, but there were a lot of good quarterbacks that year, like Sonny Jurgensen of Duke, Milt Plum of Penn State, Paul Hornung of Notre Dame, Len Dawson of Purdue, and myself. As a result of that game I was the consensus All America. It meant a lot as far as my being drafted, and it meant a lot as far as a lot of things. That kind of determined my direction. I didn't know if I could play pro football, and I didn't know if I wanted to play. But I knew that if I got drafted high enough and they wanted me, that I'd play. I just didn't know what I was going to do, but then I realized the possibilities and I said, 'Let's go.'"

Brodie beat Southern California two years out of three. Although he is inclined to call the 28-20 win in 1955 the best game he played and the most meaningful game personally, he looks back on the 27-19 win in his senior year with fond memories.

"Stanford isn't on a par with USC as far as personnel goes, but in any given game because of the way they play, Stanford has an even chance to beat USC. And the Trojans know it. I used to love to play USC," he said. "You get these little opinions about other teams, and you categorize them. I just thought USC was a team of big, slow, dumb jerks. Well, there's nothing I'd rather play than a team of big, slow, dumb jerks. Obviously they weren't, but that was my impression of what they were about. So I could hardly wait. I can remember Monte Clark, who became a real close friend of mine, was playing defensive tackle for USC—he and George Belotti. They came in, and I

217

remember I was going to throw the ball. I pumped it and ducked under them. On the way back to the huddle I said, 'You know, you guys will never change, you dumb suckers.' It got them so mad, and I was just sitting there laughing at them. Well, you frustrate the heck out öf your opponents, and I don't know what there was to it, but it always was my viewpoint. I didn't care if they knew it or not. It was just fun to play them. That was the day I remember laughing my head off.''

Stanford's Rose Bowl hopes were dashed by three conference losses by a total of four points. One was the Oregon State game in which the Indians made only one of three extra point tries and lost 20-19. Brodie completed 19 of 31 passes for 223 yards in that contest. The week before, UCLA had capitalized on a blocked point after touchdown for a 14-13 win.

The final loss was a 20-18 setback by California which saw the Indians lose the ball on the Bears' seven yard line on one occasion and a Brodie-to-Camera touchdown pass called back on a penalty on another.

Lou Valli, a 176-pound junior halfback from San Jose, turned in the all-time single game rushing effort that day in a valiant bid to bring Stanford out on top for a break-even season. Valli carried the ball 23 times for a net 209 yards, a 9.1 yard average, and a new Big Game record. This stole the spotlight from Brodie and California quarterback Joe Kapp. The mark still stands as a Stanford record.

"Brodie did an excellent job for us, particularly his senior year," Taylor said. "He was outstanding. When the pro scouts were looking at him and asking me whether he would do all right in the pros, I wasn't quite sure. I thought he had tremendous ability as far as a passer was concerned, but I wasn't sure if he was strong enough physically to take the beating in the pros. But he played 17 years. How wrong can you be?"

There never were any regrets on Brodie's part regarding the decision to attend Stanford. "I've been all over the country, and I've seen every campus that has a reputation for being pretty, and they're not even in the same league with Stanford," he said. "If a guy has an avenue to get into Stanford and he doesn't go, I think he has wasted a super opportunity because this is the place. The air is clean; there's a difference in the atmosphere. You never get the feeling somebody is standing around behind you. There are so many diversified things to do. I just don't see where there's a weakness."

Paul Wiggin, Stanford tackle who later played 11 years with the Cleveland Browns, was named on the *Sporting News* All America team and was selected on the AP, UPI, and Hearst second teams. Brodie was a consensus choice, being picked on the *Look, Collier's*, INS and NEA All America first teams and second team on the UPI, *Sporting News*, and Hearst teams.

Wanted: Good Kicks

Two missed conversions cost Stanford a chance to go to the Rose Bowl in 1957, which was to be Taylor's last year as Stanford coach. Chuck had informed Al Masters he did not want to stay in coaching and, with the approval of President Wallace Sterling had been offered the newly created position of assistant athletic director.

The Indians lost three conference games and finished with a 6-4 overall record. The loss that proved most costly was the 27-26 defeat by Oregon before 56,000 fans at Stanford Stadium—the biggest crowd ever to attend a game in this series. A victory would have given Stanford a tie for the championship with Oregon State. As it turned out, Coach Len Casanova's Webfoots tied the Beavers for the conference championship and, although Oregon had lost to Oregon State, they got the bid to Pasadena because the Beavers had gone the year before.

Each team scored in every quarter in the Stanford-Oregon game, but Stanford missed its first and last points after touchdowns while Oregon missed on only its last opportunity. Jack Douglas, who had passed to Jeri McMillen for Stanford's first touchdown, moved the Indians 71 yards to the Oregon nine yard line before being stopped shortly before the final gun.

Failure to kick extra points also cost Stanford the Washington State game as the Cougars claimed a 21-18 victory. The Indians had an 18-0 lead at half time and held an 18-7 advantage with three and a half minutes left in the game, but could not hold it. Washington State's Bob Newman completed an 87-yard pass for a touchdown to make it 18-14, and the Cougars recovered an on-side kick at the Stanford 47 and added

Jack Douglas, quarterback 1955-57.

another score with 44 seconds left to play. The Stanford defense played a big role in two of the Indians' scores. Center John Thomas blocked a kick and recovered on the Washington State 17 to set up Stanford's second touchdown at the end of the first quarter, and tackle John Kidd recovered a fumble on the Cougars 29 to give the Indians the opportunity for a third score in the second period. After missing kicks on the first two PAT's, Stanford tried a pass the third time but, although Douglas' toss to McMillen was complete, he was stopped short of the goal.

There were other highlights during the season. Joel Freis caught two touchdown passes from Douglas in Stanford's 20-6 win over UCLA. Jack Taylor returned a pass interception 67 yards for a touchdown and Lou Valli broke loose for a 60-yard run to the Spartan 10 to set up a score in a 46-7 win over San Jose. In the game against Northwestern Valli ran 48 yards to the Northwestern 15 after taking a reverse from McMillen on a punt return in the first quarter, as the Indians beat the Wildcats 26-6 in a nationally televised game.

And Stanford's kicking improved. The Indians wound up their season by making nine straight extra-point kicks in their last three games. They made all five in handing Southern California a 35-7 lacing, the worst beating Stanford had administered USC since the series began in 1905; made two in a 24-14 loss to Oregon State; and made two more to edge California 14-12.

Halfback Al Harrington suffered a broken jaw in the third quarter of the game with Southern California, which limited his action in the final two games to kicking extra points. Chris Burford, a sophomore who developed into one of Stanford's all-time great ends as a junior and senior, caught a 12-yard pass from Douglas for Stanford's final touchdown. Roy Stephens, McMillen, Chuck Shea, and Jim Byrer accounted for the other scores against the Trojans.

Freis and Eric Protiva blocked California conversion attempts to give Stanford victory in the Big Game, 14-12. Douglas and Shea played major roles in the Stanford offense; Douglas took the Indians to the Bears' one at the final gun—after gaining good field position by recovering an on-side kickoff attempt by California.

It was prior to the Big Game on November 23, 1957, that the Block S Society dedicated the "Pop" Warner memorial fountain, an attractive structure containing a bronze portrait of Warner outside Stanford Stadium.

Joel Freis, leading role in 1957 Big Game win.

222

Jack Curtice Takes Over

Jack Curtice of Utah and Bob Blackman of Dartmouth were the leading candidates to replace Taylor. The Stanford Board of Athletic Control finally settled on Curtice and on January 16, 1958, signed him to a five-year contract.

"We had Bill Corbus, Bob Reynolds, Frankie Albert, and Chuck Taylor in for a meeting with Curtice, and everyone was impressed with his background," said Cliff Burnhill, a member of the BAC and former president of the Stanford Alumni. "He had been a successful coach at West Texas State and University of Utah, and he taught the same type of wide open offense which had characterized Stanford under Taylor.

"Reynolds took Curtice down to Los Angeles to meet the leading Stanford alumni in that area, and everybody liked him."

Curtice was colorful, folksy, and witty, but his attempt to use the same approach he had employed at West Texas State did not work. The Cardinals posted a 2-8 record in 1958 and scored only 96 points, allowing 226 as the Stanford defense failed to hold any of the opponents under two touchdowns. Stanford wound up leading the Pacific Coast Conference in passing offense, but was last in rushing offense, rushing defense, and total defense.

"Jack had an idea of using a combination of the Oklahoma defense on one side of the line and another defense on the other side," Chris Burford recalled. "He junked the whole thing after Washington State beat us 40-6 in the first game. Curtice was a terrific offensive coach, but I think he tried to do too much of the coaching himself instead of assigning things to his assistants. He had a good staff of assistants in Leon McLaughlin, Andy

Everest, Pete Kmetovic, Dutch Fehring, Herm Meister, and Bob Ghilotti, but they were afraid to do anything. When Curtice came over to a group of players he would take over instead of letting the assistants go ahead. I never knew just what my responsibilities were, even at the end of my junior season. Sometimes he'd even change the defense on a Friday afternoon before a game.

"We had a good passing attack, but we didn't have any backfield speed. One of Curtice's standing jokes was that the reason we didn't run the sweeps was that we'd be penalized for delay of the game. One of the big problems Curtice had was that he didn't have players who were willing to give the dedication it took to win. The ball club didn't have the feeling it could win like Stanford does now. Football is a mental game, and if the desire is high enough a team can overcome a lot of deficiencies. Another thing was that we never had the depth to compete with USC or the other top teams."

Key personnel in the 1958 season were Bob Nicolet and Dick Norman, who shared the quarterback duties, and pass

Jack Curtice, who succeeded Taylor as Stanford coach, with co-captains Ed Cummings and Gary Sargent.

receivers Chris Burford and Irv Nikolai.

Burford was recruited out of Oakland High School by Burnhill, an Oakland lawyer, and now is a partner in the same office with his benefactor in Walnut Creek, California. Also a partner there is Chuck Morehouse, a former Stanford guard, who was recruited out of Alameda High by Burnhill.

In Stanford's first game of the season, Washington State capitalized on two fumble recoveries in the opening minutes of the game to claim an early lead. The only Cardinal score came as the result of Phil Burkland's recovery of a Washington State fumble in the end zone, and Washington State romped to a 40-6 win at Pullman.

Things did not get any better the next week when Rice invaded Stanford Stadium and handed the Cardinals a 30-7 setback. "We figured we'd really get them at Stanford," Burford said. "The year before we had gone to Houston, and they had beaten us 34-7. By the end of the first quarter we were just wilted by the heat and humidity. But we thought it would be different at home. But we had a heat wave that day and the temperature was about 98. Several of our players had heat prostration, and we wilted like flies. Rice thought it was great. They even brought their long-sleeved jerseys."

Then Stanford put everything together to defeat Washington 22-12. The Cardinals spotted the Huskies a touchdown in the first five minutes, and then dominated the game the rest of the way, rushing for 249 yards and completing 16 of 32 passes for another 132. Rick McMillen ran five yards for a second-quarter score and romped 20 yards for a touchdown in the third period after Nicolet intercepted a Washington pass and returned it to the Huskies 25. Roch Conklin recovered a fumble on the Washington 40 in the fourth quarter, and Nicolet passed 14 yards to McMillen to the one and then one yard to John Bond for the touchdown.

The Cardinals had a bad case of fumble-itis and lost four of seven bobbles as the Air Force registered a 16-0 win. But Stanford enjoyed its best offensive effort of the season in its 21-19 win over UCLA in Los Angeles. The Cardinals rushed 223 yards and completed 16 of 28 passes for 201, for a total of 424 yards. Sid Garber passed 22 yards to Burford for a touchdown the first time the Cardinals had the ball, and Nicolet hit Burford for 32 to help set up a second score.

The Cardinals came close to upsetting the Rose Bowl-bound California Bears but lost 16-15. Stanford hit 23 of 43 passes for 279 yards but managed to run for only 74 in its loss to California. With 1:30 left to play Norman completed four passes in a 78-yard drive, including a 21-yard toss to Joel Freis, to pull the Cardinals within a point of the Bears. But Face's attempt to run for two points failed.

Earlier in the game a two-point conversion attempt had also failed. Norman's pass to Nikolai was touched by Face and ruled incomplete after Stanford's first touchdown. Face then gave Stanford a 9-8 lead in the second quarter with a 27-yard field goal, and the Cards had advanced to the California 20 in the third period with the help of Nicolet passes to Face and Freis. But four straight passes fell incomplete to halt the drive. Then the Bears marched 80 yards in 16 plays; Jack Hart, Wayne Crow, Joe Kapp, and Billy Patton alternated on running plays, never taking to the air. On the conversion, however, Kapp passed to Crow for two points and California had a 16-9 lead. Stanford's final drive left the score 16-15.

Bad breaks and key injuries were blamed for the poor season. Due to injuries, Curtice started a different backfield combination in each of the first eight games. Quarterbacks Nicolet and Norman and pass receivers Burford and Nikolai had excellent records in the 1958 season. Nicolet led the conference in passing with 77 completions in 146 attempts for 724 yards while Norman was second with 76 completions for 133 tries and 717 yards. Pass receiver Burford earned All-Conference honors and was the No. 1 pass receiver with 45 catches for 493 yards, while Irv Nikolai was second with 32 for 343.

The Norman-to-Burford combination gave promise of things to come in the 1959 season. Burford ended up third in the nation in pass receiving. The big end played 540½ minutes in 10 games. Only four members of the Vow Boys ever had played more time for Stanford, and they participated in 11 games. Despite the fact that they split the quarterback duties, Nicolet ranked seventh nationally in passing and Norman, eighth. Stanford was seventh nationally in team passing with an average of 258.1 yards per game.

All Offense, No Defense

Despite the adversity he encountered at Stanford after being so successful at West Texas State and Utah, Curtice never lost his sense of humor, except for one occasion. "He was one of the most warm-hearted guys I've ever known," said Fehring, who joined the Stanford staff in 1956 and served as an assistant until 1967 when he switched to scouting. In addition, he was head baseball coach through 1966. "Jack was here at a bad time when the material wasn't the best. But even after a defeat, when everybody was feeling low, I can remember Andy Everest, who had played for Jack at Texas Mines, would get out a ruler and start beating on a desk, and Jack would do a soft shoe dance, and we'd be off and running, making plans for the next game."

The one time Curtice was not in a jovial mood came one Friday night when the Stanford football team was quartered at the President Hotel in Palo Alto before a game. "There wasn't a room big enough to handle the squad so we'd meet in the cold garage in the basement for a chalk talk," Morehouse recalled. "They'd bring in a blackboard, and the players would sit around on cars. It was cold down there.

"A couple of the players always got a room on the street— about the sixth floor—and had made a science of dropping water balloons on pedestrians on the sidewalk. One of them was an engineering major, and they'd time a balloon to see how long it took to land. Then they'd calculate how long it took the pedestrian to walk from under the theater marquee to the spot where the trial balloon had landed.

"One night they didn't recognize Curtice and bagged him. He called the entire squad down to the garage. He was mad and

228

wanted to know who was responsible."

"I was the team captain, and he wanted me to find out who had done it and tell him," Burford said. "I was in the middle. I had respect for the coach and always got along with him, but I also felt I couldn't turn against my teammates."

Stanford finished the 1959 season with a 3-7 record, but it could just as easily have been 7-3 or 8-2. "We had at least four games that could have gone our way, where we lost by three points or less," Burford said. "We could score on anybody, but the trouble was we couldn't stop anyone. We led the nation in passing offense as a team. Dick Norman was the leading passer and I was the top receiver. Ben Robinson was No. 4, and Skip Face tied for second in scoring with 100 points."

Norman became the second man of all time to net more than 2,000 yards in total offense in 10 games or less—he led the nation with 2,018 yards. He completed 152 of 263 passes for 1,963 yards and 57.8 percent. The number of completions and yards were the greatest in history against major competition at that time. Norman's performance gave Stanford its third individual passing title in seven years. Bob Garrett previously had won the honor in 1953 and John Brodie in 1956. Stanford was No. 1 in team passing with an average of 227.8 yards per game.

Burford caught 61 passes for 756 yards, tying the national record for catches, and giving him a two-year mark of 106 receptions.

Quarterback Dick Norman set NCAA passing record in 1959 game with California with 34 completions in 39 attempts for 401 yards.

Norman's spectacular performance against California, 34 completions in 39 attempts for 401 yards, set NCAA single game marks which still stand. But despite this, California won 20-17. Stanford had a chance to tie with 3:21 left to play, after fighting from its own 45 to the California 10 but went for a touchdown instead of taking a field goal.

Norman completed five of seven passes as he led the Cardinals' drive and then on the final play ran for five yards at right end.

"We didn't want a tie," Burford declared. "Curtice went for victory. He was enthusiastic and never willing to settle for a tie. Norman tried to get out of bounds to stop the clock at the end of the game, but his knee hit the ground in bounds, and the final seconds ticked off before we could get off another play.

"Actually Dick's performance that day was even better than the 34 for 39. It should have been 36 of 41," said Burford, who caught 12 passes from Norman that day. "Three of his passes were grounded to stop the clock, and I caught two that were called back on penalties. To show you the quality of the pass defenses that day, Wayne Crow of California, who wasn't noted as much of a passer, completed his first seven tosses, including one for 48 yards to Gael Barsotti for Cal's first touchdown."

Stanford lost its opening game in the 1959 season to Oregon 28-27 because the Cardinals went for a two-point conversion and a win instead of letting Face, who kicked 19 of 20 PAT's, put his toe to the ball. Mac Wylie ran 38 yards for the first Stanford touchdown and Norman passed 35 yards to Dick Bowers for a second. With one minute left, Norman passed to Ben Robinson for 11 yards and a score, but his pass to Burford for the two-point attempt was deflected just before the Stanford end could grab the ball.

The Cardinals uncorked an amazing passing attack in a second half thunderstorm to throw a scare into Wisconsin, which wound up the season by going to the Rose Bowl to face Washington. After spotting the Badgers a 16-0 lead in the game at Madison, Wisconsin, the Cardinals took to the air despite heavy rain, and Norman whipped a 54-yard scoring pass to Burford to start Stanford rolling. He wound up with 219 yards on 18 completions in 27 attempts for the game which Wisconsin won 16-14. "The rain was so heavy that you couldn't see the action in some parts of the game films," said Chuck Morehouse.

Stanford had a 21-12 lead over Southern California at the half, but the Trojans, who have a reputation for being a strong second half team, scored twice in the fourth quarter for a 30-28 win. The best the Cardinals could do was a single touchdown. This time it was not the failure to convert that beat Stanford as Face kicked all four extra points.

Burford caught touchdown passes of nine and 13 yards from Norman as the Cardinals picked up 207 yards through the air on 16 completions in 32 attempts. "Those two touchdowns gave me a bit of extra pleasure," Burford said, "because when I was in high school I had written to USC inquiring about going there. One of the assistant coaches wrote back that they weren't interested in me, that they already had filled their quota of players. I only caught one pass all season when I was a sopho- more, but it was for a touchdown against USC."

Stanford registered a 54-38 victory over San Jose State in a game that turned out to be a football fan's dream. "That shows what kind of a defense we had," Burford observed. "We had to score 54 points to win." The combined total of 92 points set a new Stanford Stadium record, breaking the mark of 82 set in the 82-0 win over Mare Island in 1923 (and tied in the 82-0 victory over UCLA in 1925). Stanford rolled up 509 yards in total offense on 224 yards rushing and 285 passing with 13 completions in 25 attempts.

Norman threw a 58-yard pass to Ben Robinson for Stan- ford's first touchdown. Norman completed another to Burford

William (Skip) Face, halfback-fullback 1958-60, had a big after- noon against Oregon State in 1959.

for 35 yards for another score on the first play after Gil Dowd had recovered a Spartan fumble on the second-half kickoff.

UCLA handed Stanford a 55-13 trouncing as Billy Kilmer directed the Bruin offense and capitalized on two Cardinal fumbles for a pair of easy second-quarter scores.

Morehouse recalled one amusing incident about the game however. "Our scholarship only covered tuition in those days," he said, "so we worked for the corporation yard to earn extra money. During the football season we cleaned up the stadium after home games, and on the Sunday after the UCLA game I was picking up papers in the section where the UCLA rooters had been seated. I looked down and there was a fellow lying under the bench. I guess he had celebrated the victory a little too much and just laid down and went to sleep and his friends left him there. He'd been there all night. We woke him up and helped him wash up a bit. He kept saying, 'How am I going to get back to Los Angeles?'"

One of Stanford's three victories in the 1959 season was a 39-22 win over Oregon State, and Burford credits a statement by Tommy Prothro, then the Beavers' coach, with helping to fire up the Cardinals. "We had been beaten by Oregon State for four straight years since Prothro had been at Oregon State, and he was quoted as saying, 'My team never will lose to Stanford.' After reading that we got mad and went up there and beat them," Burford said. "It was a good example that you never should say anything about an opponent before a game that might get him fired up."

Face had a big afternoon against the Beavers, scoring three touchdowns, kicking a field goal, kicking four conversions, and scoring a two-point conversion for 27 points. The other points came on a 57-yard pass from Norman to Burford.

One of the least amusing things to happen to Burford occurred during spring drills before the 1959 season. "Homer Smith, who now is head coach at Army, decided to have us practice recovering a loose ball one afternoon before Coach Curtice showed up," Burford said. "He lined us up in pairs and threw the ball between us. My instinct as a receiver was that if I couldn't catch the ball the best thing was to knock it down to prevent an interception. I reached out with my left hand to knock the ball down and my hand slid under the face guard of the other player, Ron Fernandes, and I broke my wrist. Luckily it was in the spring and I was ready to play by fall."

Curtice thought it would be a good idea to invite some of the staunch alumni to make trips with the team when it was traveling by charter, and on one occasion invited one of the old grads to give the half-time talk to the team. When the squad filed into the locker room at half time and started looking around for Connie Jarvis, the Cardinals' veteran trainer, they could not find him. Finally he showed up and was asked where he had been. It turned out that the alumnus Curtice had invited to give the half-time pep talk had become so excited about the assignment of talking to the team that he was hurrying too fast and fell down some stairs. Jarvis had to be dispatched to revive him.

A Winless Season

There were very few occasions for Curtice's folksy humor to shine through during the 1960 season, which turned out to be one of total disaster. Stanford still had Dick Norman at quarterback and Skip Face at fullback, but the supporting cast lacked experience and the squad was hit by a number of costly injuries. As a result, the Cardinals posted their first winless season since Marchie Schwartz encountered similar adversities in 1947 and went 0-9. This time the Cards were 0-10.

Curtice had 18 lettermen returning, but only five of them were starters from the 1959 campaign. One of his biggest problems was that all of the top receivers—Burford, Robinson, Dick Bowers, and John Bond—had graduated. This quartet had caught 129 of 176 passes for 1,775 yards in 1959. Candidates for left end included Vic Preisser and Bob Peters, who had played for the Braves or reserve squad, and Chris Jessen, up from the frosh. At right end Curtice had Rich Hearney, a non-letterman; Steve Pursell from the Braves; and Chet Hinshaw from the freshmen. The result was that Norman did most of his throwing to his backs. Face was the leading receiver, catching 29 passes for 270 yards, and Mac Wylie grabbed 25 for 377.

"Generally speaking, we had some pretty good athletes," recalled Chris Cottle, a center on the 1960 team and now district attorney in Santa Cruz County. "Going both ways it was pretty tough, particularly in terms of depth. The team morale was pretty low after the third or fourth game, and when we lost to San Jose State (34-20) that was horrible.

"I was so depressed after the San Jose game that I went into the locker room and just sat there. I wound up getting

234

locked in. That was the low point of the season. We had some outstanding athletes, but we didn't have any black athletes, and that was at a time when blacks were excelling. In terms of speed, compared to other teams, we just couldn't compete.

"The fact that Stanford was a good academic school attracted a lot of top athletes. That and the fact that football wasn't the overall important thing. A good education was the No. 1 priority. A lot of athletes who came to Stanford weren't on scholarship because all scholarships were based strictly on need. This was true only at Stanford. The academic picture was to push people, and that placed you in a difficult position. I remember going to a German professor and asking if I could make up an examination later because I was going on a football trip and would miss class the day of the exam. The professor told me that if I wasn't there to take the exam I would get an F."

Stanford came closest to winning in its opening game with Washington State, losing a 15-14 decision at Spokane. The Cardinals held a 14-0 lead at the half, but the Cougars tallied a pair of quick touchdowns in the fourth quarter to win. Garner Eckstran intercepted a flat pass by Norman and ran 60 yards for Washington State's second score. A two-point conversion by Washington State's Keith Lincoln after the first touchdown was the margin of victory.

Three Norman passes and a 24-yard run by Face gave Stanford a first quarter score against Wisconsin and a 7-0 half-time lead over the Badgers. The only other time Stanford ever held the lead in a game the rest of the season was at the end of the third quarter of the Oregon State game seven weeks later when the Cardinals had a 21-19 edge. But they lost that one 25-21. They also lost that Wisconsin game 24-7, although Norman and Rod Sears completed 21 of 43 passes for 267 yards.

Cottle never played on a winning team against USC. "The games always were pretty close, however," he said. "We lost by one point as freshmen and beat UCLA and Cal. Then the next two years, with the same players, we lost to all three."

Everything Stanford tried against USC backfired in 1960 as the Trojans registered a 21-6 win. On the fourth play of the game one of Norman's passes was intercepted by Jerry Trayham of USC and returned 35 yards for a touchdown. Later in the first quarter the Cardinals had a fourth down on the Trojan 34, and Norman tried to pass for the necessary four yards. The play

235

lost a yard and USC took over and marched for another score.

Stanford's only points came after Don Peter recovered a Trojan fumble on the USC 29. Norman passed to Steve Pursell for 20 yards to the one yard line, and Hal Steuber tallied the touchdown.

Norman needed only 146 yards to become the all-time leading passer in Stanford history going into the Oregon game at Portland, but he completed only five of 15 tosses for 27 yards. The Ducks, who were 14½ point favorites, capitalized on the passing of Dave Grosz and the running of Cleveland Jones, Dave Grayson, and Jerry Tarr for a 27-6 win.

The 1961 *Quad* cited costly injuries and a lack of speed for the collapse of the 1960 Stanford team. The situation never was more obvious than the week before the Oregon State game. C. B. Simon, a starting tackle, was out with a shoulder injury. Guards Ron Fernandes, Chuck Morehouse, and Errol Scott were sidelined along with end Vic Priesser. The only guards Curtice had were Don Peter and Tom Walsh. Starr Rounds, a sophomore center, was moved to guard to provide some backup strength.

Oregon State was an 11-point favorite in the game, which was played in the rain. It turned out to be a see-saw affair with the battered Cardinals giving Coach Tommy Prothro's Beavers a real battle. Oregon State scored with only 1:54 left in the first quarter, but Stanford tallied in three plays as Norman hit Face with a 15-yard pass, and he ran another 41 yards for a touchdown with only five seconds left in the period.

Stanford held a 14-13 lead at the half and had a 21-19 edge after three quarters, but the Beavers took a 25-21 lead with 6:36 left in the game. With Gil Dowd doing yeoman work and Norman completing a left-handed pass to Dale Ostrander for 15 yards, the Cardinals marched from their own 28 to the Oregon State four.

Here fate struck a cruel blow at Stanford. Face took a pitchout at left end and scored with 1:58 remaining, but the touchdown was nullified by a clipping penalty. Stanford was set back 15 yards, and the Beaver defense braced to hold off the threat.

The only thing the Cardinals could salvage from the loss was that Norman, who completed nine of 14 passes for 131 yards, had set a new Stanford school career passing record of 3,604 yards to break John Brodie's old mark of 3,594.

Although it matched a pair of lacklustre teams the Big Game attracted a crowd of 76,200, only a few hundred less than the capacity of Memorial Stadium in Berkeley. Stanford was 0-9 and California, 1-7-1.

The Bears were a three-and-a-half point favorite and quickly established themselves as the superior team by driving 74 yards to the Stanford four yard line. Then Randy Gold whipped a pass to Steve Bates in the end zone for a Bears touchdown. It was the only pass Gold threw during the game.

California marched 97 yards for another score and a 14-0 lead after halting a Stanford threat on the Bears' three yard line. The Cardinals pushed over a third-quarter touchdown and appeared headed for another as Norman used screen passes to Wylie to guide Stanford from its own 12 to the California six. But the Bears braced, and Face had to kick a 29-yard field goal to make the score 14-10. That was as close as the Cardinals could come to overtaking California.

"We knew California planned to smash our tackles," Curtice said. "During recent weeks we've had so many injuries at that position we couldn't find a way to cope with the situation."

Norman, who led the nation in passing the year before, dropped to ninth place as he completed 95 of 201 passes for 1,057 yards and only four touchdowns. Face, who had tied for second nationally with 100 points in 1959, tallied only 47 in 1960. The highly recruited fullback from San Marino wound up as Stanford's leading pass receiver with 29 catches for 270 yards and was second to Dowd in rushing yardage with a net 430 in 96 carries. Dowd gained 477 in 116 tries.

"Rick McMillen was an outstanding athlete, and one of our better backs," Cottle recalled. "One day in practice Rick ran the wrong way on a play. Curtice chewed him out and told him to get himself together. On the next play Rick ran the wrong way again. Curtice couldn't believe it. A little while later McMillen ran the wrong way a third time. Curtice didn't say a word. Rick never did it in a game though. That was one time there was a little humor during practice. Usually they were dull and not much fun. The coaching staff lacked the knack of making it fun."

A fine group of sophomores headed by quarterback Steve Thurlow moved up to the varsity in 1961 to provide a much needed lift. Thurlow was considered one of the best prospects

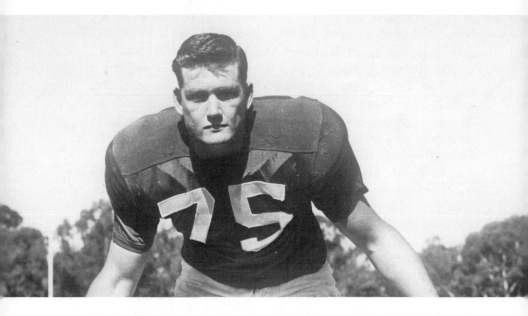

First visit to Los Angeles Coliseum awed Al Hildebrand, 1961-63 tackle.

in Stanford history. At this stage he was farther advanced than some of the great quarterbacks of the past at a comparable period. But he was stricken with mononucleosis in midseason and sidelined for the rest of the campaign. Curtice wound up splitting the quarterback assignment among Rod Sears, Chuck Butler, and Jim Smith as the Cardinals posted a 4-6 record.

Butler faked a draw play and threw a 47-yard touchdown pass to Larry Royse in the fourth quarter as Stanford edged Tulane 9-7 in the season opener to snap an 11-game losing streak. The next week at Corvallis, the Cardinals exploded after a scoreless first half to blast Oregon State 34-0. The Beavers dominated the first half but were unable to score, once driving to the Stanford three where Terry Baker fumbled and Al Hildebrand, a sophomore tackle, recovered for the Cards. In the second quarter Baker skirted right end, reversed his field, and ran 51 yards to the Stanford 34 before being shoved out of bounds. The Beavers got to the three yard again that time before Baker missed on a field goal.

Sears threw a 22-yard pass to Steve Pursell for one touchdown and set up another with a 39-yard toss to Royse in the third period to give Stanford a 14-0 lead. Tyce Fitzmorris ran

29 yards, and Ken Babajian and Thurlow added other scores in the final quarter.

"I can remember thinking that everything was working that day," said Cottle. "The running, the passing, the defense. I wondered why it was that we were doing the things we did every week, and yet we were winning? We had our spirits up for the games, but I think it was the Monday, Tuesday, and Wednesday attitude that killed us. Friday was too late to get up for the game."

After winning their first two games of the season the Cardinals invaded East Lansing, Michigan, to face Michigan State, which had a good team and was nationally ranked. Stanford trailed only 7-0 at half time and capitalized on a Spartan fumble to trail only 7-3 in the third quarter after Stan Lindskog kicked a 40-yard field goal. It was a clear example of Stanford being worn down because of a lack of depth the rest of the way as Michigan State rolled to a 31-3 win.

"Curtice told us to hold the score down," one of the players recalled. "What he meant was to hold their score down. He had us convinced we couldn't win."

Stanford developed a good running game to defeat San Jose State 17-6, rushing for 235 yards while gaining only 68 on six pass completions in 12 attempts. The next two weeks were nonproductive. Washington capitalized on a pass interception and a fumble recovery for a 13-0 win at Seattle. UCLA posted a 20-0 victory as Kermit Alexander returned a short field goal attempt 94 yards for one Bruin score. Walker ran a pass interception back 27 yards for another.

Stanford had a slight edge in statistics the next week against Oregon, but could not handle Mel Renfro as the Webfoots tallied a 19-7 win.

"Renfro had a broken bone in his foot so he was only in the game for five plays," said Bob Burke, a sophomore end from Coos Bay, Oregon, who went on to law school and now is an attorney on the Peninsula. "He came in for one play in the first quarter and scored on a four-yard play on which he actually dove over the head of our defensive halfback. He ran a couple of plays in the second quarter and then came back on the last play of the half and took a pitchout and threw a 39-yard pass to Burleson for a touchdown.

"After we had scored in the third quarter he took the kickoff and ran it back 94 yards for a touchdown. He was only in for five plays but he was responsible for three touchdowns."

Stanford fumbled three of the first four times it had the ball against Southern California and yet trailed the Trojans only 7-0 after the first quarter. And that score came on a 69-yard run by quarterback Pete Bethard. Ben Wilson, a 238-pound fullback, added a pair of touchdowns, and the Trojans rolled to a 30-15 win.

"That was my first game in the Los Angeles Coliseum and it scared me when I came out of the tunnel and saw all those people in that big stadium," said Al Hildebrand. "On one play that big Wilson came through my position, and the next thing I knew I was on my back in the end zone with Wilson laying across my chest. I never believed USC was mortal after that. They had counter-plays that looked just like the one they had run before, but one time it would be a run and the next time a pass."

"We always were in the game with USC for the first half, but their depth would start to pull us down in the third and fourth quarters," said Thurlow. "Half of our ball club was from Southern California, so we always played our best against USC. But we always had a negative attitude or a defeatist attitude. We lacked the mental toughness and never felt we were as good as USC. A lot of us came to Stanford because we wanted to go to a good school and still play football. But we still used to fantasize about how we possibly could go to the Rose Bowl."

A number of theories were advanced for Stanford's dismal showing during the Curtice era, among them one that football was progressing rapidly and Stanford was not keeping pace.

A different idea was offered by Burke. "At that time Stanford wasn't doing a lot of recruiting. We had a few good athletes, but we didn't have the financial support they've had in more recent years. There were no junior college transfers to help fill in any weak spots, and football was not the most important thing on the campus. Actually, it was a bad time. There was talk of de-emphasizing football. Stanford was wrestling with the idea of whether it wanted to play big time football, and the student body wasn't backing the team."

Another theory which was advanced was that the team was suffering because there were only a couple of black players on the squad. Many of the alumni apparently were against the idea of having blacks on the team, but the feeling among the players was that the presence of blacks might have solved Stanford's problem of not having a real good running back.

240

A number of players who performed under Curtice expressed the feeling that personally Jack was a "nice guy" but that he and Stanford were not meant for each other. "He wasn't accustomed to recruiting the type of player who could get into Stanford," said one former player.

"Our passing game held us together somewhat," said George Honore, an end from San Jose. "We didn't have good pass protection, so most of our passes had to be short ones."

A muddy field did not bother Stanford in the 1961 Big Game as 79,000 turned out to watch Jim Smith lead the Cardinals to a 20-7 victory in Stanford Stadium. Hal Steuber, Stan Lindskog, and Gary Sargent, who had been injured during a good part of the season, played prominent roles in the win which gave Stanford a 4-6 season.

Smith completed five of seven passes during the game, for a total of 43 yards. His first two completions—to Frank Pati-

George Honore, leading receiver in 1961.

tucci for 19 yards and to Lindskog for 16—played a big role in Stanford's first touchdown drive, which was capped when Ken Babajian scored on the first play of the second quarter. Another pass—this time to Chris Jessen for 11 yards—and Gary Craig's 24-yard romp around right end with a pitchout produced the second score a few minutes later.

California, fighting to salvage something from a disappointing season which had yielded only a tie with Missouri and a victory over Washington, drove to the Stanford three early in the third period. But Jim Pierovich fumbled and Jim Shroyer recovered in the end zone for Stanford. Later in the quarter Stanford moved 76 yards in four plays for another touchdown. Lindskog swept around left end and down the sidelines for 49 yards. Then after gaining two up the middle, he went around left end again for 21 yards to the California four. Craig scored from there.

The win over the Bears proved to be Stanford's only victory in the Athletic Association of Western Universities' race and gave the Cardinals a tie for fourth place with California in the five-team conference.

Honore was the only Stanford player named on the All-AAWU first team, with fullback Ed Cummings earning second team recognition. Honore finished as second leading pass receiver in the conference with his 22 catches for 225 yards. Stanford's passing game produced only 901 yards for the season, an average of 90 yards per game. Yet that was good enough to rank the Cardinals second to USC in the conference. The running game yielded a net 1,472 yards as Babajian and Craig finished the leading rushers with 189 and 185 yards respectively.

A couple of weeks before the start of preseason drills Craig wrote a letter to Curtice, asking permission to report late because he had taken a summer job selling pots and pans and was doing very well. He explained that he would like to skip the first week or two of practice because he could use the money.

The 1962 season turned out to be Curtice's best, but it still did not save his job.

"The Big Game with California turned out to be one of our best games," said Patitucci, a big end from Montebello. "We won the game, but Curtice still lost his job. We were behind 13-3 at the half, and Curtice sent Weaver in at quarterback for Thurlow in the second half. We had been moving the ball on the ground, using fundamental plays.

242

Ed Cummings, 1962 co-captain and defensive star.

"Curtice liked to use the double pass, and it was at this point that he sent in the play after we had run the ball from our own 20 to the California 25. In the huddle everyone was asking why he would call that play when we had been running so well? Weaver threw a lateral to Chris Jessen who then passed to Bob Howard for a touchdown. It turned the whole game around and we won 30-13."

The 25-yard pass by Jessen not only was the only pass he threw during the game—and the season—it was the only one of his career.

Lindskog's 39-yard field goal had given Stanford a 3-0 lead late in the first quarter, but California scored twice in less than five minutes before the end of the half, but the Bears never recovered from the shock of Jessen's pass.

Weaver, a third string quarterback, threw three touchdown passes in the final 20 minutes of the game. Jessen caught one for 11 yards late in the third quarter, and Patitucci and Howard grabbed the others from eight and 18 yards in the final period. Marv Harris had recovered a fumble to start one of the drives, and Ed Cummings intercepted a pass and returned 15 yards to the California 29 to set up the other.

Stanford had launched the season with victories over Tulane and Michigan State. It then lost three in a row before beating UCLA and suffered two more defeats before finishing up with wins over San Jose State and California.

"We stayed in the infirmary on the Tulane University campus because there was a possibility the two black players on our squad might make the trip," explained Burke. "They couldn't stay in any of the hotels in New Orleans, so the arrangements were made for the infirmary. As it turned out they didn't go, but the team voted to stay in the infirmary anyhow. Steve Pursell found a microphone which was used to make announcements on the different floors and started doing some imitations of the coaches, thinking the mike was turned off. What a surprise he had when the coaches came roaring upstairs to see what was going on. His voice was going all over the building."

The Cardinals beat Tulane 6-3. J. D. Lodato took a pitchout and skirted left end for 30 yards and a touchdown early in the third quarter, after Chapple had recovered a Tulane fumble. Otherwise, Stanford's offense did not do much.

Thurlow's passing and the running of Lodato and John Paye were the keys in the Cardinals' 16-13 upset of Michigan State. Stanford's first score followed a 36-yard pass from Thurlow to Howard after Tony DeLellis had recovered a Spartan fumble. Paye ran 33 yards for the second score, after Thurlow had passed to Patitucci for a 25-yard gain and to Howard for an 11-yard gain. Lindskog's 26-yard field goal provided the winning points.

Patitucci intercepted a bobbled pitchout and ran 82 yards for a touchdown to highlight Stanford's 17-7 triumph over UCLA in Los Angeles. The Bruins had taken the opening kickoff and marched to the Cardinals' eight where UCLA's Kermit Alexander fumbled Larry Zeno's pitchout. Patitucci intercepted and ran the length of the field to score.

"I had knocked Alexander down on the play or Patitucci never would have made it," said Al Hildebrand, a 6-5 end-tackle from Houston, Texas. "Frank had a 20-yard lead by the time Alexander got to his feet, but Kermit made up half of that distance in the first 15 yards he ran."

244

Frank Patitucci, out of breath after 82-yard interception return.

Thurlow chuckled as he recalled the play. "Patitucci was leaning forward and striding in perfect form for the first 40 yards or so," he said. "Then he began to straighten up, and the last 30 yards he was leaning backwards and gasping for air. Alexander finally caught him at about the two yard line, but the momentum carried them into the end zone."

Lindskog's 25-yard field goal gave Stanford a 10-0 lead before the Bruins scored on a play almost identical to Patitucci's. Allen Curr was hit hard on a pitchout and fumbled. The ball was caught in mid-air by Bob Jones of UCLA, who ran it back 81 yards for a touchdown.

Stanford became the first Pacific-8 school to play in the Palouse since 1958 when the Cardinals invaded Spokane to face Washington State. The experience was not a pleasant one as the Cougars registered a 21-6 win, although Stanford piled up 238 net yards to 84, and 12 first downs to six.

Washington State's James Paton blocked Lindskog's attempted quick kick on the first play of the second quarter, and Gery Gehrmann recovered in the end zone for a touchdown. The Cougars added two quick scores at the start of the third quarter. Ken Graham ran the second half kickoff back 92 yards for a touchdown. Then a pass from Dave Mathieson to Gerald Shaw resulted in a score, after Clete Baltes had intercepted a Thurlow pass at the Stanford 28.

A Cal Man Takes Over

"When the decision had to be made for a new coach in 1962 there obviously were a number of candidates," Chuck Taylor related. "At that particular time John Ralston was riding a crest of success at Utah State. I had known a little about him when he was at the high school level across the bay. All of the reports we kept getting were that he was a tremendously dedicated person. Of course he had great running teams at Utah State which didn't affect me an awful lot because I had a faint suspicion that our quality and material here would have to be in the other direction. But John convinced me that he had the ability to be flexible in the utilization of the material. Although the first few years were a bit grim he did eventually move into the passing style and turned out to be successful."

Ralston was hired just before the start of 1963 spring practice, the last official act of Al Masters, who was stepping down as director of athletics. Thus Taylor and Ralston came in together as athletic director and football coach. They also quit together nine years later, Taylor to enjoy semi-retirement, and Ralston to move into the professional ranks as coach and general manager of the Denver Broncos of the National Football League.

Ralston was born in Oakland but attended elementary and high school in Norway, Michigan, before enrolling at the University of California, where he played linebacker on two Rose Bowl teams. "I always wanted to coach," Ralston said. "I knew at the age of 11 what I wanted to be. It's just a lot of fun for me. I never worked a day in my life. It's like trying to build a bigger house, taking a program and having the thrill of seeing it

247

develop. I always was anxious to get back to the Bay area, and although I'd had four wonderful years at Utah State, it was a chance to move to a bigger school when the Stanford opportunity came along."

Ralston won only three games his first season but never had another losing season. He wound up with Rose Bowl titles in his final two years.

"We had some real trying moments," he observed. "Recruiting was brutal. I don't know how many games we could have turned around in those early years, but things didn't work out like they had at Utah State. We were getting a few good athletes, but we lacked depth. It was the era of Dave Lewis at quarterback, and we didn't use him properly."

New athletic director Chuck Taylor (left) and John Ralston, newly appointed Stanford coach, discuss plans for 1963 season.

Guy Rounsaville, who had played under Curtice as a sophomore, noticed a big change under Ralston although the results were not much different the first season. "It was as different as night and day," stated Rounsaville. "You went on impulse under Curtice. Ralston was organized. He also had a different outlook on recruiting and set out to get proven players from the junior colleges. He stressed the J.C.'s. It was a different atmosphere."

Weaver, the hero of Stanford's 30-13 victory over California the previous year, had impressed Ralston in spring drills. And as a result, Thurlow, who had started practically every game in 1962 and shared the quarterback duties with Weaver, was moved to right half, a shift designed to take advantage of his running ability.

"It was a terrific break for me," said Thurlow. "Because of the shift I was drafted by the New York Giants. I never would have made it in the pros as a quarterback."

Weaver was injured in the third quarter of the UCLA game, the third game of the season, and Dick Berg, a sophomore, inherited the quarterback duties for the remainder of the season.

Patitucci and center Marv Harris earned All-Conference recognition as Stanford finished in the Pacific-8 cellar with a 1-4 record, beating only arch-rival California 28-17 within the conference. The Cardinals were 3-7 overall, with the other two victories coming against San Jose State and Notre Dame.

"We beat Notre Dame 24-14 on national TV and, even though Notre Dame wasn't up to its usual standards that year, it had to be a big win," said Bob Burke. "Dutch Fehring had scouted them against USC and UCLA the previous two weeks, and they had beaten both teams. (The only games the Irish won that season.) He came back and told us, 'you don't have a chance. They're big, fast, mean, and smart, but on a given day any team can beat any other team.'"

The Irish scored with the opening kickoff and held a 14-10 edge at half time, but Stanford dominated the second half. Thurlow scored two touchdowns and passed to Ray Handley for another. Braden Beck added a 30-yard field goal to complete the scoring.

Thurlow and Beck also played leading roles in the victory over California as Ralston launched a string of four straight wins over his alma mater. Thurlow rushed for 124 yards and scored

249

two touchdowns while Beck kicked three field goals as Stanford came from behind in the second half to whip the Bears.

Beck kicked a 36-yard field goal in the second period, a 48-yarder early in the fourth (to give the Cardinals an 18-17 lead), and a 46-yarder to conclude the scoring. Chapple, Harris, Bob Nichols, and Patitucci contained the California offense and held Craig Morton to eight completions in 18 pass attempts for 120 yards. Stanford relied on its running game to pick up 214 net yards in 63 carries, while throwing only nine passes, completing three for 42 yards.

California got on the scoreboard first with a field goal in the opening quarter, but Beck tied the score in the second. Stanford went ahead 9-3 early in the third period when a bad snap from center in a punting situation gave the Cardinals the ball on the Bears' six yard line. But California regained the lead 10-9 and pushed its advantage to 17-9 on a 69-yard punt return by Tom Blanchfield at the end of the quarter.

Fullback Babajian's touchdown and Beck's second field goal put Stanford back in front. A California fumble led to another Cardinal score before Lodato intercepted a Morton pass to provide the opportunity for Beck's final kick.

Ralston had expressed optimism that he would take Stanford to the Rose Bowl within four years after taking over the coaching duties. He made progress in that direction in 1964 as the Cardinals finished fifth in the Pacific-8 race with a 3-4 record and a 5-5 mark overall. Although he was unable to beef up the offense which scored only 150 points, Ralston did improve the Stanford defense by limiting opponents to 138 points. Handley was named on the All-Conference offensive team, and Gary Pettigrew, Chapple, and co-captain Dick Ragsdale were selected for the defensive unit.

Ralston installed Lewis, a 6-2, 200-pound sophomore who was an Indian of the Chuckchansi Tribe, at quarterback, but things did not really jell until after midseason. The Indians won three of their last four games as Lewis led Stanford to a 21-3 victory in the Big Game in one of the Tribe's best all-around performances of the year. The Bears held a 3-0 lead at half time, but Stanford came to life in the third quarter and dominated the second half.

Bob Blunt returned the second half kickoff 37 yards to the Stanford 40, and Lewis took the Indians the rest of the way in just six plays. The key play was a 46-yard pass to end Mike Con-

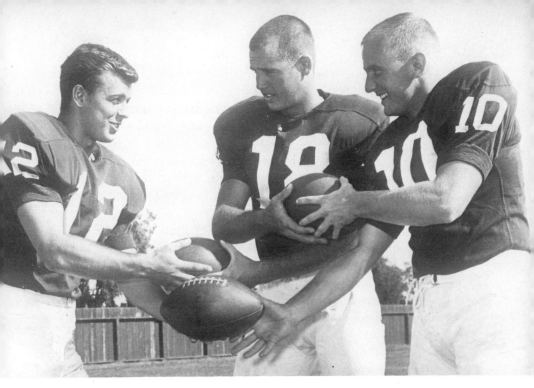

Stanford had three quarterbacks in its starting backfield at the beginning of the 1963 season with Dick Ragsdale (left) moving to left halfback, Steve Thurlow (center) to right half, and Clark Weaver handling the signal calling.

nelly, who had been shifted from quarterback to split end because of a hand injury which interfered with his taking the snap from center.

Stanford added two fourth-quarter touchdowns. Lewis scored on an 11-yard keeper in the opening minute. Then John Guillory, a sophomore defensive back, intercepted a pass and returned to the Bears' 39. With a second down and 10 on the California 11, Lewis passed to Fergus Flanagan on a tackle-eligible play for the touchdown.

Beck kicked nine field goals and 15 extra points during the season to lead Stanford's scoring and tie for third in the conference race with 42 points. He kicked a 27-yard field goal in the final 13 seconds to bring the Cardinals from behind for a 10-8 victory over Oregon, knocking the Ducks from the undefeated ranks. Stanford held Oregon to 33 net yards rushing and 40 passing while piling up a total of 374 yards, 201 of them coming on passes as the Indians completed 18 of 29 attempts. Beck also kicked the winning points in a 10-8 win over stubborn

San Jose State. The other victories came over Rice 34-7 and Oregon State 16-7.

Lewis got his big chance at quarterback against the Beavers and picked up 67 yards with his running to add punch to the Stanford ground game. Blunt accounted for one of the Indians' scores with a 24-yard romp. Stanford blew another excellent opportunity when it failed to get into the end zone in four running plays from the one yard line after Handley had raced 40 yards.

The Indians came close in four of their other five games. Their only bad loss was a 28-6 thumping by Notre Dame at South Bend. The Cardinals bowed to Washington State 29-23, UCLA 27-20, Washington 6-0, and Southern California 15-10.

Ralston came up with a pair of good running backs, Ray Handley and John Read, in 1965 to supplement Stanford's passing game, and the Indians improved their season record to 6-3-1. The best they could do in the conference, known as the Athletic Association of Western Universities (AAWU) was another fifth place finish with a 2-3 mark. Stanford did not play Washington State or Oregon State.

Stanford led the conference in total defense, allowing 236 yards per game, and was second in both rushing defense and passing defense, giving up only 96 yards per game through the air. The Indians were fourth in both rushing and passing offense but wound up third in total offense. Their passing, however, could account for an average of only 136 yards per game. Handley, who had set a Stanford single season record of 936 yards the year before, wound up with 654 net yards to place fifth in the league in rushing yardage. Read was eighth with 553 yards. Lewis finished second in passing with 94 completions in 183 attempts for 1,257 yards and led the conference in punting with a 44.9-yard average for 29 kicks.

The season was marked by the fact that Stanford played all three of the service academies, making the Indians only the second university ever to face all three in one season. Stanford bested Army 31-14, the Air Force 17-16, and tied Navy 7-7. Also on the plus side were wins over San Jose State 26-6 and Tulane 16-0 and conference victories over Oregon 17-14 and California 9-7.

Big plays of the season came in the 26-6 win over San Jose State in the opening game. Rubin returned a punt 62 yards for a touchdown in the second quarter, and Lewis passed to Blunt for a 71-yard touchdown play in the fourth period. Donn Renwick intercepted a Spartan pass and returned 43 yards to the San Jose six to set up another touchdown, and DeSylvia kicked field goals from 23 and 25 yards.

Stanford had a big edge in statistics in the Big Game but had to come from behind to win. The Indians out-rushed the Bears 228 yards to 109 but lost an excellent scoring opportunity in the second period when Handley fumbled on the California one and Paul Hoeber recovered for the Bears. After a scoreless first half Terry DeSylvia kicked a 24-yard field goal in the third quarter for Stanford, only to have California move 62 yards in six plays early in the final period to score. The Bears completed six passes during the game, and two of them were during this drive as Jim Hunt hit Tom Relles for a 15-yard gain and then tossed to Lloyd Reist for a 28-yard gain to the Stanford four. Relles punched over to put the Bears ahead 7-3.

It took Stanford 11 plays to punch over the winning score after returning the next kickoff to the 30. A Lewis to Bob Conrad pass was good for 18 yards to the California 11, and Handley made up for his earlier fumble by blasting through the mid-

Halfback Bob Blunt and quarterback Dave Lewis, counted on to lead Stanford to a successful 1965 season.

dle for the remaining yardage.

Stanford bottled up Heisman Trophy winner Mike Garrett for three quarters as the Indians played Southern California to a scoreless deadlock. But the Trojan star broke a 77-yard run for a touchdown in the fourth period. Then Rod Sherman intercepted a Lewis pass and swept end for 25 yards and another score, for a 14-0 victory. Stanford's only scoring opportunities came in the first quarter when DeSylvia missed on a 41-yard field goal attempt and in the fourth period when he failed on a 35-yard attempt. The Indians stopped USC on the Stanford two in the third period after the Trojans had marched from their own 10 to a first down on the Indians' six. Garrett got four yards in three tries, and on fourth down Troy Winslow picked up one.

Lewis used the tackle-eligible play twice to beat Oregon 17-14. The Ducks held a 7-0 lead at half time as the result of a second quarter touchdown. But Lewis passed to tackle Blaine Nye for 13 yards for a Stanford score after Dale Rubin had returned a punt 48 yards to set the stage. DeSylvia kicked a 19-yard field goal for a 10-7 lead after Bill Ogle had recovered an Oregon fumble on the Ducks' six.

Lewis passed to tackle Fergus Flanagan for nine yards and a fourth quarter touchdown, after Oregon had driven 58 yards to go ahead 14-10. Stanford completed 18 of 31 passes for 206 yards but had five fumbles and lost the ball each time to stall its offensive efforts.

DeSylvia made seven of 10 field goal attempts during the season and, as in the California and Oregon games, it was his kicking that brought the Indians out on top in the 17-16 win over the Air Force at Colorado Springs. The 150-pound senior from Portland, Oregon, kicked a 29-yarder in the closing seconds after the Indians had marched from their own 20 to the Falcons' 12.

The Air Force had driven to the Stanford 18 earlier in the fourth quarter, but Monty Mohrman and Bill Ostrander tossed the Falcons for losses, and an Air Force field goal attempt was wide. Stanford trailed 9-0 at the half but staged an 84-yard drive to score in the third period as Handley scored from the

Stanford's all-time career rushing leader, Ray Handley, who gained a net 1,768 yards with a best single season of 936 in 1964.

two; Lewis had passed 15 yards to Bob Blunt and 19 yards to Handley to move the ball into scoring position.

The Falcons' Barnes ran the kickoff back 98 yards for a touchdown, but Stanford came back with a 91-yard drive that was capped by a 13-yard scoring pass from Lewis to Blunt.

Ralston faced the 1966 season with a great deal of optimism. He had 25 lettermen returning from the previous year, including six starters from the offensive unit and six from the defense. "I thought it would be a good team," Ralston said. "It had a little flavor of the old and some good young personnel. We had Gene Washington, a sophomore quarterback, plus Chuck Williams, a transfer from Ventura Junior College, and Mark Marquess, who was up from the freshman squad."

Among the new men Ralston was counting on to bolster the line were George Buehler, a 241-pound tackle; Malcolm Snider, 226-pound guard; Greg Broughton, a fullback; and John de la Forest, 224-pound guard.

Gene Washington was recruited out of Long Beach High

Terry DeSylvia made seven of 10 field goal attempts in 1965.

School as the greatest quarterback prospect to enroll at Stanford in years. He had quarterbacked an undefeated freshman team and displayed such great promise in spring drills that Ralston had shifted Dave Lewis, the starting quarterback in 1965, to left halfback. But Washington had rough times during the season, and Lewis returned to share the quarterback duties.

Stanford wound up at the bottom of the AAWU standings again with a 1-4 record, again beating only California among conference teams. The Indians had a break-even season of 5-5 with non-conference wins over San Jose State 25-21, Tulane 33-14, Illinois 6-3, and Air Force 21-6. Passing, which was Stanford's trademark, failed miserably. The Indians were fourth in the conference, averaging only 125 yards per game. Washington completed only 35 of 102 attempts for 479 yards and had 11 interceptions. Lewis completed 28 of 52 passes but gained only 395 yards. End Bob Conrad accounted for more than half of Stanford's catches with 45 for 545 yards to rank third in the AAWU. Jack Root, who rushed for 571 yards on 136 carries, produced almost one-third of the Indians' rushing offense, which yielded an average of 167 yards per game—fourth best in the conference.

Stanford started in impressive fashion against San Jose State in the season opener, taking the opening kickoff and marching 67 yards to a touchdown. Washington passed 23 yards to Tim Abena for the score. But the Cardinals had to come from behind to win 25-21 as Danny Holman had passed the Spartans into a 21-10 lead after three quarters.

Two 58-yard drives in the first six minutes of the fourth quarter brought the Cardinals from behind, after a pass interception and a fumble recovery put San Jose State in good position for its first two scores. Stanford showed more of its old-time passing form by completing 21 of 31 passes for 234 yards, but three interceptions and eight penalties for 72 yards helped stall scoring bids.

In Stanford's 33-14 victory over Tulane the highlights were Bill Shoemaker's three field goals—from 40, 25, and 50 yards—and a 90-yard run off tackle by Lewis. The next week, however, Shoemaker managed to convert only a 21-yard field goal as Oregon claimed a 7-3 win. Shoemaker missed on a 31-yard attempt and had a 42-yard field goal try blocked. Another Stanford scoring threat was halted by a pass interception after the Cardinals had moved to the Webfoots' 16.

Sub-quarterback Chuck Williams hooked up with halfback Bob Blunt on a 75-yard touchdown pass to put the Cardinals back into their game with Washington. This was the first play after the Huskies had taken a 16-7 lead by capitalizing on a pass interception in the third quarter. Don Martin's 35-yard field goal pushed the Huskies ahead 19-14, but the Cardinals responded with a 68-yard drive to take the lead 20-19. Only four minutes remained, but that was plenty of time as Washington, aided by a 50-yard gain on a pass from Tom Sparlin to Dave Williams, advanced to the Stanford five. With less than 20 seconds showing on the clock, Washington's Martin kicked a 22-yard field goal to give the Huskies a 22-20 triumph.

Stanford made sparing use of its passing game in defeating California 13-7 for the sixth straight year. The Cardinals threw only seven passes and completed four for 44 yards. California had little success through the air, completing only four of 19 attempts for 31 yards.

Safetyman Dave Nelson's interception of a pass and 25-yard return to the California 40 set up Stanford's first score. The drive took nine plays and included one pass and six running plays by Root, who scored from the three. The other scoring drive covered 54 yards in three plays, with Jon Huss reeling off 28 yards to get it started and Greg Broughton capping it with a 17-yard jaunt. California's only score came in the second quarter on a 58-yard punt return by Don Guest.

Outlook Is Brighter

"We were getting better players, and we got a little bit smarter," Ralston said in looking back on the 1967 season. "I thought we could get as many good players as USC, but there aren't that many good ones. There are certain areas where Stanford has real appeal, like Montana, Washington, Oregon, and Chicago, and we got several outstanding players there. And we always did better than average in Southern California."

With Chuck Williams and Mark Marquess available to handle the quarterbacking, Ralston had moved Gene Washington to flanker in spring practice to take advantage of his speed and pass-catching ability. It was a good move as Washington led the conference in receiving with 48 catches for 575 yards, but he caught only two touchdown tosses. Williams was second in the Pacific-8 Conference, the new name adopted by the AAWU in September, 1966. He had 76 completions in 153 attempts for 923 yards, with seven touchdown passes.

Stanford wound up with a 5-5 overall record and a 3-4 mark in the conference for a fourth place tie with Washington. One of the big problems seemed to be that the Indians averaged only 117 yards per game with their passing game, sixth best in the league, while their running game averaged 175 yards with fullback Nat Kirtman accounting for more than one-third of the rushing yardage with a net 573 yards. Stanford was able to score only 157 points while allowing 179.

Washington was the only Stanford player to earn All-Conference honors on the offensive team, but tackle Blaine Nye

259

Gene Washington led Pac-8 in receiving in 1967 and 1968.

and linebacker Marty Brill earned recognition on the defensive unit. Offensive tackle Malcolm Snider, who gained All America honors the following year, was elected to the Pac-8 second team. Linebacker Don Parish, a junior who had been shifted from defensive end, was named "Player of the Week" for his performance against UCLA, while Williams earned "Player of the Week" recognition for his play against Washington.

In the season opener Kirtman turned in one of the longest kickoff returns in Stanford history with a 98-yard sprint against Oregon State. The Beavers had just scored on the second play of the second quarter when Kirtman exploded. But that was the extent of Stanford's scoring. All the scoring came in the second quarter, and Oregon State took a 13-7 win as Mike Haggard kicked field goals from 22 and 28 yards.

Williams threw touchdown passes of 43 yards to Gene Washington and five yards to Jim Cross in Stanford's 14-7 win over the Huskies at Seattle. The Indians' defense gave up 255 yards rushing to Washington but proved tough when its goal line was threatened. Dick Oliver intercepted a pass and returned it 45 yards to stop a Washington march which had reached the Stanford 24 in the first quarter.

Other drives were stopped at the 33, 29, and 25 before the Indians made their best defensive stand by halting the Huskies on the four yard line in the fourth quarter. Linebacker George Jugum had intercepted a Williams pass and returned it 27 yards to the Stanford 13. However, the middle of the Indians line threw Tom Manke for a one-yard loss on a fourth down keeper play when the Husky quarterback tried to pick up one yard for a first down.

Donn Renwick and Tom Massey also had pass interceptions for Stanford as the Huskies managed only one completion in 10 attempts. Massey ran 23 yards to the Washington 35 with a pass interception in the fourth quarter, but the Indians were unable to capitalize on the opportunity.

Stanford came up with its top offensive performance of the season to defeat Washington State 31-10, after spotting the Cougars a 10-0 lead in the first quarter. Williams completed six passes in a 76-yard scoring drive in the second quarter with Washington catching a seven-yard toss for the touchdown 40 seconds before the end of the half. That tied the score 10-10, Bill Shoemaker having kicked a 32-yard field goal midway in the period.

Pat Preston picked off a Washington State pass at the Cougar 31 to set up a Stanford score by Jack Root in the third quarter, and the Indians got another on a 10-yard pass from Williams to Cross before the period was over. Williams completed his third scoring pass of the day in the fourth quarter on a seven-yard pitch to Shoemaker after Kirtman had returned a Washington State punt 39 yards to the Cougar 14. A personal foul moved the ball to the seven and the Indians scored on the first play.

Williams and Marquess had one of the best passing days of the year as they completed 15 of 25 attempts for 138 yards.

The Indians had another good passing day against UCLA, completing 16 of 29 throws for 221 yards, and adding a net 229 yards rushing for a big edge in the statistics. But the Bruins walked off with a 21-16 victory as Gary Beban's faking and Mike Garratt's running proved too much for the Stanford defense to contain consistently. Parish, Nye, and Brill played outstanding games on defense, but just when it appeared the Indians had checked the Bruins, Beban or Garratt would break loose for a good gain to keep things moving.

Stanford tied the score at 7-7 in the final minute of the first quarter when Williams faked into the line on a fourth down and one situation and then threw a 39-yard pass to Shoemaker for a touchdown. Shoemaker put Stanford ahead with a 27-yard field goal, but touchdowns by Beban in the second and third periods gave UCLA a lead the Indians could not overcome. Stanford added a touchdown in the fourth quarter and was on the Bruins 16 at the end of the game, but three of Williams' passes went incomplete.

Co-captains of the 1967 team Jack Root, Marty Brill, and Don Swartz.

The passing game was off, but the running attack was working both times as Stanford squeezed by Kansas 21-20 and San Jose State 28-14. The Indians rushed for 240 yards against 64 for the Jayhawks, but Kansas offset this edge with a couple of spectacular kick returns. Junior Riggins returned the kickoff following Stanford's second touchdown 87 yards for a Kansas score. Don Shanklin ran Bob Reinhard's punt back 47 yards for a touchdown early in the third quarter to give the Jayhawks a 17-14 lead. Stanford had 12 players on the field at the time of Shanklin's run and still could not catch him.

A 16-yard run by Marquess, Kirtman's 30-yard romp on a draw play, and another 15-yard gain by Marquess accounted for most of the yardage as Stanford moved 80 yards with Root scoring from the one to put the Indians back in front 21-17. Then Bill Bell's 28-yard field goal, his second of the game, brought Kansas to within a point of Stanford with 6:01 left in the third quarter.

Both teams had chances to score in the fourth period. The closest Stanford could get was the Kansas 27 where Shoemaker missed on a 45-yard field goal attempt. Kansas reached the Stanford 16 late in the game, but Bell was wide right on a 32-yard attempt.

San Jose State's Danny Holman had a big day as he completed 25 of 42 passes for 294 yards against the Indians. But he had three interceptions, and the third of these thefts killed any hopes the Spartans had of surprising Stanford. Holman had passed to little Frank Slaton for 26 yards and a touchdown earlier in the fourth quarter to make the score 21-14. The next time San Jose got the ball, Holman moved the Spartans to a first down on the Stanford 10, but his next pass was intercepted by Bob Rinker in the end zone and returned to the Indians' seven. With Kirtman reeling off gains of 13 and 23 yards, Stanford moved upfield to the Spartans' 33. Then Kirtman completed the 93-yard march by blasting through the middle, almost untouched, for the touchdown that sealed Stanford's 28-14 win.

Defensive improvement was responsible for Stanford's strong late season showing. Blaine Nye, Tom Hazelrigg, Don Parish, Malcolm Snider, George Buehler, and George Crooks were leading performers in the defense.

The Big Game was not one of Stanford's better efforts of the season. Fumbles played a big role in California's 26-3 victory. The Indians fumbled three times and the Bears recovered all three, turning the first one into a 23-yard field goal by Ron Miller and another into a fourth period touchdown.

The only thing Stanford salvaged from it was that Gene Washington caught 10 passes to edge Cal's Wayne Stewart for the Pacific-8 pass receiving title with 48 catches for the season. Stewart, who had five receptions in the game, was second with 45.

The game was a strange one for three quarters, with Stanford holding a 3-2 lead at half time and California claiming a 5-3 edge at the end of three quarters. Stanford's only scoring came on a 33-yard field goal by Shoemaker in the first quarter. California's two points in the first half came early in the second period when Dick Oliver of the Indians intercepted Gary Fowler's fourth down pass at the goal line and then downed the ball in the end zone.

California broke the game open with three touchdowns in the fourth quarter. Fowler's 30-yard punt return to the Stanford 45 just before the end of the third quarter played a big role in the first of the scores. A 35-yard pass from Randy Humphries to Wayne Stewart moved the Bears to the 10. On the first play of the final period Stewart outfought Dave Nelson of Stanford to take a pass from Humphries for the touchdown.

A Stanford fumble on the first play after the next kickoff was recovered by Mike McCaffrey of the Bears on the Indians' 21, and two plays later Humphries completed his second touchdown toss with a 21-yard aerial to Jim Calkins. Humphries sneaked over from the one yard line with six seconds remaining in the game as the Bears snapped a six-game losing streak to the Indians.

Stanford had only two scoring opportunities in its game with Southern California, and both of them were nipped by pass interceptions by Mike Battle. The Trojans, on their way to the Rose Bowl for the second straight year, romped to a 30-0 victory as Steve Sogge passed to Earl McCullouch for 28 and 29-yard touchdowns. O. J. Simpson, a junior tailback from San Francisco, took a break from his ball-carrying duties to take a pitchout and pass nine yards to Steve Dale.

Surprisingly, the Trojans outpassed Stanford, completing 14 of 27 for 196 yards while the best the Indians could do was 11 of 22 for 148 yards. USC rushed for 264 yards compared to Stanford's 55.

Nat Kirtman, his 98-yard kickoff return not enough.

What Does It Take?

A sophomore quarterback by the name of Jim Plunkett arrived on the scene in 1968, and things began to change as far as the Stanford football picture was concerned. Plunkett had the motivation to become a great quarterback, and he took the Indians along with him.

"We can learn so many great lessons from Jim Plunkett," Ralston said. "I remember when he was a senior in high school in San Jose he was named the All-Northern California quarterback, but when he went to an all-star game the coaches told him the other quarterback was far superior and asked Jim where he would like to play. He said he had played a little defensive end as a sophomore and that he would play there. He played 58 minutes in the game and played like a mad man.

"You trace these two young men over a five year period, and you find that the other player went to a rival institution and played 27 minutes in his entire intercollegiate career. Plunkett emerged not as regular quarterback, not as an All-Coast or All America, but, as a senior, the No. 1 athlete in the country in college football, winner of the coveted Heisman Trophy.

"After his freshman year, a rather mediocre year, I interviewed Jim, as was our technique following spring practice, and I said, 'Jim, we've got two senior quarterbacks, and we've got a junior. It looks like a redshirt year for you, or maybe we'll have to change your position.'

"'Coach,' he said, 'tell me what I've got to do. I want to play quarterback.'

"I told him, 'You don't roll out and throw the ball. We're a roll out team. You don't move and throw on the move well

Sophomore Jim Plunkett gets set to unlease 64-yard touchdown pass to Jack Lasater.

enough. I suggest you go home this summer and maybe get some guys and throw the ball some, like 100 or 200 times a day.' If I said 200, they tell me he maybe threw 1,000 times a day. He worked for a construction company, but when he got home he went down to the park and threw the ball.

"When he came back that fall we couldn't believe it was the same guy. Then we did decide to redshirt him because we did have the superior players. We came around after that year, and we wondered why we did it. He was obviously the best one by midseason, but we held to it, even after an injury to our top quarterback.

"He came in as a sophomore and in the initial game completed 10 of 13 passes for 277 yards and four touchdowns. Jim continued from that point, never satisfied, always with a vision of what he had set in mind for Jim Plunkett. Every spring when the other guys were heading for Santa Cruz, he took a sack of footballs and went out to the field to throw into a net. He'd take a five step drop and he'd throw with all he had. He strengthened that arm until he'd make the ball vibrate in the air he could throw it so hard.

267

"What a thrill it was to take him all the way through. And then his senior year, he'd been elected co-captain, and one of the writers asked him, 'Which would you rather do, win the Heisman Trophy or go to the Rose Bowl?'

"He didn't hesitate one second. 'Go to the Rose Bowl,' he said, 'because I can do that with my team.'

"Yet in all the goal-setting we learn to take on one thing at a time. He was able to accomplish both goals. He took his team to the Rose Bowl, and he won the Heisman Trophy."

For all of his heroics, and despite the fact that he set a new conference record by passing for 2,156 yards his sophomore year, Plunkett was accorded only honorable mention on the All-Pacific-8 Conference team. The first team honor went to USC's Steve Sogge. Gene Washington, who set conference marks with 71 catches for 1,117 yards, and tackle Malcolm Snider were named on the first offensive team, and linebacker Don Parish was selected on the defensive team. Plunkett, guard George Crooks, end Stu Kelner, and defensive guard George Buehler were accorded honorable mention.

Plunkett's debut came in a 68-20 romp over San Jose State. These were the most points scored by Stanford since 1949 when the Indians had beaten Hawaii 74-20. Although he played only about half of the game, the big Stanford sophomore threw for 277 yards and four touchdowns. Washington also gave an indication he would have an outstanding year as he grabbed five passes for 170 yards and three touchdowns, one of them a 79-yard shot from Plunkett. Another was for 51 yards, and Plunkett also fired a 66-yard TD pass to Lasater.

Then Stanford rolled over Oregon 28-12 at Eugene as Plunkett hit 14 of 26 passes for 227 yards and three touchdowns. "I was a little disappointed with some aspects of the game, but Plunkett made the difference," said Ralston. "He's our equalizer. He always seems to make the right play at the right time. You really have to give credit to center John Sande for the way he handled George Dames today. Dames shut off our running power, but not once did he get to our passer. Sande did a fine job for a sophomore, and he must be considered one of the bright surprises of this early point of the season."

"Ralston always was an optimistic, fired-up type of guy," said Buehler. "He just enjoys coaching. He's sincere, and not putting on a show. I can remember before the USC game my senior year, everyone was nervous. Ralston told us to go out and have fun. It kind of amazed me. But he knew you can't win if you're too tight."

Stanford came closer to beating Southern California than it had in 11 years, but O. J. Simpson, who became the Trojans' second Heisman Trophy winner in four years, proved too much for the Indians. Simpson gained 220 yards on 47 carries and scored three touchdowns to lead USC to a 27-24 victory before 81,000 fans at Stanford.

From the very start the game was a crowd-pleaser, full of brilliant plays and near-misses. Stanford had a golden opportunity in the opening minutes when Parish jarred Simpson loose from the football and recovered on the USC 46. A Plunkett-to-Washington pass carried the Indians to the Trojan 13, but the threat stalled and Horowitz missed the first of three successive field goal attempts, all wide to the right.

Ayala's 32-yard field goal in the second quarter gave the

Malcolm Snider, a 1968 All America tackle.

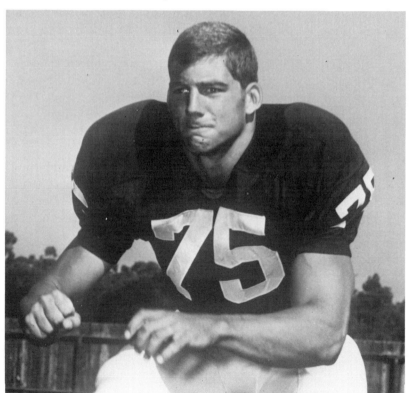

Don Parish, an All America linebacker in 1969.

Trojans the lead, but after that they would have to come from behind three times before finally putting the Indians away for good.

Stanford's Bubba Brown, a shifty junior college transfer, cut through a gaping hole in the left side and romped 51 yards for a second quarter touchdown to put Stanford in front. Then Simpson's first score of the afternoon returned the Trojans to a 10-7 lead, but Steve Horowitz kicked a 38-yard field goal with 40 seconds left in the half to tie the score at 10-10.

Stanford marched 90 yards at the start of the third period to again move in front, with Jack Lasater catching a 27-yard pass from Plunkett for the touchdown. Then a pass interception by Gerald Shaw gave USC the ball on the Stanford 46, and Simpson swept around right end and went all the way to tie it up again. Plunkett, who completed 14 of 30 passes for 247 yards, went 10 yards on a perfectly executed option play for another brief Stanford lead that failed to hold up.

The Indians held a 24-17 lead with five minutes left in the third quarter, only to have USC tie the score as Simpson tallied on a four-yard plunge, after a 52-yard pass from Sogge to Jim Lawrence had advanced the ball to that point. Then Ron Ayala kicked a 34-yard field goal with 3:09 remaining in the game to give the Trojans their winning margin.

Don Parish, George Buehler, and Pat Preston were outstanding on defense for the Indians in that game. Parish had 23 tackles, and Ralston said after the game: "Without doubt Parish is the best linebacker I've ever been around. With Parish on his feet we have a defense." Buehler had 15 tackles and was named Pac-8 defensive "Player of the Week." Simpson was named offensive player.

Injuries and pass interceptions almost proved fatal as Stanford had to come from behind to tie Washington State 21-21 at Spokane. The Indians lost tight end Bob Moore with a hamstring muscle pull, Jack Lasater with a shoulder separation, and Buehler with a leg injury. Plunkett completed 14 of 30 passes for 222 yards, but the Cougars stopped four Stanford drives with interceptions.

There was a little more than six minutes remaining to play when Plunkett hooked up with Washington on an 11-yard touchdown pass for the tying score. It was Washington's eighth catch of the game and gave him a total of 110 yards.

Plunkett had another outstanding game against UCLA, but Stanford failed to take advantage of its opportunities and dropped a 20-17 decision to the Bruins. Plunkett hit on 25 of 43 passes for 272 yards, with Washington making 13 catches for 114 yards, and Bubba Brown carrying 18 times for 114 yards. But it all went for naught as the Indians managed to collect only three points out of five drives which reached the UCLA one, two, six, seven, and 17 yard lines.

A 49-yard punt return by Jim Kauffman led to Stanford's first score with Plunkett rolling inside left end from the two yard line. Mark Marquess, who had been converted from quarterback to split end, caught six passes for 56 yards during the game, and one of them was a 10-yard reception for a touchdown in the second quarter to give Stanford a 14-0 half-time lead.

But the Bruins came from behind to win in the final four minutes when Bill Bolden hit Ron Copeland on a 50-yard pass play to the Stanford three and Greg Jones punched into the end zone. UCLA had gotten back into the ball game by scoring twice in the third quarter, the first touchdown coming on a 65-yard "bomb" from Bolden to halfback Gwen Cooper.

"That UCLA defeat was the lowest moment we had had," said Ralston. "We had won our first three games and had played well against USC in losing 27-24, and tying Washington State

271

21-21. There were all sorts of mistakes. There were coaches' errors and there were players' errors in the UCLA game, but we rallied back to win our last three games."

But before the last three wins came a game with Oregon State. The Beavers' great running power and a wet field were too much for Stanford to handle on November 2 at Stanford Stadium. Plunkett passed for 214 yards by completing 18 of 34 passes, but could only produce one touchdown, a 35-yard throw to Washington in the last seven minutes of the game. Meanwhile, All America fullback Bill Enyert and halfback Billy Main proved to be almost unstoppable with their inside and outside ground attack. Enyert carried 34 times for 164 yards while Main gained 126 yards in 18 carries as the Beavers registered a 29-7 win. Main scored on runs of 24 and 20 yards while Bob Mayes, Beaver wingback, romped 55 yards to score on a reverse.

One of the wins was a 35-20 victory over Washington in which reserve quarterback Don Bunce came off the bench to rally the Indians after the Huskies had taken a 7-0 lead in the first quarter. Plunkett was shaken up on the first play of the second period while running an option from the Washington 11. He was hit at the six and lateraled to Howie Williams, who continued for the touchdown.

Bunce threw only seven passes, but he completed five of them for 137 yards and three touchdowns. He capitalized on a pass interception by Kauffman in the second quarter to throw a three-yard touchdown pass to Howie Williams. One of the throws he failed to complete, however, was intercepted by George Jugum of the Huskies who ran it back 85 yards for a score that gave Washington a 14-14 half-time tie.

In the third period Bunce rolled out to his right and pegged a long pass to Washington who had beaten Al Worley, the Huskies' All America defensive back. The play was good for 80 yards and a go-ahead touchdown. Stanford added two more scores in the fourth quarter. One came after Stu Kellner recovered a Washington fumble on the Stanford 49; the other came after Buehler pounced on a Husky fumble at the Washington 28—Bunce passed 28 yards to Washington, who made a diving catch in the corner of the end zone. One of the defensive standouts for Stanford was co-captain Kellner who blocked two field goal attempts, recovered a fumble, and made ten tackles.

Plunkett enjoyed one of his best afternoons of the season when he led the Indians to a 20-0 win over California in the Big

Game at Berkeley. Stanford dominated every phase of the game, gaining 189 yards rushing and 241 passing for a net total of 430 compared to California's 126. Actually the game was not as close as the score would indicate. Plunkett completed 17 of 31 passes for 241 yards and ran for an additional 34. Gene Washington caught seven passes for 90 yards, running his total to 71 for the season to set a new Pacific-8 record. A fierce pass rush, led by Don Parish who was named Pac-8 "Player of the Week," plus a tight Stanford secondary held California to eight completions in 29 pass attempts. All told, the Indians had five interceptions, with Dennis Moore and Tom Massey collecting two each and Parish one.

A three-yard pass from Plunkett to tight end Bob Moore produced Stanford's first touchdown in the opening quarter. Greg Broughton, who turned in one of the best efforts of his career, carried 28 yards on a draw play to set the stage for a second period touchdown. Washington, on a flanker reverse, went the final 17 yards behind blocks by George Crooks and Dan Lightfoot. Bill Shoemaker accounted for the other scoring with 20 and 33-yard field goals in the second and fourth quarters.

Plunkett wound up the 1968 season with 142 completions in 268 attempts for .529 percent and 2,156 yards. He threw 14 interceptions and also had 14 touchdown passes. He led the league in all departments except percentage, and set new conference marks for yardage and TD passes. Plunkett also was tops in total offense with 2,203 yards. The Indians, who led the Pac-8 in passing offense with an average of 251.6 yards per game and total offense with a 428 yard average, finished the season with a 6-3-1 mark overall and a 3-3-1 in the conference for third place.

Practice Pays Off

Stanford headed into the 1969 season with what Ralston called "guarded optimism." It was all based on the fact that a number of highly skilled players, including Plunkett, Lasater, Moore, center John Sande, and linebackers Don Parish and Pat Preston, returned from the previous season. The question mark was the defensive line, which was made up largely of sophomores or juniors who had not seen too much action the year before.

Plunkett had ranked 10th nationally in 1968 in passing. He had led the Pacific-8 and became only the third passer in conference history to gain more than 2,000 yards in a single year. And he improved on that record as a junior, completing 197 of 336 passes for 2,673 yards and throwing for 20 touchdowns.

Stanford came close to achieving Ralston's dream of a Rose Bowl invitation, posting a 7-2-1 record overall and a 5-1-1 mark in the conference that gave the Indians a tie for second place with UCLA. The two losses were classic games. Purdue scored a 36-35 win at Lafayette, Indiana, on October 4. Southern California claimed a 26-24 victory the following week in Los Angeles. USC's Ron Ayala beat Stanford for the second straight year, this time kicking a field goal on the last play of the game.

The only other blemish on the Indians' record was a 20-20 tie with UCLA. "We should have beaten UCLA," said Bob Moore, a 6-3, 220-pound tight end from Klamath Falls, Oregon, who now plays with the Oakland Raiders. "It was a disappoint-

Tight end Bob Moore races under pass from Plunkett.

ment, the culmination of a lot of disappointments. After the game a bunch of the players—Jim Plunkett, Jack Lasater, Ron Kadziel, and some others—got together and talked about the outlook for our senior year. We felt we were going to beat those guys. We didn't know what it was going to take, but we were willing to go to almost any extreme. As a result, quite a few of the key players stayed around the campus that summer and worked out together. It was group concentration.

"That loss to USC was unreal. Steve Horowitz had kicked a field goal to put us ahead and everyone was on the field jumping up and down, but I had an eerie feeling there still was a lot of time left. (There was 1:03 left.) When Ayala kicked his goal everything went blank. It didn't hit me until sometime later."

There were 83,000 in the Coliseum that night, and they were not disappointed. It was a typical Stanford-USC battle with Plunkett being matched against the Trojans' Clarence Davis, who had inherited Simpson's tailback spot. Neither let the fans down. Plunkett completed 25 of 37 passes for 296 yards and two touchdowns. Davis carried 39 times for 198 yards.

Plunkett passed Stanford into a 12-0 lead with a three-yard scoring toss to Moore in the first period and a 12-yard screen

Bubba Brown off on a 33-yard touchdown run against Oregon.

pass to Howie Williams in the second. But USC scored twice in the last 1:02 of the half to claim a 14-12 edge at the intermission. The first score came after the Trojans recovered a fumbled punt on the Stanford 37. The second came with 27 seconds left in the half when Tyrone Hudson intercepted a Plunkett pass and raced 57 yards down the sidelines to score.

Horowitz put the Indians out in front with a 28-yard field goal early in the third quarter, only to have Jimmy Jones whip a 19-yard scoring strike to Gerry Mullins for a Trojan touchdown and a 20-15 lead. Bubba Brown scored for Stanford, but Ayala put USC in front 23-21 with 3:23 remaining. At this stage Plunkett hit little Randy "Rabbit" Vataha with a 67-yard pass to the USC 21. But three plays gained only one yard so Horowitz kicked a 37-yard field goal for a 24-23 Stanford lead, and the Indian bench erupted in pandemonium.

There were only 55 seconds on the clock when the Trojans lined up on their own 32 yard line following the kickoff. But Jones marched them to the Stanford 24, and Ayala kicked a 34-yard field goal—exactly the same distance as the year before when he beat the Indians 27-24. There was no time remaining as the ball barely cleared the crossbar.

Stanford's receivers had a busy evening with Williams making seven catches for 68 yards, Lasater five for 55, Moore five for 53, and Vataha four for 100.

The loss to Purdue the previous week had been just as exciting, but lacked the importance of the Southern California game. It was a matchup between Plunkett and Purdue's Mike Phipps that produced one of the greatest passing duels of all time. Between them the two quarterbacks threw 85 passes without a single interception. Plunkett hit 23 of 46 for 355 yards and four touchdowns, but Phipps went him one better and completed 28 of 39 for 429 yards and five touchdowns.

Stanford had what appeared to be a comfortable 35-21 lead after three quarters. Then Phipps threw touchdown passes of 21 and 19 yards to Johnny Bullock and Stan Brown respectively; then he completed his thirteenth straight pass with a two-point conversion to Greg Fenner to give the Boilermakers the victory.

Jackie Brown brought the kickoff back to the Stanford 41 and Plunkett marched the Indians into Purdue territory only to fumble after a 17-yard run on an option play. Bob Moore, who had eight catches for 99 yards, caught two touchdown passes.

Williams and Kadziel were on the receiving end of the other scoring tosses.

Vataha was Plunkett's leading target when the Indians came from behind to tie UCLA 20-20. The little wide receiver caught five passes for 105 yards and two touchdowns as Plunkett made good on 26 of 44 attempts for 263 yards. The Bruins took the opening kickoff and scored, but Stanford matched it with a touchdown the first time it had the ball with Vataha taking a 15-yard pass for the six points. Plunkett hit Vataha again in the second quarter with a 28-yard toss, and Horowitz added a 30-yard field goal for a 17-6 lead at the half.

Dennis Spurling intercepted one of Plunkett's passes and returned to the Stanford 13 to set up a Bruin score in the third quarter. UCLA took the lead 20-17 on the second play of the final period when Dennis Dummit sneaked over after getting the Bruins into position with a 31-yard pass to Gwen Cooper. Stanford's Horowitz kicked a 27-yard field goal to tie the score and had a chance to win it for Stanford in the final four seconds when he had another opportunity from the 27. But Vince Bischof, a defensive end from nearby Cupertino, broke through to block the attempt.

Plunkett had a career high for passing yardage as the Indians edged California 29-28 in a wild Big Game before 80,000 at Stanford Stadium. Big Jim threw for 381 yards to top his previous high of 355 against Purdue, as he completed 22 of 41 attempts. Lasater caught four passes for 111 yards, and Vataha had four for 95. It looked like Stanford might make a runaway of the game as the Indians scored 17 points in the first six-and-a-half minutes, but it turned out to be a real cliff-hanger.

Everything broke in Stanford's favor at the outset. It took the Indians only six plays to bag their first score as Howie Williams took a pass from Plunkett and scampered 20 yards to complete a 47-yard play. California fumbled four plays later, and on second down Plunkett passed to Lasater who shook off two tacklers and scored on a 62-yard play. Pat Preston recovered another Bear fumble, and Horowitz kicked a 25-yard field goal. All of this happened with only 6:27 elapsed in the first quarter.

California got back into the game with a touchdown late in the opening quarter and another midway in the second period before Horowitz kicked a 34-yard field goal to give the Indians a 20-14 half-time lead. Plunkett was 14 for 25 for 310 yards at

278

Steve Horowitz kicks 30-yard field goal against UCLA.

the intermission.

After a scoreless third period, Horowitz booted a 25-yard field goal to boost Stanford's lead to 23-14 two minutes into the fourth quarter. But California's Dave Penhall exhibited some passing talent of his own to bag a pair of quick touchdowns for the Bears. A 55-yard pass to Ken Adams paved the way for the first and a 37-yard toss to Jim Fraser led to the second as the Bears took the lead 28-23.

'Stanford took the kickoff at its 20 with five minutes left in the game and methodically hammered out an 80-yard march for the winning points. Plunkett crossed up the California defense, which was expecting passes, by using Bubba Brown and Howie Williams on running plays. He threw only twice in the drive, completing one toss to Williams for nine yards and one to Lasater for 10. Brown completed the 12-play march by slamming over from the four.

Penhall almost matched Plunkett's statistics as he hit 23 of 36 passes for 321 yards. Stanford finished the afternoon with 563 total yards, while California had 464. Brown was the leading rusher for the Indians as he collected 97 yards on 20 carries. Fowler topped the Bears with 106 in 15 tries.

Throwing a soggy football in Seattle did not bother Plunkett. The big Stanford quarterback connected on 24 of 35 tosses for 323 yards as the Indians registered a 21-7 win over the Huskies. Plunkett dazzled Washington in the second quarter by moving the Indians 79 yards in eight plays and completing five straight passes in the process, including a perfect 26-yard

Randy Vataha leaps high to pull down pass against UCLA.

scoring strike to Vataha which produced a touchdown.

Fans who like offense found the game with the Air Force one which satisfied their appetite. Stanford wound up with a 47-34 victory as Plunkett enjoyed another good day with 22 completions in 38 attempts for 278 yards and two touchdowns. Bubba Brown also threw a 23-yard touchdown pass to Vataha in a switch from the normal pattern, and Vataha tallied a second time on a 63-yard punt return. Horowitz kicked field goals from 19 and 46 yards. Three touchdowns and a field goal in the second quarter gave Stanford a 24-17 edge at half time, and the Indians sewed up the win with a 16-point outburst in the fourth period.

Ralston had been concerned about his defensive line at the start of the season. His six-man defensive front consisted of Jack Schultz, a converted running back, and Jeff Siemon, a sophomore, at ends; Dave Tipton, a junior college transfer, and Bill Alexander, a junior non-letterman, at tackles; sophomore Pete Lazetich and converted linebacker Tim McClure at guards.

Stanford wound up with the second best rushing defense record in the Pac-8, allowing opponents an average of 110 yards per game. Don Parish won All America honors at linebacker, and Pat Preston was not far behind. Parish had been a fullback as a freshman, but Jack Root and Greg Broughton had that position sewed up when he came up to the varsity, so he was moved to linebacker. It was a move Ralston never regretted.

Parish and Rich Keller gained All-Conference defensive honors, while Plunkett, Bob Moore, and John Sande were named on the offensive unit.

Moore never had played tight end prior to spring practice in 1968. At Klamath Falls (Oregon) High School he had played quarterback as a freshman and then had been a halfback and defensive end. Drafted by the New York Mets as a pitcher and offered a bonus contract when he graduated, he passed it up to concentrate on football.

Moore liked to catch passes, but he looked at his position as more important in other ways. "A tight end can put a lot of pressure on the defense," he said. "If I can get a deep back or a safety to cover me while a wide receiver is opened up for a score, then I'm really pleased about it. Of course I want to catch as many passes as possible, but if you score two touchdowns and miss two important blocks you can't feel very well about the way you've played."

Sande, who had started every game as a sophomore in 1968 when the previous year's regular Tom Giallonardo was injured in an auto accident, had been recruited by some 25 schools. "I chose Stanford because I want a good education in law, and I want to go to the Rose Bowl," he said.

Family Involvement

"I remember so many things about the individuals, it overshadows the team," Ralston observed as he reviewed his years at Stanford. "We had some great moments, but nothing takes the place of achievement. I remember Plunkett's dedication, the play of Joe Neal in 1963 and 1964. Then in 1964 Notre Dame butchered us. There were no holes open, no blocks, but Ray Handley threw himself into the line in an attempt to gain yards. Steve Thurlow did a superb job against California in 1963, and Dave Lewis was outstanding in the 1965 game against California.

"You see players achieve, like Bob Bittner, a 195-pound tackle, who was up against Ron Yary, USC's All America. But Yary couldn't knock Bittner off the spot. That's the reason you're in it, the personal achievement of players."

The 1970 season also produced some personal achievement for Ralston as he finally realized his goal of producing a Rose Bowl team.

Most people consider Stanford's 24-14 victory over Southern California the highlight of that season. After all, the Indians had not beaten the Trojans since 1957—a string of 12 straight losses. However, Ralston rated the 29-22 victory over Washington the peak of the season.

"It was a real emotional game, and was the biggest thing of the year because it clinched the conference championship and the right to play in the Rose Bowl after eight long years," Ralston said. "My family was deeply involved—my wife Patty, twin daughters Terry and Sherry, and my son Larry. We had been through low moments, but there had been constant progression.

283

During that Washington game my daughters stood behind the screen at the north end of the stadium and cried the entire game. My wife got up and left the stadium and walked around outside. She could tell by the noise from the crowd how the game was going.

"The thing about the 1970 season was that we won the big ones. We got over the top against USC; that game was a classic for hitting. There were a lot of great plays, with the Stanford defense producing a couple. The players got confidence they could beat USC and they did it."

Beating Southern California was a thrill for the Stanford players, but there were more to come following the victory over Washington and the 27-17 triumph over Ohio State in the Rose Bowl. "Beating USC was tremendous after a lot of frustrations," said Plunkett. "But I think there was more jubilation in the locker room after the Washington game. Both games meant a lot to us, but it's hard to say which meant the most. USC came first, and we had had so many disappointments against the Trojans before.

"That night game in Los Angeles my junior year was the biggest disappointment of my college career. (Stanford lost 26-24 on a 34-yard field goal by Ron Ayala on the last play of the game.) In fact, every game with USC was frustrating until 1970. We had come so close in 1968 and 1969 we were determined that final year. Bob Moore, Jack Lasater, Jody Graves, and I all had redshirted together and were a close group, and there was more dedication. The defense was a very close knit unit with a lot of camaraderie that paid off. Basically it was the same group as the year before, so it was better. But they worked real hard."

An indication of Stanford's potential came in the season opener with the University of Arkansas at Little Rock in a nationally televised game. The Razorbacks were the nation's fourth ranked team after a 9-2 season in 1969, losing only to Texas 15-14 and Mississippi 27-22 in the Sugar Bowl. Arkansas was not prepared for Stanford's explosive start which saw Hillary Shockley, a 220-pound fullback, romp 43 yards for a touchdown, breaking two tackles at the five yard line. A few minutes later Vataha returned a punt 28 yards, and Plunkett capitalized on the situation to move the Indians 51 yards in four plays, two of them being a 31-yard pass to Demea Washington and a 17-yard scoring toss to Lasater.

Before the end of the period Shockley had added another touchdown to cap a 67-yard drive in 13 plays. Eric Cross, a sophomore halfback, boosted Stanford's lead to 27-0 when he returned a punt 61 yards for a touchdown early in the second quarter.

Joe Ferguson, a sophomore quarterback, finally got the Arkansas offense moving and then gave way to Bill Montgomery who led the Razorbacks to a pair of touchdowns to make the score 27-14 at the half.

Shockley got his third touchdown and what proved to be the winning score in the third quarter, carrying the ball five straight times to complete an 86-yard, 15-play drive. Arkansas ground out a touchdown just before the end of the third quarter, and then added another mid-way in the final period as the strength-sapping heat and humidity began to tell on the Stanford team.

Arkansas surged back and, with less than a minute left in the game, had a third down and one on the Indians' four yard line. Bill Burnett tried the middle but was hit by Jeff Siemon, Stanford's great linebacker, along with Tim Robnett. After a time out the Razorbacks isolated Chuck Dicus, their outstanding end, to the left, but Montgomery faked and rolled left on the option. Montgomery never looked for Dicus, however, as he tried to make it by himself. Siemon and Mike Simone moved up to stop him, and the measurement showed he was one foot short of the first down. Stanford had held for a 34-28 victory and was on the way to the Rose Bowl and Plunkett, to the Heisman Trophy.

Shockley was the workhorse of the Stanford backfield, carrying the ball 23 times for 117 yards and three touchdowns. Plunkett completed 22 of 39 passes for 262 yards, and Jackie Brown caught 11 passes for 130 yards. Siemon led the defense with 16 tackles.

Stanford's Rose Bowl hopes had been derailed by Southern California the two previous years, so the game with the Trojans was considered a "must" game for the Indians. Even a "bomb threat" failed to dampen the enthusiasm that October 10 afternoon.

A statement by Stanford's President Richard W. Lyman was broadcast prior to the game. It read: "Ladies and Gentlemen: You have been informed that a bomb threat has been made against this game. You are aware of the precautions that

285

have been taken, both in anticipation of such a threat and in response to it. If there are further developments to report, you will be told of them. No one is disposed to ignore such threats, in view of events elsewhere in the country. On the other hand, blackmail and threats must not be allowed to paralyze a nation or an institution. If it once becomes established that such tactics can succeed, we shall have magnified enormously the capacity of a malicious few to sabotage society. We have decided, therefore, that the game will continue as scheduled. By your presence here you are indicating that you feel the same. Thank you."

The 86,000 fans in Stanford Stadium saw the Indians score a 24-14 victory to hand the Trojans their first loss in regular season play since 1967, a string of 25 games. It was one of the most satisfying wins for Stanford since 1951 when Chuck Taylor's team defeated the Trojans 27-20.

Southern California, led by Clarence Davis, boasted what was generally regarded as the most awesome rushing attack in the country. The Trojans were averaging 343 yards per game rushing, 538 yards in total offense, and scoring 39 points per game. Davis, who had gained 198 yards against Stanford in 1969, was backed up by Lou Harris, Mike Berry, and Ron McNeill.

"We will need the kind of effort we saw in the first quarter of the Arkansas game and the third quarter of the Oregon game," Ralston said. "And we'll have to make it last 60 minutes. For the past two weeks we have gotten off to a bad start and we can't afford that against the Trojans. If we can hold them to 350 yards it might be a real good effort on our part."

Stanford did not quite achieve Ralston's goal, allowing the Trojans 383 yards. But the Indians did limit USC to 105 yards on the ground, more than 200 yards below their average. Twice Stanford shut off scoring threats inside the 10 yard line with brilliant defensive play.

In the second quarter, after Stanford had taken a 14-0 lead, the Trojans drove to the Indians' one yard line where they faced a fourth down and goal situation. Berry, on his only carry of the game, tried to pinch through the left side but was met by Stanford's Larry Butler, 232-pound junior guard, who stopped him six inches short of a touchdown.

The Trojans reached the Stanford 19 in the third quarter, but Siemon intercepted a Jimmy Jones pass on the nine. Then

Hillary Shockley breaks loose for good gain against Air Force.

in the fourth quarter USC marched to a first down on the Indians' three. Three plays picked up only two yards and, on fourth down from the one, Jones tried to roll out and circle left end. Jim Kauffman, the Stanford rover back, diagnosed the play perfectly, and threw Jones for a two-yard loss.

The Stanford defense, led by Siemon, Dave Tipton, Butler, Pete Lazetich, Greg Sampson, Kauffman, and Charles McCloud, sacked Jones and Mike Rae five times. Siemon had 15 tackles and was called by Ralston "the greatest I've ever coached."

Plunkett completed 19 of 31 passes for 275 yards and put Stanford on the scoreboard late in the first quarter when he led Bob Moore on a perfect "seam" pattern pass for a 50-yard touchdown. Moore made an over-the-shoulder catch at the 18, broke a tackle, and continued into the end zone. Cross had given the Indians good field position with a 10-yard punt return to the Stanford 47.

Cross provided even better position in the second quarter with a 47-yard return to the USC 19. Jackie Brown scored from the one after reeling off a 14-yard run to the two.

Even a clipping penalty which set them back to the 11 after USC had scored early in the third quarter failed to take the steam out of the Stanford offense. Randy Vataha caught

287

three passes for gains of 8, 13, and 34 yards, and Demea Washington caught one for 19. Jackie Brown added another 19 yards on a pitchout before Brown tallied his second touchdown.

After twice being denied by Siemon and Kauffman, the Trojans took advantage of a pass interception to score with 4:37 left in the game to close the gap to 21-14. However, the Indians cooled any USC hopes when Steve Horowitz kicked a 36-yard field goal, after a 22-yard pass from Plunkett to Moore had helped Stanford advance to the USC 19 with a minute and a half remaining.

All kinds of names have been attached to outstanding football teams or combinations. But the one selected for the Stanford defensive line was most unusual. The name was "Thunderchickens," a title selected by Lazetich, 236-pound guard from Billings, Montana.

"We need some identity," Lazetich said. "With Plunkett and the offense setting all those records, we were getting tired of just being called the defensive line. Tipton really looks like a big chicken the way he runs around flailing his arms. Where I come from in Billings, there's a motorcycle gang called the Thunderchickens. They're wild and reckless and run all over the place just like we do. That's why I picked the name."

Pete Lazetich "needed some identity."

Ralston was a bit leary when the Thunderchickens decided to wear white shoes for the important game with Washington at Stanford Stadium. "What difference does it make what color of shoes they wear?" asked Virgil "Doc" Marvin, the veteran Stanford equipment manager. "Let them wear white shoes if they want."

The white shoes had to spend a lot of time on the field in the second and third quarters that afternoon. After scoring three touchdowns in the opening period, Stanford failed to do much on offense until midway in the final quarter. Then Plunkett hit Vataha on a perfectly thrown pass for 15 yards and a touchdown to give the Indians a come-from-behind 29-22 win.

Things did not look too good for Stanford when Jim Krieg of the Huskies ran the opening kickoff back 95 yards for a touchdown, but less than four minutes later Plunkett threw a six yard pass to Jackie Brown to tie the score. Two minutes later the Indians had another score when Plunkett hurled a 33-yard pass to Vataha, and then rifled a nine-yard touchdown to Lasater. Before the first period was over Plunkett had connected for his third touchdown pass on a 27-yard toss to Moore following Schultz' pass interception and return to the Husky 34.

Little Sonny Sixkiller put Washington in front late in the third quarter when he scampered nine yards for a touchdown after being forced out of the pocket. The Huskies had recovered a fumble on the Stanford 14 to gain this position.

"We were behind 22-21, and then zingo—Plunkett whipped a pass to Vataha—and we were out with the Pacific-8 championship," Ralston said. "My wife was out in the parking lot, but she could hear the crowd reaction and she knew we were on the plus side. We got together as a family afterwards, and the five of us talked about the eight years of obsession and dedication."

In addition to his four touchdowns, Plunkett wound up with a total of 268 yards passing on 22 completions on 36 attempts. Vataha had six receptions for 111 yards; Moore, six for 82; and Brown, five for 41. Sixkiller, under pressure from the Thunderchickens, hit 18 of 41 attempts for 158 yards, but Stanford had three interceptions.

The defense had another tough assignment when Stanford visited Los Angeles for a meeting with UCLA. The Thunderchickens sacked Bruin quarterback Dennis Dummit five times while holding UCLA to a net 25 yards rushing, with Lazetich and Tipton spending considerable time in the Bruin backfield. However, Dummit managed to complete 18 of 35 passes for 244 yards, but the UCLA touchdown was the result of recovering a Shockley fumble on the Stanford 15. Three plays later Marv Kendrick dove over for the score. The Cards won 9-7.

For the first time in 18 games Plunkett failed to throw a touchdown pass as all of Stanford's scoring came as the result of field goals by Horowitz from 38, 35, and 30 yards. A 44-yard pass from Plunkett to Vataha set up the second one, while a 42-yard completion by the same combination set the stage for the final score with less than five minutes to play. Plunkett hit 18 of 37 passes for 262 yards, and Jackie Brown picked up 107 yards in 26 carries for his best-ever performance as Stanford rushed for 219 yards.

It took Plunkett and the Indians a while to get warmed up for their game with Oregon at Eugene in the conference opener. After trailing the fired-up Webfoots 3-0 at half time, Stanford stormed back to score the first five times it had the ball in the second half for an easy 33-10 victory. A 58-yard kickoff return by Cross was instrumental in the first touchdown. Plunkett passed eight yards to Vataha for the second, after contributing a 24-yard run on a key play in an 80-yard drive. Reggie Sanderson's 82-yard kickoff return and Plunkett's 15-yard run on an option play added a third score in the third quarter. Jackie Brown took a swing pass from Plunkett for 23 yards to account for the fourth touchdown of the period.

A 29-yard run by Brown, who gained 92 yards for the game, and a 26-yard Plunkett-to-Vataha pass added a final score in the fourth period.

Plunkett, who completed only nine of 25 passes in the first half, wound up with 18 for 38 and 250 yards and three touchdowns. The Stanford defense limited Oregon to a net three yards rushing.

Stanford had not beaten Washington State in the Northwest since 1956, but the Cougars were no match for the Indians as Plunkett established a new NCAA career passing record in a 63-16 romp at Spokane.

Plunkett played only half of the game, but completed 10 of 14 passes for 275 yards. One of them was a 96-yard scoring toss to Vataha in the second quarter, which not only set a new Stanford touchdown pass record, but pushed the Indians' passing star past the NCAA career record of 6,568 held by Steve

Dave Tipton shakes ball out of grasp of Cal's Gary Fowler.

Ramsey of North Texas State. Plunkett finished the game with a career total of 6,630 yards and finished the season with a total of 7,544 yards—almost 1,000 yards ahead of Ramsey's mark.

Jim Sweeney, Washington State coach, came to the Stanford dressing room after the game to personally congratulate Plunkett. "Plunkett is the best college football player I have ever seen," Sweeney said. "The best way to play Stanford is to balance your people against theirs so that you can take them on. You can't squirm around the way we have to, because Plunkett is so experienced he will pick you apart."

Plunkett became the first man in college football to pass for 7,000 yards during his career as he hit 13 of 26 passes for 210 yards in a 48-10 win over Oregon State. He had three touchdown throws, one for 70 yards to Lasater; the others were for nine yards to Moore and 12 yards to Sanderson. Kauffman contributed a 37-yard pass interception return for a touchdown, and the defense, led by Phil Satre, sacked Beaver quarterbacks Jim Kilmartin and Ralph Keck five times.

After wrapping up the conference title with the win over Washington, Stanford lacked the same kind of determination in its final two games: they lost to the Air Force 31-14 and California 22-14. It started snowing as the Stanford plane touched down at Colorado Springs Friday afternoon and continued most of the night. It was a cool 26 degrees when the Indians trotted onto the floor of Falcon Stadium for the kickoff. Charles McCloud, a sophomore from Houston, Texas, took one look at the white stuff and observed: "There's no way I can play in this."

McCloud and Benny Barnes had been two of the pleasant surprises of the season for Coach Ralston. They had taken over starting roles after Miles Moore and Mike Ewing suffered injuries. Moore had suffered a neck injury 10 days before the start of the season and was out for the year. Ewing had a muscle pull which limited his action.

The Air Force, battling for a bowl bid of its own, capitalized on the passing combination of Bob Parker to Ernie Jennings for three touchdowns. The Falcon defense dropped Plunkett four times and held him to 17 completions in 35 attempts for 182 yards and no touchdowns.

Plunkett threw touchdown passes of 38 and 74 yards to Vataha and Brown, respectively, in the Big Game; he completed 20 of 37 passes for 280 yards. But Dave Penhall hit 18 of 26 tosses for 231 yards, and Randy Wersching kicked three field goals to spark the California victory before 76,800 fans at Berkeley.

"Losing to California as a senior was a big disappointment," Plunkett said. "I never had lost to them before, and I didn't know what it meant to be beaten by Cal. It really did me in. However, the biggest disappointment I ever had was losing that night game to USC my junior year."

Plunkett closed out his career by leading the Pacific-8 Conference in passing and total offense for the third straight year, completing 191 of 358 passes for 2,715 yards and 18 touchdowns, and an average of 246.8 yards per game. He added 183 yards rushing for 2,809 yards total offense.

His 7,544 yards passing and 7,887 yards total offense were career NCAA records as well as conference marks. In addition, he set new Pac-8 season standards of 336 pass attempts, 197 completions, 2,673 yards passing, 20 touchdown passes, 389 plays total offense, and 2,786 yards total offense for 10-games in 1969. For 11 games in 1970 he made 358 pass attempts, 2,715 passing yards, 2,898 yards total offense, and 436 plays total offense.

Plunkett, who was eligible for the professional football draft after his junior year because he had redshirted during the 1967 season, had turned down a lucrative pro contract to play his senior year in a bid to take Stanford to the Rose Bowl.

"That was something I had been shooting for ever since I first saw the Rose Bowl game on TV in 1962," the star quarterback of the New England Patriots recalled. "My plans started then, and there never was any question in my mind about staying at Stanford and playing my senior year. Coach Ralston, all of our coaches, and my teammates had been building something at Stanford for a couple of years. If I had left I would always have had the feeling that I had let them down before our goals were reached. Besides, we are always telling kids today not to drop out, to finish school, to set targets, and to work towards them. What would they think if I dropped out for professional football?"

Plunkett's record-setting season earned him a flock of honors, but the big one was the Heisman Trophy, the award which goes annually to the "outstanding college football player" in the country.

"I am honored to receive this award," said Plunkett, the

Jim Plunkett looks at the Heisman Trophy he won as college football's outstanding player in 1970.

first Stanford player to become a Heisman winner, when he arrived home from New York following the announcement. "It means a great deal. It's a fine way to end a career in college, and I'm glad I stayed the extra year. I am very grateful to my teammates and coaches and, I think, more happy for everyone else than myself.

"Right now I feel like I'm in an emotional knot. I can't say enough about the guys I played with at Stanford. I developed a lot of wonderful friendships."

On hand to greet Plunkett was Dr. Richard Lyman, president of Stanford University. "It means a lot to Stanford to have a Heisman Trophy winner," said Dr. Lyman. "But it means more to have Jim Plunkett. He has done it the hard way. He has shown ability to come back."

Also greeting Plunkett were Coach Ralston, and teammates Jack Schultz, Jack Lasater, Bob Moore, and Bill Meyers. "This is just a tremendous thing," Ralston stated. "Everyone connected with Stanford is very proud of Jim's individual achievements. I didn't think we held up our end of the deal after winning the conference title, and began to feel that maybe we had let him down. But Jim never failed to hold up his end. We all take a great deal of pride in this tremendous achievement."

Plunkett received 510 first place votes, 285 second, and 129 third, for 2,229 points in the Heisman voting by 1,059 electors across the nation. Runner-up was Joe Theismann, Notre Dame quarterback, with 1,410 points. Archie Manning, Mississippi quarterback, finished third, followed by Steve Worster, Texas fullback; Rex Kern, Ohio State quarterback; Pat Sullivan, Auburn quarterback; and Jack Tatum, Ohio State cornerback.

The Associated Press was the only All America selector to pass over Plunkett, selecting Theismann and placing Jim on the second team. But Plunkett was the choice of UPI, *Sporting News*, Football Writers, Football Coaches, Walter Camp, and NEA; the Maxwell Award winner; and "Player of the Year" choice in most quarters.

John Sande, a starter at center for three seasons at Stanford, was named on the second offensive units of the UPI and NEA All America teams, yet he only received honorable mention from the Pacific-8. Joining Plunkett on the first team All-Pac-8 were end Bob Moore, flanker Randy Vataha, defensive lineman Dave Tipton, and linebacker Jeff Siemon.

295

Back To Fundamentals

Stanford was an 11-point underdog when it lined up against Ohio State in the 57th Rose Bowl on January 1, 1971. Very few of the experts gave the Indians much of a chance against Woody Hayes' Buckeyes who had gone through the season undefeated. Further, the team boasted six All Americas—fullback John Brockington and end Jan White on offense and guard Jim Stillwagon and backs Jack Tatum, Mike Sensibaugh, and Tim Anderson on defense.

"We worked like hell preparing for Ohio State," Ralston declared. "The losses to the Air Force and California proved we had lost our fundamental edge. In the California game we had a couple of third and one situations, and we didn't come close to knocking them out.

"We went back to the grass roots—fundamentals—with double practices. It was like starting all over."

Ralston ran into some opposition from his players, however, when the squad moved to Long Beach for its final week of drills. Before the game, co-captains Plunkett and Schultz, along with Ron Kadziel and Demea Washington, confronted the coach with player demands.

"The players felt the coaches were working us too hard and being too tough on us mentally after the season we had had," Plunkett explained. "There was an early curfew, and the players weren't being allowed to use any of the 10 Rose Bowl cars which had been placed at the disposal of the team. Coach Ralston let up some, but he would not compromise his principles. It was a difficult thing. I think he felt responsible for the losses in the last two games of the season himself."

Center John Sande, ready for meeting with Jim Stillwagon in 1971 Rose Bowl, and Plunkett.

"The only thing you'll remember about this game is the score," Ralston told his players, and although he eased up a bit on their nighttime activities, he continued to work hard on the pregame preparations.

"We had watched Stillwagon in the Ohio State films and never saw him in a bad play in 1,600 feet of film," Ralston observed. "We planned to have guards Dan Lightfoot and Terrell Smith work with Sande, the center, in blocking Stillwagon and preventing him from putting a rush on Plunkett."

Sande was looking forward to the confrontation with the Buckeye All America. "I think we are blocking better now than we have all season," he said during the final week of drills. "We broke down in the final two games because we got behind and they knew we were going to pass. I think we are in an ideal situation for this game. We are the underdogs, and a lot of people don't give us much chance. But remember, we played some of our best games when we were underdogs this season."

At half time, as the Stanford team filed into its locker room, Sande stopped Ralston and said: "Don't worry coach, I can handle Stillwagon alone."

Before the game Ralston had said that, in order to win, Stanford must not allow Ohio State to dominate both the offense and the defense. The Indians got away to a tremendous start by scoring a touchdown and a field goal the first two times they had the ball, to take a 10-0 lead. The touchdown was set up by a reverse that sprung Eric Cross for a 41-yard gain to the 18 on Stanford's first offensive play. Plunkett passed to Moore on the next play for a touchdown, but the score was nullified by a penalty. Then Plunkett made 13 on a quarterback draw, and after a penalty against the Bucks, Stanford's Jackie Brown slid off right end for four yards to score.

Horowitz kicked a 37-yard field goal when the Indians were stopped at the 20 on their next series.

The Buckeyes' powerful, ground game swung the momentum in favor of Ohio State for the remainder of the first half; the Big 10 champions held a 14-10 advantage at the intermission.

Steve Horowitz kicked a 48-yard field goal to pull Stanford within a point, at 14-13, but Fred Schram matched it with a 32-yard goal for the Buckeyes—and a 17-13 advantage.

The third quarter had been a big one for Ohio State during the 1970 season, the Buckeyes scoring 90 points while holding their opponents to nine. But Stanford's defense—led by Tipton, Kadziel, Bill Alexander, Siemon, and Schultz—turned things around in the second half, and Schram's field goal was the only points Ohio State could muster.

Stanford tallied another touchdown in the fourth quarter. After Stanford took a 20-17 lead, Ohio State abandoned its running game in a bid to catch up. But Schultz intercepted a Kern pass on the Buckeye 25 and the Indians added a final touchdown in four plays. Vataha took an 11-yard pass to start the move and covered the final 10 on a pass from Plunkett. Stanford had a 27-17 victory, a victory that sent half of the record crowd of 103,839 wild with excitement and plunged the Ohio State rooters into deep despair.

Two of the big plays of the game for Stanford had occurred early in the fourth quarter. One came on the first play of the final period when the Indians stopped the Buckeyes on the Stanford 20. Ohio State had fourth down and inches to go for a first down. Brockington, a 220-pound fullback who had rushed for 1,040 yards in nine games and had been ripping the Stanford defense all afternoon, was called on to get the necessary yardage at right tackle. But Stanford's Kadziel met him head on and threw the All America back for a one-yard loss. It was after this that Stanford drove 80 yards in 13 plays to score, with Plunkett picking the Buckeye secondary apart with four pass completions of six to 10 yards.

The second big play gave Stanford game control. It looked like the Indians might be stalled when Vataha was dropped for a nine-yard loss on a flanker reverse, but Moore came up with a big catch. With third down and 16 at the Ohio State 37, Plunkett drilled a 35-yard pass to Moore, and the big tight end made a brilliant catch between Sensibaugh and cornerback Don Lamka. The two Buckeyes had Moore pinched between them, but he took the ball away from them for a first down on the two.

"Vataha was my primary receiver, but he was double or triple covered," Plunkett said. "I looked around for someone else who was open. Moore wasn't open, but he caught it anyway. On the play I had called, the tight end normally would stay in and block while the wide receivers would run curl patterns. As we were walking to the line of scrimmage, just off the cuff, I told Bob he'd better go out. I don't know why I did it."

"It was a broken play," Moore recalled. "I went to the far

Defensive back Jim Kauffman and linebacker Ron Kadziel, who made big play in Rose Bowl game with Ohio State.

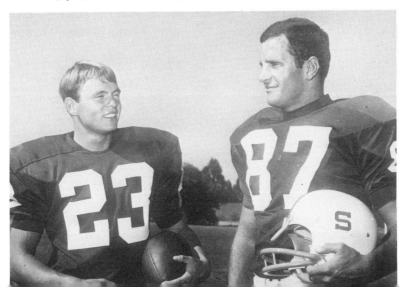

corner and turned around. I was surprised when I saw Jim scrambling. I lost sight of the ball for a moment, and then it was there. At the moment it happened I didn't realize the significance of that catch. I was so intense on winning the game. The next play was a sweep around my side, and I moved out. The linebacker came outside with me, and I hooked him. I felt better about that play than the catch.

"The papers did everything to humiliate us. I had dreamed of playing in the Rose Bowl for three years and didn't want to be embarrassed. The feeling after the game was that winning was a lot more satisfying than everyone had thought it would be. It hit you. We were fortunate we were prepared that way."

"We played so well we were hard to stop," Plunkett said. "That day I don't think anyone could have stopped us. Ohio State was a very good team, but this was a tremendous thrill for us. That's where I had set my goals, and when I got there I wanted to play well; I hated to plan all those years and then not have a good game. I was happy for Coach Ralston. He had taken a lot of criticism from the press and other coaches who said Stanford had the best material but didn't win."

In the game Ohio State ran for 364 yards but gained only 75 yards with its passing game, completing seven of 20 attempts. Stanford offered a more balanced attack, running for 143 and gaining 265 through the air as Plunkett completed 20 of 30. Moore caught five of his passes for 113 yards while Washington grabbed six for 80 and Vataha, six for 51. Plunkett, surprisingly, was one of Stanford's leading ground gainers with a net 26 yards, although he was dropped for losses of 23 yards. Cross, on his one run, tied Brown as the most productive runner with 41 yards. Shockley added 35.

Schultz, who lived in South Pasadena, said he had waited outside the Rose Bowl as a kid, hoping someone would take him inside. "I never made it until today," he said. "I always wondered what it was like. Now I know. It's great. Our team always won the big ones. We were no different today."

"Heroes were many on this day of days for the Big Red," wrote the *Pasadena Star-News*. "But nobody contributed so much as the magnificent Plunkett, the peerless passer. No matter what Ohio State did on defense, Plunkett countered with shrewd audibles on the line of scrimmage. His strong arm pierced the vital holes in the previously unviolated Buckeye Barricade.

"Center John Sande of Stanford was another of the Indians' heroes. All he did was completely shut off Ohio State's great middle guard, Jim Stillwagon."

Plunkett, as might be expected, was selected for the Helms award as the "most valuable player" of the game.

"It was the result of a lot of hard work and preparation," Ralston said. "Dave Tipton was a man possessed, and Demea Washington was outstanding. Moore and Vataha were very unique guys. It had become such a challenge. But the only reason Stanford was there was because of Plunkett. You never had the feeling you couldn't put points on the scoreboard with Plunkett in there."

Only Pressure Was Time

There were a lot of holes to be filled when Ralston started preparing for the 1971 season. Graduation had taken 11 lettermen from the offensive unit and an equal number from the defense. Missing on offense were Plunkett, Moore, Vataha, Lasater, Horowitz, Lightfoot, Sande, Smith, Washington, Charles Saibel, and reserve quarterback Jesse Freitas, who had decided to transfer to San Diego State rather than ride the bench another season. Eight of these who were missing had been starters.

Vataha, Moore, and Lasater had been responsible for most of Stanford's pass receptions in 1970: Vataha catching 48 for 844 yards; Moore, 34 for 562; and Lasater, 19 for 282. Together they had grabbed 12 of the 18 touchdown passes Plunkett had thrown.

Gone from the defense were starters Schultz, Kauffman, Alexander, Kadziel, Dennis Moore, and Tipton. Also gone were Graves, McClure, Merrill, Ewing, and Mark Brown, all of whom had seen a lot of action.

Ralston had a good nucleus of lettermen returning, however. Most important, he had an outstanding quarterback available in Don Bunce, a 6-1, 196-pound senior, who had served as a back-up quarterback to Plunkett in 1968 and 1969 but had decided to sit out the 1970 season to save his eligibility. A gifted athlete, Bunce had the ability to break a game open either with his passing or his running. He had demonstrated his ability in the 1968 game with Washington when he came off the bench when Plunkett was shaken up and directed Stanford to a 35-20 win.

"It had been tough to redshirt Bunce his senior year," Ralston remarked. "He lived only six doors from me."

"I don't think there was any pressure on me because I was following Plunkett," Bunce stated. "The only pressure I felt was that I only had one year in which to do the things I wanted to do. It was time pressure."

By the end of the season Bunce had proven that his decision to wait for his chance to play first string was a good one. He had completed 162 of 297 passes for 54.5 percent, 2,265

Coach John Ralston is hoisted on shoulders of linebacker Jeff Siemon and tackle Bill Meyers (75) after 27-17 win over Ohio State.

yards, and 13 touchdowns. And he had directed the Indians to another 9-3 season and a second consecutive Rose Bowl.

"I think the key game that season was the one with Oregon State at Corvallis," Bunce said. "That one really gave us the confidence to come around. I can remember more individual plays about that game, but the one that stands out was one just before the end of the first half when I hit John Winesberry for a touchdown that got us back to 24-10."

Bunce was scrambling for his life on the play. A couple of big Oregon State linemen appeared to have him collared when he ducked under their arms and fired a 46-yard scoring pass to the fleet Winesberry with only 59 seconds left in the half.

The Indians were a rejuvenated team in the next half. They scored once in the third quarter and twice in the fourth for a 31-24 victory in one of the greatest comebacks in Stanford history. Bunce threw a 67-yard TD pass to Miles Moore in the opening minutes of the third quarter. Stanford had a third down and eight on its own 33, but Bunce noticed a switch in the Beaver defense and took advantage of it.

"I checked the defense as I came up to the line and noticed the defensive back was playing Miles one-on-one so I called an audible, switching to a short post pattern. We had studied films and noticed that they did that occasionally. It was an ideal situation for Moore."

Midway in the fourth quarter Randy Poltl, an outstanding strong safety for the Cardinals, literally stole the ball from Jerry McBurney of the Beavers. Eight plays covered 46 yards for a touchdown, but Stanford's bid to take the lead on a two-point conversion was denied when Steve Brown, Oregon State's brilliant linebacker, intercepted Bunce's pass in the end zone.

Bunce said, "That's another thing I remember about that game—throwing three passes to that middle linebacker."

Trailing 24-23 with 8:41 left to play, Stanford again called on its "Chicken" defense which checked Oregon State with only one more first down. Roger Cowan shook the ball loose from Dave Schilling with a hard tackle and recovered on the Beavers' 41. Bunce ate up five minutes of the clock with a methodical drive that took 11 plays and was capped when Brown dove over from the one yard line with only 53 seconds left in the game. To put some added pressure on the Beavers—in case they managed to score in the time remaining—Bunce passed to tight end Glen Stone for two points for a 31-24 win.

Quarterback Don Bunce, "no pressure replacing Plunkett."

Bunce was named the "outstanding offensive player" of the game on the strength of his 21 completions on 33 passes for 254 yards. Larry Butler and Mike Simone led the Stanford defense with 16 and 15 tackles respectively, but yielded "player of the game" honors to Brown of the Beavers, who had three pass interceptions in addition to the one on the conversion attempt and 20 tackles.

One of the key additions to the Stanford roster in 1971 was Rodrigo "Rod" Garcia, a 5-9, 155-pound soccer-style kicker from Cerritos Junior College. In the 1971 Stanford football brochure Garcia is listed as one of three place-kickers "who might see action." He ended up kicking 14 field goals in 27 attempts. Seven of his misses were from 40 yards or farther.

Stanford had opened the season with three impressive victories, beating Missouri 19-0, Army 38-3, and Oregon 38-17.

Garcia made his debut by kicking 44 and 28-yard field goals as the Indians handed Missouri its first shut out in 37 games and four years at Columbia, Missouri. Shockley bulled his way 45 yards for one touchdown and Bunce passed 26 yards to Winesberry, a fleet sophomore flanker, for another.

After the Missouri game the Indians continued on to New York and spent a week at Bear Mountain preparing for the Army game at West Point. Bunce baffled the Cadets as he passed for three touchdowns in the first half. The last one came with only seven seconds remaining. Army, apparently thinking Stanford would run out the clock, was caught off guard as Bunce hit Moore on a 75-yard scoring bomb down the left sideline. Garcia added a 46-yard field goal on his only attempt that day.

Stanford had to face Washington and Southern California back-to-back, a tough assignment, and to make matters worse, the Indians also had to play both games away from home. But the Stanford defense was never better than in these two games.

"We went up to Seattle, and there was a standing-room-only crowd," Ralston recalled. "But the Thunderchickens chased Sixkiller all over the stadium. The 17-6 score was not

The Thunderchicks, Stanford's defensive front four, of Greg Sampson, Larry Butler, Pete Lazetich, and Roger Cowan.

impressive, but we really owned them that day."

"We knew Washington had a good team and that the game was a crucial one for both of us," Bunce said. "They were supposed to be unbeatable by the pass. Our defense played one of its best games that day, and Benny Barnes did a super job as he dropped Sixkiller a couple of times on a safety blitz and had three pass interceptions."

The Thunderchickens made life miserable for Sixkiller, dropping him for 40 yards in losses and intercepting four passes and deflecting eight others as he wound up completing only 12 of 46 tosses.

Bunce did not have an extraordinary afternoon, hitting only nine of 24 attempts, but one of them was a needle-threading toss of 20 yards to Winesberry in the corner of the end zone for a first-quarter touchdown. Reggie Sanderson added a 20-yard scoring romp and Garcia kicked a 47-yard field goal as the Indians put all of their points on the board in the first half for a 17-0 lead.

Stanford invaded Los Angeles the following week to battle the Trojans, who were undefeated but had been tied by Nebraska 21-21. The game in the Coliseum, on a rainy night with accompanying lightning and thunder, was "no contest" as the Indians posted a 33-18 victory. All of the Trojans' scoring came in the fourth quarter after Stanford had a comfortable 20-0 edge.

Utilizing a new "power I" offense, Stanford took the opening kickoff and moved 63 yards in 13 plays with Bunce scoring on a bootleg play from the two. Garcia's 43-yard field goal made it 10-0 in the second quarter. The count quickly jumped to 17-0 after Robnett's pass interception which he returned 37 yards to the USC one.

After a scoreless third quarter, Garcia added a 45-yard field goal before the Trojans got on the scoreboard via a 54-yard pass from Mike Rae to Edsel Garrison. But Stanford responded with an 80-yard scoring play. Bunce rolled around left end for 11 yards and pitched to Sanderson who ran the rest of the way untouched.

"I was surprised we could run on them the way we did," Bunce said. "We took it to them, and it primarily was our running game that did it. I didn't have any touchdown passes that night, but I remember it was the first game I was called on to knock down somebody on a pitchout."

307

Stanford had more trouble than expected with Washington State the following week and wound up on the short end of a 24-23 score. Riding the crest of a 3-0 record in the Pacific-8, the Indians appeared to have gained control in the third quarter when they moved 67 yards with the second-half kickoff to score in nine plays. A 24-yard field goal by Garcia, following Winesberry's diving catch of a 42-yard pass from Bunce, gave Stanford a 20-14 edge late in the quarter. But Don Sweet kicked a 27-yard field goal on the final play of the game to give the Cougars a stunning upset victory.

One of the most spectacular plays of the game was executed by Stanford on the kickoff following Washington State's second touchdown. Miles Moore took the ball on the Indians' three and returned to the 12. There he reversed to Winesberry who outran the Cougars for 88 yards to complete the 97-yard scoring play.

A 20-9 win over UCLA virtually wrapped up the Rose Bowl bid for the Indians. "It was a big game for us and a big one for Miles," Bunce observed. "He caught six passes for 109 yards, including a 29-yard touchdown in the fourth quarter. I just threw it up in the air and hoped he would get under it. I didn't see what happened too often on my passes in that game. I usually was lying on my back on the ground."

Garcia contributed 33 and 46-yard field goals, which were set up by interceptions by Barnes and Poltl. Barnes also set up Stanford's game-clinching touchdown with an interception which he returned to the Bruins' 29.

Stanford suffered an embarrassing 13-12 loss to San Jose State as Garcia, who had established a new Pacific-8 record of 14 with his two field goals in the UCLA game, missed on five attempts against the Spartans. Garcia's last try came with 17 seconds remaining; Bunce had guided the Indians to the San Jose State three before the Spartans braced. Garcia had had his first attempt of 52 yards blocked but had missed the other three to the left. This time, kicking from the 10 in what amounted to a regular PAT attempt, he missed to the right.

"There was a lot of talk before the California game that if we lost to the Bears we wouldn't go to the Rose Bowl," Bunce revealed. "We had lost to Duke (9-3), Washington State (24-23),

Miles Moore grabs 29-yard scoring pass from Bunce out of hands of UCLA defender.

and San Jose State (13-12) and the players sort of felt that if we lost to the Bears, we didn't deserve to go to the Rose Bowl. It was one of the most boring games of the season with our defense holding them scoreless."

Actually, the Thunderchickens never permitted California to penetrate past the Stanford 43 yard line during the game in which they held the Bears to 38 net yards rushing and 85 yards passing.

Jackie Brown enjoyed his biggest day of the season as he rushed for 56 yards and caught seven passes for 119, earning "offensive player of the game" honors. Bunce completed 18 of 24 passes for 211 yards. Blocks from Moore and Sanderson cleared the way as Brown raced 58 yards with a swing pass from Bunce for Stanford's first touchdown just before the end of the first half.

The season ended with Bunce the only member of the Stanford offensive unit to earn All-Pacific-8 honors, but Lazetich, Butler, and Siemon were named on the defense.

Stanford, which always had been noted for its passing, wound up second to Washington in that department in 1971, with 2,424 yards to the Huskies' 2,606. But the Indians ranked first in the conference in total offense with 376.6 yards per game. They were also No. 1 in rushing defense (116.5 yards per game), No. 1 in pass defense (103.8), and No. 1 in total defense (220.4). Individually, Bunce was tops in passing with 206.8 yards per game and first in total offense with 229.4. Garcia was second in scoring with 66 points on 14 field goals and 24 extra points. Moore was third in pass receptions with 38 for 816 yards while Barnes shared league honors in pass interceptions with seven.

The Thunderchickens and linebacker Siemon drew most of the attention for Stanford's defensive play, but the work of the defensive secondary also played an important role in Stanford's success. Bob Gambold, who had played quarterback at Washington State, had been in charge of the defensive backs in 1970 and was defensive coordinator in 1971. Jack Christiansen, former San Francisco 49er coach who had been an All-Pro defensive back with the Detroit Lions, worked with Plunkett and the offensive backs in 1970, but he switched to defense in 1971.

The Stanford defense allowed opponents to complete only 39.7 percent of its pass attempts. The quartet of McCloud, Rob-

Open field as Jackie Brown swings upfield.

nett, Poltl, and Barnes had allowed only four touchdown passes to be completed and had intercepted 21 passes, better than one for every five completions.

Another Rose Bowl Upset

Ralston credited a change in his coaching philosophies for his success in putting Stanford into the Rose Bowl two consecutive years.

"One of the greatest mistakes I used to make was trying to do too much, particularly during games," he said. "Now I delegate things in a large way to my assistants. I have some outstanding people on my staff, and I set standards and goals and then get out of the way.

"Up until the 1967 season I called all the plays. I used to be the guy wearing the headphones and right in the center of things. I got so involved that when I had to make a key decision I didn't make it well. Some key errors on major decisions prompted me to change.

"During the game I concentrate on four things," Ralston explained. "The most important is the matter of scoring combinations—what would happen if we went for a two-point conversion and they went for one, for example. I also make all of the kicking decisions, make suggestions about sticking to or modifying the game plan, and go around encouraging the personnel. I'm the cheerleader part of the time."

Occasionally Ralston would call a play when he had a hunch that something different would work. It was such a hunch, and the desire to get some momentum going, that caused him to order a fake punt at the Stanford 33 yard line midway in the fourth quarter of the 58th Rose Bowl game with Michigan on January 1, 1972. It was a spectacular game which saw the Cardinals pull out an almost impossible 13-12 victory.

Stanford's 9-3 record and 6-1 mark in the Pac-8 Confer-

312

ence had put the Cards into the Rose Bowl again, but it looked like another mismatch. Michigan was 11-0 and had scored 409 points while holding opponents to 70. Stanford had managed to score only 248 points and had given up 123 while suffering upset losses to Duke 9-3, Washington State 24-23, and San Jose State 13-12.

The Wolverines had three All Americas in offensive guard Reggie McKenzie, linebacker Mike Taylor, and defensive back Tom Darden. They also had a pair of outstanding ballcarriers in tailback Billy Taylor, a three-year All-Big 10 who had rushed for 1,215 yards and a 5.6 yard average, and fullback Ed Shuttlesworth, a power runner who had gained 815 yards and had lost only two all season.

One of the Stanford players keenly looking forward to the game was Mike Simone, senior linebacker from Garden Grove.

Linebacker Mike Simone, a chance to play in Rose Bowl.

Simone had missed the Rose Bowl game the year before because of a locked knee cartilege, making him a very disappointed young man.

"Having won last year--won't lessen our desire to win this one," Simone said. "I know everyone felt after last year's Rose Bowl game it would have been all in vain to do all that work and lose. It's the same way this year. It is like starting the season all over, and we have been very successful along that line in the past."

There was a much more relaxed attitude about the Stanford squad as it prepared for the meeting with Michigan, and Ralston fell into the same pattern. "I'm much more relaxed as a coach now," he said. "I appeal more to the pride of my players. I don't set down many hard and fast rules any more. When you make things hard and fast, you are in trouble. Last year, for example, we had a curfew the entire time we were in Long Beach preparing for the Rose Bowl. This year we didn't have one until Wednesday night before the game. I didn't have any problems either."

Michigan, No. 4 in the grid polls, had been established as a 10-point favorite, but the odds did not worry Stanford. They only presented a challenge, and the Cardinals had been at their best when responding to such challenges. Bunce was second in

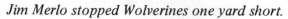

Jim Merlo stopped Wolverines one yard short.

the nation in total offense, passing for 2,265 yards and running for 248—for a total of 2,513.

The Wolverine defense, however, was one of the best in the country, allowing only 63.3 yards per game rushing and a total of 179.7 yards per game.

"We can't just stand back and pass against the Michigan defense," Ralston said. "We have to be able to run the ball too." Ralston had inserted some special tricks for the game but had decided to go basically with "the stuff that got us here."

Ralston's hunch play of a fake punt was the turning point in the game. Michigan had taken a 3-0 lead early in the second quarter on a 30-yard field goal by Dana Coin, but Garcia had tied the score with a 42-yard field goal late in the third quarter. Then Michigan marched 71 yards in 17 plays to score for a 10-3 lead.

The Michigan defense had tightened up to shut off Bunce's passing, and the Indians had fourth down and 10 at their own 33. Steve Murray went back in punt formation, but the ball was snapped to Jim Kehl who was in a blocking position some three yards behind center Dennis Sheehan. Kehl handed the ball forward between the legs of running back Jackie Brown, who hesitated momentarily while Kehl completed his fake of running left.

Then Brown took off on a sweep around the right side for 31 yards to the Michigan 36. From there Bunce passed to tight end Bill Scott for 12. Then Brown, who had scored twice against Ohio State the year before, blasted through right tackle for 24 yards and a touchdown to tie the score at 10-10.

Another big play had come early in the third quarter. The Wolverines had taken the second-half kickoff and marched to a first down at the Stanford eight. Two plays gained four yards, and Simone, who played an outstanding game at linebacker, dropped Fritz Seyferth for a one-yard loss on third down. Michigan went to Billy Taylor on fourth down, but Jim Merlo, the other member of Stanford's trio of outstanding linebackers, and Benny Barnes nailed him a yard short of the goal line.

Michigan got a safety and a 12-10 lead with 3:18 left in the game when Jim Ferguson, Stanford's sophomore safetyman, made a mistake and tried to run a missed field goal attempt out of the end zone. Ferguson was supposed to stay in the end zone and run to his right to see if a lane opened up before venturing out. Instead, he ran to the left and got out to the two yard line before he was hit by Shuttlesworth and forced back into the end zone. Judge William Quimby of the Big 10 ruled it a safety, a decision which met with a lot of dispute in the press box.

Stanford was forced to give up the ball on a free kick, but the Thunderchickens, who had been outstanding all afternoon, took the ball away from the Wolverines at the Cardinals' 22 with only 1:48 left to play. Bunce, using his two-minute offense without the benefit of a huddle, completed five of six passes—each of the five for a first down—to move Stanford to the Michigan 17. He hit Scott for 13 yards, Winesberry for 16, and had one throw fall incomplete. Then he hit Miles Moore for 11, Sanderson for 14, and Winesberry for 12. Bunce then called on Sanderson and Brown for running plays to further run down the clock. With 16 seconds remaining, Garcia booted a 31-yard field goal to give Stanford an almost unbelieveable 13-12 win.

"That last series was something we always had planned for if we needed a touchdown in the closing minutes of the half or the game," said Bunce, who was voted "Outstanding Player of the Game" after completing 24 of 44 passes for 290 yards. "Really all I called were simple pass patterns. We had one basic pass play and one run. The passes were variations of the same play; I just threw to different receivers, sometimes the second-

Rod Garcia's 31-yard field goal in final 16 seconds gave Stanford 13-12 victory over Michigan in 1972 Rose Bowl game.

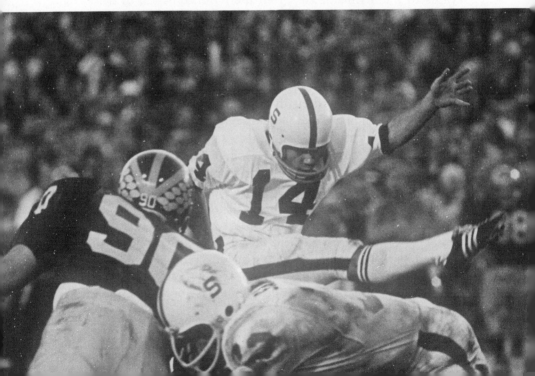

ary and other times the third receiver. The receivers made some great catches.

"It was the first time the series ever had gone. I felt in the huddle before the first play that I should say something about keeping cool, but when I looked up and saw those determined faces I knew nothing need be said. Really I was getting tired, but I had to admire the work of the offensive line.

"After we got past midfield I felt we were in Garcia's range. It was poetic justice that it should happen that way. It had to happen. I never have played in a more exciting game than that one, and that proved to all of us that we could compete."

"It was a tremendous effort by a great football team," observed Ralston. "You can't say enough about our defense. Stopping Michigan on the goal line on those key plays was something. You don't stop Michigan like that too often. Our passer and receivers were superb."

"I was pretty confident since I had gotten one off well," said Garcia of his game-winning boot. "I'd have preferred a touchdown because it would have been easier on me. But I thought it would end up with me having to kick a field goal. Hey, don't talk to me. Talk to Lazetich and the defense."

Ralston said that before Garcia was sent in for the final field goal attempt one of the Stanford players came up to him on the sidelines and said: "Coach, please don't talk to Rod." During the San Jose State game Ralston said he had talked to Garcia during the game, trying to calm him down. Garcia had missed five field goal attempts against the Spartans.

"The first time you win a Rose Bowl game I think is probably the greatest moment in a coach's life," Ralston remarked. "The second time you win you don't have the feeling of old hat when you win one like this. But at the same time I think I got a greater thrill from a personal standpoint, though I couldn't be prouder of our Stanford team."

Lazetich, one of the leaders of the Thunderchickens, called the game the best defensive effort of the year for the Indians. "It was better than our game against Washington because Michigan was such a powerful running team," he said.

Change Of Command

There were a couple of major changes on tap for Stanford in 1972. On January 5 Ralston announced he was leaving the Farm to accept a five-year contract as head coach and general manager of the Denver Broncos of the National Football League.

A few months later, President Richard W. Lyman ruled the university should drop the nickname of Indians and use only Cardinals in referring to its athletic teams. The action was taken after a small group of students protested the "Indians" nickname, declaring it was demeaning.

Ralston, who compiled a 55-36-3 record in his nine years at Stanford, said he had been considering a move since a few days after his Stanford team had upset Ohio State in the 1971 Rose Bowl. "I've always been one of those who starts out to build a house, and after you've taken it a certain distance find you can't build it any more. My goal at Stanford originally was to produce a national championship. I feel that we've fallen a little bit short there, though we've gone three years of having our football team in the top 10 of the country, and the back-to-back Rose Bowl wins might indicate that maybe we've done as much as we can at the present time."

Athletic director Chuck Taylor said Stanford would move as quickly as possible to name a successor. "It is imperative that we name a coach as soon as possible so that there is no loss of continuity," Taylor said.

The Stanford Board of Athletic Control did not take long to act. It had two top candidates for the head coaching job in Mike White, a graduate of California who had joined Ralston's

318

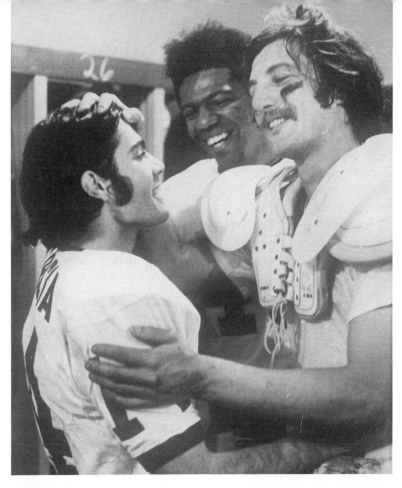

Garcia receives congratulations from wide receiver Miles Moore and tight end Bill Scott after his 31-yard field goal to beat Michigan.

staff in 1964 and had served as offensive line coach, and Jack Christiansen, a former professional star and head coach of the San Francisco 49ers for five years before coming to Stanford in the spring of 1968.

As offensive coordinator, White had the top recommendation for the job, but opted to accept a multi-year contract as head coach at California. Christiansen, who was in Denver to talk to Ralston about an assistant's post with the Broncos, was offered the job and accepted.

"I'll tell you, it's going to be a lot of hard work. It's a tough act to follow with the success we've had at Stanford the last four years," Christiansen said. "It's a great challenge and a great opportunity."

One of the features about Ralston's reign at Stanford had been his staff of assistants. "It was a great stroke to get Christiansen on the staff," Ralston said later. "Three of my assistants now are head coaches at three of the four major universities in California: Christiansen at Stanford, White at California, and Dick Vermeil at UCLA. That was one of my good fortunes, assembling good people."

White took three members of the Stanford staff with him to Berkeley so Christiansen had to set about lining up several new assistants. He had a stroke of luck when he landed Norb Hecker, who had been defensive coach of the New York Giants for five years, and George Seifert, defensive backfield coach from Oregon. Dave Currey and Ray Handley were retained from Ralston's staff. Bob Jones was added as offensive coordinator and Pete Kettela, as receiver coach.

Christiansen, with a professional background, elected to

Jack Christiansen accepts job of succeeding Ralston as head coach.

continue the wide-open type of offense Ralston had employed. Although he had 31 lettermen returning, the new Stanford coach faced a big problem rebuilding the defensive unit which had been hard hit by the graduation of Lazetich, Butler, and Greg Sampson from the line; Siemon, Simone, and Phil Satre from the linebacker ranks; and defensive backs Benny Barnes and Tim Robnett.

On the plus side was the fact that Christiansen had a capable quarterback to take over for the departed Bunce. Mike Boryla was big and rangy and, although he had been used sparingly behind Bunce, had shown in two spring games that he was capable of handling the passing assignment.

Christiansen also had an established field goal kicker in Garcia; a good running threat in Winesberry; and some good receivers in Cross, Miles Moore, Bill Scott, and Winesberry. One of his biggest problems involved the rebuilding of the offensive line which had been decimated by the loss of center Dennis Sheehan, guard Doug Adams, and tackles Bill Meyers and Tim Schallich.

"They say things run in cycles, and if that is true there isn't a one of us around here who feels that our cycle is over," Christiansen stated. "From top to bottom, this is probably the most evenly balanced Pacific-8 race we've ever seen. It's hard to discount any single team. Just because we have been in the Rose Bowl twice in a row, I don't think anyone should discount us either."

There had been six quarterbacks on the freshman squad when Boryla came to Stanford, and he had been switched to flanker. Among the others, Steve Murray had been shifted to safety and Pat Moore, to strong safety. A former All-State back in Colorado, Boryla had moved back into the quarterback picture with an impressive showing in spring drills. But because of Bunce's durability and the many close games, Boryla did not see much action in 1971.

Stanford backers were encouraged by Boryla's performance in the season opener with San Jose State. The Cardinals romped to a 44-0 victory to avenge the 13-12 setback of the previous year. Boryla completed 22 of 33 passes for 229 yards and two touchdowns. Winesberry, shifted from flanker to running back, romped 85 yards and linebacker Terry Pape ran 30 yards with a pass interception for additional scores.

Winesberry broke through tackle and, with blocks from

Mike Askea, Bill Reid, and Younger Klippert, turned in the longest run of the year for the Cardinals. "Winesberry's touchdown run ruined us," said San Jose coach Dewey King. The Spartans had been holding their own until that time.

Scott Laidlaw, a sophomore fullback, made his debut with a five-yard gain the first time he carried the ball. Two plays later he ran for 32 yards and then caught a pass for another 18 to personally account for 55 of the 62 yards in a five-play touchdown march. Garcia kicked a 42-yard field goal, and flanker Eric Cross caught six passes for 41 yards and two touchdowns in the easy win.

A 48-yard field goal by Garcia and a 12-yard pass from Boryla to tight end Bill Scott was the extent of Stanford's offense in a 10-6 win over Duke at Durham, North Carolina. But the Cardinal defense was outstanding as it gave up only one touchdown, although the Blue Devils had first downs at the Stanford two, one, four, and eight yard lines. On another occasion Duke had a fourth and one at the 12 and failed to make the yardage. Dennis Bragonier, senior safety from Hayward, was named the Pac-8 defensive player of the week for his performance which included 18 tackles, a pass interception, and a fumble recovery.

John Winesberry, 85-yard run against San Jose State.

Winesberry had one of his finest games at Stanford when he ran for 135 yards in 29 carries, caught four passes for another 50 yards, and scored three touchdowns in a 41-35 victory over West Virginia. Stanford collected a total of 486 yards—258 rushing and 228 passing—with the Broyla-to-Cross combination clicking for two touchdowns. The Mountaineers made it interesting by scoring 21 points in the fourth quarter and pulled off the most exciting play of the game when Artie Owens took a reverse on a kickoff and ran 96 yards to the Stanford two before being pulled down.

With three wins under their belt the Cardinals took on Southern California before 84,000 at Stanford Stadium, and things looked pretty bright for the first half. Stanford got a break in the first three minutes when James Ferguson recovered a fumble by Rod McNeill of the Trojans in the end zone for a touchdown. Garcia kicked field goals of 49 and 35 yards to offset touchdowns by Anthony Davis and Sam Cunningham and produce a 13-13 tie.

Then things began to go sour. Boryla threw a 60-yard pass to Cross for a touchdown, but the play was called back on an illegal procedure penalty. When Dave Ottmar went back to punt, the ball sailed over his head to the Stanford five where it was recovered by James Sims of USC. Anthony Davis scored with 51 seconds left in the half, for a 20-13 Trojan lead.

Stanford finished with a minus 16 yards rushing, gaining 64 yards but losing 80. And although the Cardinal defense held Davis to 60 yards in 20 carries, he scored two touchdowns and the rest of the Trojan ballcarriers piled up 232 yards.

In the next game Boryla put on a dazzling passing display as Stanford bounced back to hand Washington a 24-0 lacing. The big Cardinal quarterback hit 24 of 44 passes for 293 yards and touchdown throws of 23 yards to Cross and 30 yards to Don Alvarado.

"That was a helluva win," enthused Keith Rowen, sophomore tackle from San Francisco. "They were undefeated at the time, and it helped make up for the loss to USC."

Just when it looked like Stanford might have things straightened out the Cardinals had to visit Eugene, Oregon, to face the University of Oregon. As might be expected, it was raining. The Cardinals had trouble getting any kind of an offensive push started and wound up on the short end of a 15-13 score. Stanford managed only five yards rushing in the first half as the Ducks took a 15-0 lead on three field goals by Hugh Woodward and an 85-yard run by Don Reynolds on an option play lateral.

"It was pretty hard to throw because of the rain and the fact that Oregon blitzed the whole game," said Boryla, now a quarterback with the Philadelphia Eagles. "I was on my back most of the day."

Garcia missed four lengthy field goals but did convert two tries. One of them was 54 yards to set a new Stanford record, breaking the old mark of 52 yards set by Beck in 1964 at Spokane. Boryla was 23 for 55 for 290 yards but had four interceptions which spoiled his attempt to pull the game out of the fire. The Cardinals were hurt again when their running game netted only 25 yards.

California's Memorial Stadium looked more like a swamp than a football field for the 75th Big Game, yet it turned out to be one of the most exciting contests of the series. The Bears scored on the final play of the game for a 24-21 win, only the third victory of the season for rookie coach Mike White.

The field was ankle deep in mud when the Bears took advantage of two pass interference calls and two pass completions in the final two minutes of the game to reach the Stanford eight yard line. There were only three seconds left when freshman Vince Ferragamo fired a pass to end Steve Sweeney in the corner of the end zone for the winning touchdown. No attempt was made to kick the extra point as wild California rooters tore down the goalposts.

"That was real frustrating," said Boryla, "because we didn't have a chance to get back on the field. We had played a pretty good game, and I thought we had won it when Reggie Sanderson bulled over from the four to give us a 21-18 lead with less than four minutes left. It was so hard to move the ball in the mud that I didn't think they could score."

Boryla had set up Sanderson's score with a 25-yard pass to Cross and a 21-yard throw to Alvarado. Stanford's earlier touchdowns had come on a 25-yard pass to Cross and a 71-yard return of a pass interception by linebacker Gordon Riegel. "Cross made a super, diving catch in the end zone on the touchdown pass," Boryla said.

Sweeney was California's leading pass receiver with four catches, but Steve Murray, Stanford defensive back, almost matched him with three interceptions.

Mike Boryla runs for daylight against USC.

The Cardinals assured themselves a winning season by thumping the University of Hawaii 39-7 in their finale in Honolulu. Cross caught 14 passes to set new Stanford and Pacific-8 single game records. He also caught two touchdown passes, giving him nine for the season and another Stanford record. Garcia booted a 31-yard field goal, his 10th of the season and his 24th over two years for another Stanford mark.

Although Cross was the leading receiver in the Pacific-8 (53 catches for 730 yards) and Boryla was No. 1 in passing (183 completions in 350 attempts for 2,284 yards and 14 touchdowns) and led the total offense (2,071 yards), neither was accorded All-Conference honors. The only Stanford player named on the offensive team was Garcia while linebacker Jim Merlo and safety Randy Poltl were selected for the defensive squad. Merlo completed the season with 164 tackles, the most by any Stanford player in recent memory. Poltl had five pass interceptions and was a standout in other departments in the secondary for the Cardinals.

After getting the coaching problem settled, Taylor eased out of the Stanford athletic picture, leaving his assistant Bob Young to handle the details for the remainder of the spring

Joe Ruetz, athletic director.

quarter. On September 1, 1972, Joe Ruetz, who had served as Taylor's line coach from 1951 to 1956, was appointed Director of Athletics and Physical Education. Ruetz, who was forced to give up coaching because of a bout with cancer, had returned to the university in 1957, joining the general secretary's office as an executive fund-raiser.

"Our goal," said Ruetz, "is the same as ever: excellence in a variety of things and a strong sports program without sacrificing academic or athletic integrity. Football is still in there with geology and pharmacology."

326

A Rebuilding Task

Christiansen was faced with a number of problems as he prepared for the 1973 football season, among them an inexperienced offensive line and a tough preconference schedule.

Still he faced the assignment with optimism. "We know exactly where we have to improve, based on our experience of a year ago," he said. "We feel that we're in a pretty good position to improve on our record of last year, and the players are certainly optimistic about our chances of doing just that. We were obviously pleased that Mike Boryla's eligibility was extended for this season, since it's comforting to start with an established and talented quarterback."

Boryla was granted an added year of eligibility because he had played only 1:06, four plays, against San Jose State during 1970 in what would have been his sophomore year. "I developed calcium deposits in my arm and didn't play any more that year," Boryla explained. "We petitioned the conference for another year of eligibility, and it was granted."

Stanford faced Penn State and Michigan in its first two games, and the only veterans Christiansen had in his offensive line were center Bill Reid and tackle Rowen. Rob Olson, a transfer from San Jose City College, was at one guard post; Bruce Blackstone, who had seen limited action the year before, was at the other; and Todd Anderson, a sophomore, was at the other tackle spot.

Another serious area of concern for Christiansen was the graduation of five of the six leading receivers from 1972: Cross, Miles Moore, Bill Scott, Sanderson, and Alverado. They had 141 catches for 1,946 yards.

Penn State, led by John Cappelletti who wound up as the Heisman Trophy winner, handed Stanford a 20-6 setback in the opener, but the Cardinals performed well except for the offense, which had a minus eight yards rushing. Boryla completed 17 of 29 passes for 189 yards.

"Our defense played exceptionally well, holding Cappelletti to 76 yards," Christiansen said. "We had almost no offense. Instead of going forward, it went sideways and backwards. It was the hardest hitting first game of the season I've ever seen, including the Arkansas game in 1970."

A blocked kick which sailed out of the end zone and a fumble recovery at the Stanford 10 were responsible for Penn State's 10-0 lead at half time.

In its next game Stanford's game plan was destroyed when Michigan scored three times in the first quarter. Michigan marched 85 yards for the first score. It then took advantage of a fumble recovery on the Stanford 15 and a low pass from center to punter Tom Lynn that gave the Wolverines the ball on the Cardinals' six for the second two scores.

Boryla hit on 19 of 32 passes for 222 yards in another good passing performance, but the Stanford running game again wound up in the red with a minus five, the result of gaining 95 yards but losing 100.

Dave Ottmar had planned to redshirt the 1973 season in order to have a chance to play regularly at quarterback instead of serving as a backup man to Boryla. But Christiansen felt Stanford had a chance to win the Pacific-8 conference and asked Ottmar to return to the squad to handle the punting. "We can't win without a good kicker," Christiansen said.

Defense was the highlight of a 23-12 victory over San Jose State. Craig Zaltosky's 68-yard punt return for a touchdown, four pass interceptions, and a goal-line stand that saw Stanford stop the Spartans on four consecutive plays at the one yard line were the keys. "The defense finally started to hit hard and played together as a unit in this game," said Roger Stillwell, a 6-6, 250-pound defensive end who earned UPI All America honors at the end of the season.

The win was a costly one for the Cardinals, however, as Winesberry injured his knee late in the third quarter and was lost for the season.

There was concern when linebacker Riegel missed the Stanford charter flight for the trip to Champaign-Urbana, Illinois, for the game with the University of Illinois. But he caught a plane to Chicago and was on hand to play a leading role in the Cardinals' 24-0 victory over the Illini. Riegel, who may have been trying to make amends for missing the plane, made 17 tackles, knocked down two passes, sacked the quarterback, and caused a fumble.

Ottmar got his chance to do some quarterbacking in the second quarter when Boryla suffered a cut eye which required five stitches and kept him on the bench the rest of the game. Dave completed 11 of 19 passes for 132 yards and put Illinois in a hole with a punt that was downed on the Illini two yard line.

After the improvement shown by the Stanford defense against San Jose State and Illinois, the Cardinals went into their Pacific-8 opener with UCLA in an optimistic frame of mind. But the Bruins changed that outlook in a hurry. Stanford managed to stop UCLA only once in the seven times the Bruins had the ball in the first half.

Kermit Johnson and James McAlister were devastating as they ripped through the Stanford line. The first time Johnson carried the ball he blasted through guard, veered left, and ran 51 yards. He had another run of 54 yards and McAlister had one of 50. Johnson averaged 15.3 yards as he gained 168 yards in 11 carries, while McAlister had 117 yards in 14 carries and scored three touchdowns as the Bruins rushed for 621 yards.

Stanford rebounded from the humiliating 59-13 loss to UCLA by defeating Washington 23-14 in Seattle in a game that started out to be a "laugher" but instead wound up as a cliffhanger as the Huskies scored twice in the fourth quarter. Garcia kicked field goals of 37, 38, and 47 yards.

The Cardinals put everything together for a 45-14 win over Washington State, gaining a little revenge for the 27-13 loss the year before when the Cougars kicked a field goal on the last play.

"This was one of those days when everything came together," said Laidlaw, who rushed for 130 yards. "The offensive line deserves credit, and that helped fire up the team. Washington State kept saying they sacked Boryla 10 times last year and were going after a record in this game. This gave incentive to our line. It was one of those days when all of our players were ready to play. Just like the coaches, we wanted to win."

"That was probably the most enjoyable game of my ca-

Fullback Scott Laidlaw, "everything came together."

reer," said Boryla, who threw five touchdown passes to set a Stanford record while completing 16 of 23 tosses for 151 yards. "We had played four games and lost three of them. But that game we came out and played well and beat Washington State badly."

Ron Inge, a speedy freshman halfback from Stockton, provided the spark and Garcia supplied the final kick as Stanford edged Oregon State 24-23 on a cold, rainy day in Corvallis.

Oregon State had taken a 12-3 lead midway in the second quarter before Inge exploded for a 96-yard kickoff return that put Stanford back in the game. The Beavers got another score on a blocked kick only 54 seconds before the end of the half, but Boryla took the Cardinals 66 yards in five plays for a touchdown with seven seconds remaining.

Boryla passed to Reggie Ishman for 14, to Bill Singler for 36, ran for 18, and passed to Singler for seven for the score. The other play was a nine-yard loss when Boryla could not find any receivers. Garcia kicked a 36-yard field goal in the rain with 4:19 left to bring Stanford from behind.

Boryla was 12 for 26 for 153 yards and moved past John Brodie into third place on Stanford's career passing list on a 27-yard pass to Eric Test late in the third quarter.

"Character, poise, call it what you want. I think our players had a lot of faith that they'd come back and they did," said Christiansen.

Garcia gave a superb exhibition of place-kicking in the Los Angeles Coliseum on November 10, but it was not enough. Stanford watched an upset slip through its fingers as Southern California scored 10 points in the last three minutes for a 27-26 win.

"That was an extremely frustrating loss," said Boryla. "We had the lead going into the last few seconds, but they scored. You never are sure you have any game won against USC. It's hard to beat them and even tougher to win in the Coliseum. We had played a good game and had played our very best."

Garcia set a Stanford and Coliseum record by booting a 59-yard field goal in the first 3:27 of the game. Then he added three from 42, 52, and 25 yards, his last effort coming with 3:10 left in the game and making the score 26-17 in Stanford's favor. But the Trojans were aided by a pass interference call that gave them a first down on the Stanford 12, and they scored, to make it 26-24 with 2:10 remaining.

The Cardinals managed one first down but then had to kick the ball away. USC had only 33 seconds and was on its own 30. Pat Haden whipped a 24-yard pass to Jim Obradovich, his first catch of the game. A pass to Anthony Davis gained four, and Haden hit Obradovich again for 25. There were only seven seconds left as Chris Limahelu lined up in the field goal formation and toed a 34-yard placement through the uprights.

It was virtually an instant replay of the 1969 USC-Stanford game in which Ron Ayala kicked a 34-yard field goal on the final play for a 26-24 win for the Trojans.

Stanford had to come from behind to whip California 26-17.

"I got hurt in the second quarter when I was knocked down," said Boryla. "My shoulder tightened up between halves, and Dave Ottmar replaced me in the second half and did a super job."

California took a 17-13 lead early in the fourth quarter on a 56-yard bomb from Steve Bartkowski to Wesley Walker. But the Cardinals took advantage of a short California punt to regain the lead and added another touchdown on some outstanding running by Laidlaw and Doug Jena with five minutes left. Laidlaw earned "Offensive Player of the Game" honors with 132 yards in 23 carries, topping Chuck Muncie of the Bears who had 129 yards for 22 carries.

Stanford finished the season with a 7-4 record, with all the losses coming from teams ranked in the top 10 in the country.

Boryla, who led the conference again in passing with 140 completions in 256 attempts for 1,629 yards and 17 touchdowns, was named on the All-Pac-8 offensive team, while end Stillwell and back Poltl were honored on the defensive unit.

Stanford also had the unusual distinction of having two All America defensive ends in the same year, as Stillwell was selected by United Press International and Pat Donovan was chosen on the Associated Press team.

Although they had a far better percentage on their completions and fewer interceptions, the Cardinals yielded the conference passing title to Washington. The Huskies averaged 195.8 yards per game while Stanford had 181.1. However, the Cardinals topped the league for the second straight year in pass defense, allowing an average of only 120.8 yards per game. Zaltosky also was No. 1 in punt returns with a 14.2 yard average for 21 returns, while Jim Kaffen tied for second in pass inter-

Ron Inge, 96-yard kickoff return helped beat Beavers.

ceptions with seven.

"It was a tough year," Boryla said in retrospect. "We started out with high hopes. We had good people, but we just didn't have the talent to match teams like Penn State, Michigan, UCLA, and USC. We started out badly, but we came back and finished strong as our offensive line matured."

333

Missing: Experienced QB

One of the trademarks of Stanford football has been its long line of talented quarterbacks.

When the 1974 season opened, however, the Cardinal passing game had to be considered a question mark. For the first time since Jim Plunkett took over at quarterback as an unproven sophomore in 1968, Stanford was without an experienced signal caller. Christiansen had three talented quarterbacks, but all were sophomores. None had any varsity experience.

Mike Cordova, a high school All America from Mountlake, Washington, had been brilliant on the Frosh-JV squad in 1973 and saw brief action with the varsity. Guy Benjamin, an outstanding passer, had missed his freshman year because of a knee injury which required an operation while Jerry Waldvogel, possibly the quickest of the three, sat out the 1973 season after playing for the Frosh-JV team the year before.

Christiansen elected to give each of his quarterbacks a chance in the four preconference games, delaying a final decision until the week of the UCLA game on October 12.

Aside from the quarterback position, Christiansen had lettermen available at every position on both the offensive and defensive teams. The only question mark defensively involved the secondary where starters Poltl, Kaffen, and Ferguson were missing from the Pac-8's top group of pass defenders. Garcia, who had kicked 42 field goals in his three years at Stanford, also was missing, but the Cardinals had Mike Langford, one of the top junior college kickers in the nation, to replace him.

"Overall, we're much stronger this season," Christiansen stated. "If we stay healthy I feel we'll definitely have a chance to win the league championship. We like to think that our November 9 game with USC may decide the Pac-8 championship. The defense should be the outstanding part of our team, and our rushing defense in particular should be very good."

Regarding his quarterback problem, Christiansen said: "All three have outstanding qualities. I feel I could put any one of them on the field and get anywhere from a good to a great job. There's no dropoff in ability when we go from one to another."

Cordova got the call for the season opener against Penn State at University Park, Pennsylvania, and turned in a spectacular second-half performance. He earned "Offensive Player of the Game" honors for the nationally televised contest as he set stadium records with 51 passes which produced 301 yards. His 23 completions tied the stadium mark.

Penn State came from behind to win that game 24-20. The Nittany Lions scored the go-ahead touchdown by marching 80 yards in the last five minutes of the game with the help of three pass completions and a pass interference call that gave them a first down on the one yard line.

Stanford had spotted Penn State a 14-0 lead in the first 18 minutes, but came back to tie the score midway in the fourth quarter. The Cardinals apparently had another touchdown a few minutes later on a pass from Cordova to Inge, but the score was nullified by a clipping penalty on the three yard line. Stanford had to settle for a 28-yard field goal by Langford.

"That game could have turned the whole season around," said Rowen, an All-Pacific Coast offensive tackle. "The team was so keyed up for that game."

It was Benjamin's turn the following week against Illinois, and he got Stanford away to a good start with a 24-yard touchdown pass to Singler. That was the only thing that went right for the Cardinals that day, however. Illinois turned a fumble into a touchdown and ran a pass interception back 33 yards for another—all within 49 seconds at the end of the first quarter. Benjamin completed 11 of 15 passes for 128 yards in the first half but was unable to generate an offensive threat after the initial touchdown.

Christiansen switched to Cordova in the second half, but he had even less success as he completed only six of 22 passes and had three throws intercepted. Illinois romped to a 41-7 win, improving by one point on the margin by which the Illini had beaten Stanford in the 1952 Rose Bowl game.

With Waldvogel getting his chance to handle the quarter-back duties, Stanford gave powerful Michigan a scare before losing 27-16. Jerry turned in an outstanding job as he completed 21 of 40 passes for 229 yards. He threw one touchdown, and Langford kicked field goals from 52, 42, and 42 yards. The Cardinals might have won except for a fumble which the Wolverines recovered on the Stanford nine midway in the third quarter, only a minute after they had scored to take a 13-9 lead.

Having played their "best overall game," the Cardinals felt they were ready for their Pacific-8 Conference opener with UCLA. The game was played in the Los Angeles Coliseum, however—an environment in which Stanford has found it difficult to win. This time it got a 13-13 tie.

UCLA's Brett White kicked a 37-yard field goal on the final play of the game (does that sound familiar?). The Bruins completed only four of 13 passes, but one of them was for 25 yards with less than a minute left to play to help put the Bruins in position for White's kick.

Pat Donovan (83) and Roger Stillwell (91), a pair of All America defensive ends.

Cordova had earned the starting quarterback role, but Benjamin came off the bench in the second quarter when Cordova was shaken up and completed five of six passes. One was an 11-yard touchdown toss to Singler which gave Stanford a 13-10 lead until White kicked the UCLA field goal.

Stanford had an 0-3-2 record when it took the field against Washington and under the scoreboard at the east end of Stanford Stadium was a sign which read: "77 percent and benched." The reference was to Benjamin, who had completed 17 of 22 passes for 77.3 percent but had played only a half against Illinois and eight plays against UCLA.

Cordova responded with his best performance since the Penn State game, completing 23 of 37 passes for 284 yards and three touchdowns to lead Stanford to its first win of the season, a 34-17 triumph over the Huskies. Lending support to Cordova's passing were field goals of 32 and 26 yards by Langford, an 87-yard punt return by Ray Anderson to the Washington 13, and two pass interceptions by Paul Skrabo.

Stanford's conference title hopes looked brighter after a 20-18 win over Washington State at Pullman. The Cardinals came up with a balanced attack that produced 155 yards rushing and 190 yards passing as Cordova went 17 for 35 and passed for two touchdowns. Langford added the other points on 24 and 47-yard field goals.

"That game was a real turnaround for us," said Rowen. "When we got Washington State in position we captured the ability to come up and win a close game. If you're used to losing, you'll lose. We had gotten into that kind of a trend by tying San Jose State and UCLA and losing to Michigan."

Inge had been sidelined with a shoulder injury for a couple of weeks but had returned for the Washington State game. The speedy sophomore came up with one of his best games as Stanford won another close one, edging Oregon State 17-13. Inge romped for 127 yards on 20 carries and teamed with Laidlaw to give the Cardinals a strong running game. Laidlaw, who scored both touchdowns, had 81 yards in 16 carries.

With their record at 3-3-2 and a conference mark of 3-0-1, the Cardinals appeared ready for their annual confrontation with USC. "We feel pretty good at this point to be at the top and tied for the conference lead," Christiansen said. "We know now that if we win our last three games we'll win the conference and go to the Rose Bowl. USC is an outstanding team and

337

we know it will take our best game both offensively and defensively to beat them."

The Cardinals were found wanting on both counts as the Trojans rolled to an easy 34-10 victory and went on to claim their third straight conference title and their seventh in nine years. USC rushed for 295 yards while Stanford managed only 80 yards rushing and 155 yards passing.

"They blew us off the field," said linebacker Forrie Martin. "And I don't care who they're up against in the Rose Bowl, they'll blow any team off the field. We played our hearts out against them, but they just didn't let up. No mistakes, no fumbles. They were amazing. It was incredible. Everytime we made a mistake, they did something right."

On an overcast day in Eugene, Cordova did not have one of his better days. But Laidlaw had the best one of his career as Stanford blanked Oregon 17-0. Laidlaw hammered out 142 yards on 21 carries and two of Cordova's nine pass completions went for touchdowns. The Stanford defense, led by All America Pat Donovan, All-Coast linebacker John Snider, Drew Palin, and sophomore Duncan McColl, checked the Ducks with 99 yards rushing. McColl, son of the former Stanford All America end, Bill McColl, was credited with nine tackles and four quarterback sackings for losses of 31 yards.

A winning season and at least a tie for second place in the Pac-8 race were on the line as Stanford clashed with California in the 77th Big Game at Berkeley. The Cardinals secured both with a 22-20 victory in a game that will rank among the most thrilling in the long series. Both sides won and lost in the final 26 seconds, and for once, Stanford had the last chance and came out on top in one of these last second affairs.

It would be hard to write a script to match the finish of this game. Stanford appeared to have the game won midway in the fourth quarter with a 19-10 lead. But California tallied a field goal and then, with less than three minutes remaining, mounted another scoring drive.

Steve Bartkowski, the Bears' great quarterback who threw 20 completions in 41 attempts for 318 yards, faced a fourth down and 10 situation at the Stanford 37. He had only one choice—to pass—and his target was Steve Rivera, who made nine catches for 205 yards that afternoon. This time his pass was good for 24 yards, and two plays later he rifled a 13-yard bullet to Rivera in the end zone for a touchdown to put California in

Mike Langford's 50-yard field goal beats California in final second, 22-20.

front 20-19.

There were only 26 seconds left to play, and most of the 71,866 fans figured the Bears had stolen the game from the Cardinals. Many of the downhearted Stanford fans made a quick exit from the stadium.

But Benjamin knew what he had to do, and he set about it. With the poise of a veteran, he picked up a first down to stop the clock with an 18-yard pass to tight end Ted Pappas. His next attempt fell incomplete, but another try to Brad Williams, cutting across the middle, was on target. Williams also knew what he had to do, and he fought his way for 25 yards before going out of bounds on the Bears' 33 to stop the clock with only two seconds remaining.

Langford, who already had booted field goals of 29 and 31

yards, then proved himself just as big a hero as Garcia had been in the 1972 Rose Bowl. He kicked a 50-yard field goal to return the victory to Stanford.

Benjamin had come in to relieve Cordova late in the third quarter of the game. California held a 10-3 lead midway through the third quarter. Coach Christiansen informed Cordova that he had one more series to get something started. "I know it," the big quarterback replied. But nothing happened, and Benjamin got the call the next time Stanford got the ball.

A 20-yard run by Tom Lynn from punt formation helped the Cardinals get started, but they had to settle for Langford's 31-yard field goal on the third play of the fourth quarter. Then Stanford got a break when a high snap from center on fourth down gave the Cardinals a scoring opportunity on the California nine. After cashing in on that situation, the Cards grabbed the momentum as Jeff Siemens intercepted one of Bartkowski's passes and returned 21 yards to the Stanford 40.

On his first play Benjamin dropped a bomb on the Bears with a pass to Tony Hill, a speedy sophomore wide receiver. The sideline pattern was good for 60 yards and a touchdown. That made it 19-10 and set the stage for the exciting finish.

When questioned about his winning kick, Langford repeated the question. "Was I nervous? I was weak-kneed. Eric (Test) told me to keep my head down and follow through, and I did. It wasn't a bad kick, but it was a little wobbly."

Joy reigned in the Stanford dressing room. "The Big Game always ranks as the No. 1 game to win," said Rowen. "There was a lot of camaraderie in the locker room after the game. We were cheering and hugging everyone. That Williams did a great job on that last pass. He bowled over Herm Edwards and was making the most of his last reception as a Stanford player."

Laidlaw, who needed 52 yards to become the third leading rusher in Stanford history, missed that goal as he collected only 22, but he was not disappointed. "I'm emotionally drained," he said. "It's a great way to end a season and a career. I can't put it in words. I was thinking about two years ago at the end of the game, but this year we had more time. I didn't think we had enough time, however."

Thus, after a disappointing start in which they failed to win in their first five games—the first time Stanford had experienced such a lack of success since 1960—the Cardinals finished strong to win five of their last six games for a 5-4-2 record. Donovan, a 6-5, 240-pounder from Helena, Montana, was named on the United Press International All America, thus becoming Stanford's 10th two-time All America. He joins the list of Ernie Nevers (1924-25), Bill Corbus (1932-33), Bobby Grayson (1934-35), Monk Moscrip (1934-35), Bob Reynolds (1934-35), Bones Hamilton (1934-35), Frank Albert (1940-41), Bill McColl (1950-51), and Paul Wiggin (1955-56).

Here Comes The Band

Pregame and half-time shows at Stanford's home football games never have been the same since the Stanford Band emerged from the dark ages of tradition in 1963 and abandoned its militaristic marching and music styles.

Awarded its independence from university control, the band became an entirely student-owned and operated organization. More commonly known as the Incomparable Leland Stanford Junior University Marching Band, the group adopted a new philosophy for a marching band—it sought to have fun.

Not only have two Rose Bowl appearances, three cross-country ventures, and several national TV appearances changed the LSJUMB's basic philosophy, it has caused other bands to change theirs. By constantly poking a satirical finger at reality and featuring fine, contemporary music, the self-styled "nattering nabobs of novelty" have established a reputation as being one of the most progressive and creative musical organizations in the country.

Whatever the feelings of the crowds for which they play, members of the band will continue to have fun with the same refreshing vigor that prompted one fan from the 1972 Rose Bowl game to write: "Thank you for making the world a bit more joyful." Another wrote: "It would seem impossible not to be caught up in the band's absolutely infectious enthusiasm."

Wherever it goes, the Stanford Band never fails to attract an audience. After the two Rose Bowl games the band remained in the stands until long after darkness entertaining a couple of thousand fans who thronged around to listen to their lively music. It is the same whether the game is at Stanford; the Los

342

Angeles Coliseum; Little Rock, Arkansas; Ann Arbor, Michigan; or University Park, Pennsylvania. When Stanford opened the 1970 season against Arkansas at Little Rock, some 75 members of the band were on hand, hitchhiking or traveling on their own—by whatever method possible. Of course the fact that the game was on national TV might have been an added lure.

There are others involved in the Stanford football program besides the coaches, the players, and the band. Behind the scenes are Dr. Robert W. Jamplis and Dr. Frederick L. Behling, who have been the team physicians since 1956 and 1959, respectively. There is Dave Blanchard, who came to Stanford in 1965 to share duties with long-time trainer Connie Jarvis and assumed the head job when Jarvis retired in 1967. Responsible for ordering, fitting, cleaning, packing, and repairing Stanford's sports equipment is Virgil "Doc" Marvin, athletic equipment manager who has been on the job for 20 years and serves as a counselor to players in addition to his many other duties.

Until he retired in 1969 to write *The Color of Life is Red*,

The Incomparable Leland Stanford Junior University Marching Band in its pre-game formation.

a history of athletics at Stanford University, Don Leibendorfer had served as the Cardinals' only sports information director, assuming the duties soon after his graduation from Stanford in the 1920s. He was followed by Bob Murphy, who gave way to Gary Cavalli in 1974 to accept the assignment as executive director of the East-West Shrine football game.

Others involved in the program are Jack Laird, alumni relations director, and Mel Nelson, superintendent of the Stanford athletic grounds. Nelson has been on the Farm since 1927, and has numerous stories to tell about his early years at Stanford — how they used to cut the grass in the stadium and on the practice fields by turning out some 300 sheep to graze before they finally acquired lawn mowers in 1930.

Stanford boasts one of the finest football turfs in the country and the secret, according to Nelson, is a regular program of aerifying and fertilizing. "The stadium hasn't been seeded since 1928," Nelson said, "but we put 50 tons of sand on the field every other year, the season when the Big Game is to be played here, and we aerify and fertilize."

Many of the Stanford football players have worked at the Corporation Yard during Nelson's tenure, and he has made friends with a lot of them. "Bones Hamilton was one of the best blocking backs I've ever seen," he said. "Hamilton, Monk Moscrip, and Keith Topping all worked here and were good workers. Chuck Taylor worked here too. He used to mow the greens at the golf course."

One of the most underrated players in Nelson's opinion was Walt Heinecke, who played center on the 1927-28-29 teams. Nelson also recalled that Bob Reynolds, tackle on the Vow Boys team of 1933-34-35, acquired his nickname of "Horse" because of a prank a couple of his teammates pulled.

"We had several horses at the yard that we used to pull wagons and do other chores around here," Nelson said. "One time a couple of the players took a horse from the yard and put it up in Reynolds' room on the second floor at Encina Hall. I don't know how they got it up there, but that's where Reynolds got the name of 'Horse.'"

Tail-gating has been a practice at Stanford for many years, but in recent seasons it has expanded until the grounds surrounding Stanford Stadium are well filled as early as 11 a.m. on a game day, as alumni and fans arrive early and set up their tables and barbecues for a pregame meal.

"It's no problem for us," said Nelson. "They clean up after themselves. The only one it might bother is the concessionaire."

Among Stanford's most loyal fans are Dan Lee, a Palo Alto restaurateur; Dan Elliott, of Newport Beach; and Gerry Rosenthal, of San Jose. Like the Stanford Band, they are likely to show up almost anyplace the Cardinals are playing.

Then there are fans like Leo Casseta who later was kicking himself for selling his 1972 Rose Bowl tickets and for turning off his radio with 26 seconds left in the 1974 Big Game. But Leo was not alone among Stanford fans who had given up on that game. A lot of Big Red rooters got up and left the stadium after the California touchdown.

But after Garcia's winning field goal in the final 16 seconds of the Rose Bowl game with Michigan and Langford's winning kick in the last two seconds of the 1974 Big Game, Stanford football followers have reason to believe the Cardinals are not beaten until the final gun.

Stanford Stadium, largest privately owned college stadium in the country, with seating capacity of 86,352.

Appendix

STANFORD'S WON-LOST RECORD

Year	Won	Lost	Tied	Points	Opps.	Coach
1891	3	1	0	52	26	No coach
1892	2	0	2	58	29	Walter Camp
1893	8	0	1	248	17	"Pop" Bliss
1894	6	3	0	100	58	Walter Camp
1895	4	0	1	34	8	Walter Camp
1896	2	1	1	30	4	H. P. Cross
1897	4	1	0	54	26	G. H. Brooke
1898	5	3	1	93	62	H. P. Cross
1899	2	5	2	61	78	Burr Chamberlain
1900	7	2	1	154	20	Fielding H. Yost
1901	3	2	2	34	57	C. M. Fickert
1902	6	1	0	111	37	C. L. Clemans
1903	8	0	3	199	6	James F. Lanagan
1904	7	2	1	206	10	James F. Lanagan
1905	8	0	0	138	13	James F. Lanagan
†1906	6	2	1	87	29	James F. Lanagan
†1907	8	4	0	138	93	James F. Lanagan
†1908	12	2	0	218	39	James F. Lanagan
†1909	8	1	0	233	22	George Presley
†1910	7	1	0	189	25	George Presley
†1911	10	3	0	235	60	George Presley
†1912	5	3	1	88	42	George Presley
†1913	8	3	0	134	149	Floyd C. Brown
†1914	10	0	0	288	43	Floyd C. Brown
†1915	10	0	1	370	64	Floyd C. Brown
†1916	9	1	0	256	109	Floyd C. Brown
†1917	1	0	0	15	11	Jim Wylie
1918	(no official schedule)					
1919	4	3	0	130	46	Bob Evans
1920	4	3	0	82	65	Walter Powell
1921	4	2	2	100	97	C. E. Van Gent
1922	4	5	0	63	96	Andy Kerr
1923	7	2	0	284	46	Andy Kerr
*1924	7	1	1	179	69	Glenn S. Warner
1925	7	2	0	231	71	Glenn S. Warner
*1926	10	0	1	268	86	Glenn S. Warner
*1927	8	2	1	151	75	Glenn S. Warner
1928	8	3	1	274	69	Glenn S. Warner
1929	9	2	0	288	53	Glenn S. Warner
1930	9	1	1	252	69	Glenn S. Warner
1931	7	2	2	160	44	Glenn S. Warner
1932	6	4	1	171	58	Glenn S. Warner
*1933	8	2	1	131	43	C. E. Thornhill
*1934	9	1	1	224	43	C. E. Thornhill
*1935	8	1	0	121	13	C. E. Thornhill
1936	2	5	2	80	109	C. E. Thornhill
1937	4	3	2	68	53	C. E. Thornhill
1938	3	6	0	67	92	C. E. Thornhill
1939	1	7	1	54	146	C. E. Thornhill
*1940	10	0	0	196	85	Clark Shaughnessy

†Rugby   *Played in Rose Bowl

STANFORD'S WON-LOST RECORD
(Continued)

Year	Won	Lost	Tied	Points	Opps.	Coach
1941	6	3	0	160	95	Clark Shaughnessy
1942	6	4	0	204	121	Marchmont Schwartz
1943 & 1944 (did not field a team)						
1945	(no official schedule)					
1946	6	3	1	222	147	Marchmont Schwartz
1947	0	9	0	73	214	Marchmont Schwartz
1948	4	6	0	164	159	Marchmont Schwartz
1949	7	3	1	366	121	Marchmont Schwartz
1950	5	3	2	188	117	Marchmont Schwartz
*1951	9	2	0	229	181	Charles A. Taylor
1952	5	5	0	187	226	Charles A. Taylor
1953	6	3	1	246	148	Charles A. Taylor
1954	4	6	0	123	229	Charles A. Taylor
1955	6	3	1	198	135	Charles A. Taylor
1956	4	6	0	218	213	Charles A. Taylor
1957	6	4	0	227	158	Charles A. Taylor
1958	2	8	0	93	226	Jack C. Curtice
1959	3	7	0	232	261	Jack C. Curtice
1960	0	10	0	111	250	Jack C. Curtice
1961	4	6	0	105	163	Jack C. Curtice
1962	5	5	0	124	174	Jack C. Curtice
1963	3	7	0	154	199	John Ralston
1964	5	5	0	150	138	John Ralston
1965	6	3	1	144	149	John Ralston
1966	5	5	0	149	146	John Ralston
1967	5	5	0	157	179	John Ralston
1968	6	3	1	268	162	John Ralston
1969	7	2	1	349	172	John Ralston
*1970	9	3	0	343	206	John Ralston
*1971	9	3	0	261	135	John Ralston
1972	6	5	0	266	183	Jack Christiansen
1973	7	4	0	244	240	Jack Christiansen
1974	5	4	2	197	228	Jack Christiansen

*Played in Rose Bowl

Significant Stanford Football Records

CAREER

(NOTE: Career records have been revised so as to include **only** regular-season statistics and **not** Rose Bowl statistics, in order to agree with NCAA national records.)

RUSHING	TCB	YG	YL	NYG	Avg.	TDs
1. Ray Handley (1963-65)	405	1838	70	1768	4.4	11
2. Bill Tarr (1953-55)	358	1675	82	1593	4.4	16
3. Bob Grayson (1933-35)	405	1705	158	1547	3.8	18
4. Scott Laidlaw (1972-74)	349	1579	36	1543	4.7	9

PASSING	PA	PC	HI	Pct.	NYG	TDs
1. Jim Plunkett (1968-70)	962	530	48	.550	7,544	52
2. Mike Boryla (1970-73)	641	338	31	.527	4,082	31
3. Dick Norman (1958-60)	597	323	32	.541	3,737	18
4. John Brodie (1954-56)	536	296	37	.552	3,594	20
5. Gary Kerkorian (1949-51)	451	243	28	.540	3,174	17
6. Don Bunce (1968, 69, 71)	360	190	21	.528	2,805	20
7. Bob Garrett (1951-53)	357	190	28	.532	2,616	28

TOTAL OFFENSE	NYG
1. Jim Plunkett* (1968-70)	7,887
2. Mike Boryla (1970-73)	3,786
3. Dick Norman (1958-60)	3,654
4. John Brodie (1954-56)	3,560
5. Don Bunce (1968, 69, 71)	3,264
6. Gary Kerkorian (1949-51)	2,989
7. Bob Garrett (1951-53)	2,388

RECEIVING	Receptions	Yards	TDs
1. Gene Washington (1966-68)	122	1,785	10
2. Chris Burford (1957-59)	107	1,262	9
3. Bill McColl (1949-51)	104	1,525	14
4. Sam Morley (1951-53)	100	1,329	13
5. Bob Moore (1967-70)	100	1,327	10
6. Randy Vataha (1969-70)	83	1,535	11

POINTS	
1. Rod Garcia (1971-73)	197
2. Skip Face (1958-60)	176
3. Steve Horowitz (1968-70)	148

PATs	
1. Steve Horowitz (1968-70)	86 (97 attempts)
2. Gary Kerkorian (1949-51)	83 (96 attempts)
3. Rod Garcia (1971-73)	71 (80 attempts)

FIELD GOALS	
1. Rod Garcia (1971-73)	42 (80 attempts)
2. Steve Horowitz (1968-70)	21 (48 attempts)

*(Note: Jim Plunkett is the all-time NCAA leader for total offense career yards.)

SEASON

TOTAL POINTS SCORED: 100, Skip Face, 1959

TOUCHDOWNS: 11, Skip Face, 1959

EXTRA POINTS: 41 (for 43), Steve Horowitz, 1969

FIELD GOALS: 18 (for 29), Rod Garcia, 1973

NET YARDS RUSHING: 936, Ray Handley, 1964

NET YARDS PASSING: 2,673, Jim Plunkett, 1969 (10 games)
2,715, Jim Plunkett, 1970 (11 games)

TOTAL OFFENSE: 2,786, Jim Plunkett, 1969 (10 games)
2,898, Jim Plunkett, 1970 (11 games)

TIMES CARRIED BALL: 197, Ray Handley, 1964

PASSES ATTEMPTED: 336, Jim Plunkett, 1969 (10 games)
358, Jim Plunkett, 1970 (11 games)

PASSES COMPLETED: 197, Jim Plunkett, 1969 (10 games)

TOUCHDOWN PASSES: 20, Jim Plunkett, 1969 (10 games)

PASSES CAUGHT: 71, Gene Washington, 1968

NET YARDS RECEIVING: 1,117, Gene Washington, 1968

TOUCHDOWN PASSES CAUGHT: 9, Eric Cross, 1972 (11 games)
8, Gene Washington, 1968 (10 games)

SINGLE GAME

MOST YARDS TOTAL OFFENSE: 416, Jim Plunkett vs. Purdue, at Lafayette, 1969

MOST YARDS RUSHING: 209, Lou Valli, vs. California at Berkeley, 1956

MOST YARDS PASSING: Dick Norman holds all Stanford and most national single-game records with 34 for 39 (87.2%) for 401 yards vs. California at Stanford, 1959

MOST TOUCHDOWN PASSES: 5, Mike Boryla vs. Washington State at Stanford, 1973 (Jim Plunkett threw 4 TD passes on three occasions)

MOST PASSES CAUGHT: 14, Eric Cross vs. Hawaii at Honolulu, 1972; 13, Gene Washington, vs. U.C.L.A. at Los Angeles, 1968

MOST TOUCHDOWN PASSES CAUGHT: 3, Gene Washington, vs. San Jose State at Stanford, 1968

MOST FIELD GOALS: 4, tie between Rod Garcia (59, 42, 52, 25) vs. USC at Los Angeles, 1973 and Bill Shoemaker (40, 25, 52, 28) vs. Tulane at Stanford, 1966

SINGLE PLAY

LONGEST TOUCHDOWN RUN FROM SCRIMMAGE: 96 yards, Bill Rogers, vs. Oregon State at Stanford, 1952

LONGEST KICKOFF RETURN: 100 yards, Bob Bryan, vs. USF, 1950

LONGEST PUNT RETURN: 80 yards, Murray Cuddeback, vs. Olympic Club, 1923

LONGEST TOUCHDOWN PASSING PLAY: 96 yards, Jim Plunkett to Randy Vataha vs. Washington State at Spokane, 1970. (SPECIAL NOTE: Coincidentally, Plunkett also cracked the NCAA Career Total Offense mark with this same play.)

LONGEST PUNT: 75 yards (dead on 1-yard line), Dave Lewis vs. California at Berkeley, 1964

LONGEST FIELD GOAL: 59 yards, Rod Garcia vs USC at Los Angeles, 1973

STANFORD ALL AMERICAS

1924 Ernie Nevers, fullback
Jim Lawson, end

1925 Ernie Nevers, fullback

1926 Ted Shipkey, end

1928 Seraphim Post, guard
Don Robesky, guard

1929 Walt Heinecke, center

1930 Phil Moffatt, halfback

1932 Bill Corbus, guard

1933 Bill Corbus, guard

1934 Bob Grayson, fullback
Monk Moscrip, end
Bob Reynolds, tackle
Bones Hamilton, halfback

1935 Bob Grayson, fullback
Monk Moscrip, end
Bones Hamilton, halfback
Bob Reynolds, tackle

1940 Frank Albert, quarterback

1941 Frank Albert, quarterback

1942 Chuck Taylor, guard

1950 Bill McColl, end

1951 Gary Kerkorian, quarterback
Bill McColl, end

1953 Bob Garrett, quarterback
Sam Morley, end

1955 Paul Wiggin, tackle

1956 John Brodie, quarterback
Paul Wiggin, tackle

1959 Chris Burford, end

1968 Malcolm Snider, tackle

1969 Don Parish, linebacker

1970 Jim Plunkett, quarterback

1971 Jeff Siemon, linebacker

1973 Roger Stillwell, def. end
Pat Donovan, def. end
Mike Boryla, quarterback
Rod Garcia, placekicker

1974 Pat Donovan, def. end

STANFORD COACHES' RECORDS

Coach	Years	W	L	T	Points	Opps.
Miscellaneous Coaches	1891–1902	52	19	11	1029	422
James F. Lanagan	1903–1908	49	10	5	986	190
George Presley	1909–1912	30	8	1	745	149
Floyd C. Brown	1913–1916	37	4	1	1048	365
Miscellaneous Coaches	1917–1923	24	15	2	674	361
Glenn S. Warner	1924–1932	71	17	8	1974	594
C. E. Thornhill	1933–1939	35	25	7	745	499
Clark Shaughnessy	1940–1941	16	3	0	356	180
Marchmont Schwartz	1942–1950	28	28	4	1217	879
Charles A. Taylor	1951–1957	40	29	2	1428	1290
Jack C. Curtice	1958–1962	14	36	0	655	1074
John Ralston	1963–1971	55	36	3	1975	1486
Jack Christiansen	1972-1974	18	13	2	707	651
TOTALS	1891-1974	469	243	46	13549	8140

351

CAPTAINS THROUGH THE YEARS

1891—J. R. Whittmore, halfback
1892—C. L. Clemans, halfback
1893—J. F. Wilson, end
1894—P. M. Downing, tackle
1895—G. H. Cochran, fullback
1896—C. M. Fickert, guard
1897—S. W. Cotton, fullback
1898—F. S. Fisher, fullback
1899—C. G. Murphy, quarterback
1900—W. W. Burnett, tackle
1901—R. S. Fisher, halfback
1902—H. S. Lee, guard
1903—L. P. Bansbach, quarterback
1904—G. H. Clark, end
1905—A. J. Chalmers, fullback
1906—E. P. Stott, five-eighths*
1907—William Koerner, forward*
1908—D. P. Crawford, side rank*
1909—M. M. Mitchell, first five*
1910—Kenneth L. Dole, side rank*
1911—Benjamin E. Erb, halfback*
1912—Louis Cass, halfback*
1913—James H. Thoburn, breakaway*
1914—Frank J. Gard, breakaway*
1915—D. B. Carroll, center three*
1916—Joseph R. Braden, breakaway*
1917—Henry S. Pettingill, rear rank*
1918—A. P. Holt. No official
    schedule played
1918—(and spring, 1919)
    Charles W. Doe, Jr., halfback*
1919—E. R. (Reg) Caughey, tackle
1920—C. A. (Art) Wilcox, halfback
1921—John C. (Jack) Patrick, fullback
1922—Dudley S. (Dud) DeGroot, center
1923—John D. (Scotchy) Campbell,
    quarterback
1924—James W. (Jim) Lawson, end
1925—Ernest (Ernie) Nevers, fullback
1926—Frederick H. (Fred) Swan, guard
1927—J. Harold (Hal) McCreery,
    center
1928—Clifford P. (Biff) Hoffman,
    fullback
1929—Donald F. (Mush) Muller, end
1930—Ray Tandy, tackle
1931—Harry H. Hillman, quarterback
1932—Ernest W. (Ernie) Caddel
1933—Appointed each game
1934—Appointed each game
1935—Robert A. (Bones) Hamilton,
    halfback
1936—Earl M. Hoos, quarterback
1937—Grant B. Stone, end
1938—Appointed each game
1939—Stanley (Stan) Andersen, tackle
1940—Appointed each game
1941—Appointed each game
1942—Appointed each game
1943, 1944, 1945—World War II
1946—Appointed each game
1947—George Quist
1948—Appointed each game
1949—Allan F. (Al) Rau, tackle,
    and James D. Castagnoli,
    center, co-captains
1950—Russell A. (Russ) Pomeroy,
    tackle, and Gordon W. (Gordy)
    White, tackle, co-captains
1951—William F. (Bill) McColl, end;
    Gary R. Kerkorian, quarterback;
    Jesse A. Cone, guard,
    co-captains

1952—Alfred D. (Al) Kirkland, tackle;
    James A. (Jim) Vick, tackle,
    co-captains
1953—Norman V. (Norm) Manoogian,
    guard
1954—Winfred E. (Win) Wedge, tackle
1955—Robert G. (Chris) Marshall,
    tackle, and William H. (Bill)
    Tarr, fullback, co-captains
1956—John R. (John) Brodie, quarter-
    back, and Paul D. (Paul)
    Wiggin, tackle, co-captains
1957—Jon A. (Jack) Douglas, quarter-
    back, and Gary C. (Gary) Van
    Galder, end, co-captains
1958—Robert A. (Bob) Nicolet,
    quarterback; Robert L. (Bob)
    Peterson, guard; and Eric V.
    (Eric) Protiva, tackle,
    co-captains
1959—Christopher W. (Chris) Burford,
    end
1960—Richard M. (Dick) Norman,
    quarterback; and Dean S.
    (Dean) Hinshaw, tackle,
    co-captains
1961—John R. (John) Butler, center;
    and Christopher C. (Chris)
    Cottle, center, co-captains
1962—Edward A. (Ed) Cummings,
    fullback; and Gary A. (Gary)
    Sargent, halfback, co-captains
1963—Marvin K. (Marv) Harris,
    center; and Clark E. (Clark)
    Weaver, quarterback,
    co-captains
1964—Richard A. (Dick) Ragsdale,
    halfback; and Guy (Rounsie)
    Rounsaville, end, co-captains
1965—Robert R. (Ray) Handley, half-
    back; and Gary L. (Gary)
    Pettigrew, tackle; Glenn Myers,
    linebacker, tri-captains
1966—Allan M. (Monty) Mohrman,
    tackle; and Albert T. (Al)
    Wilburn, end, co-captains.
1967—John M. (Marty) Brill, line-
    backer; John P. (Jack) Root,
    fullback; Donald E. (Don)
    Swartz, center, co-captains
1968—Malcolm P. (Mal) Snider,
    tackle; Stuart L. (Stu) Kellner,
    end, co-captains
1969—Don E. (Don) Parish, linebacker;
    Patrick P. (Pat) Preston, line-
    backer, co-captains
1970—Jim Plunkett, quarterback;
    Jack Schultz, strong safety,
    co-captains
1971—Don Bunce, quarterback;
    Jackie Brown, running back;
    Jeff Siemon, linebacker,
    tri-captains
1972—Younger Klippert, offensive
    guard; Charles McCloud, defen-
    sive back, co-captains
1973—Appointed each game
1974—Appointed each game

*Rugby

352

STANFORD GAME BY GAME RECORD

1892 (Spring)

10	Hopkins Academy	6
22	Berkeley Gym	0
6	Olympic Club	10
14	California	10

1892 (Fall)

14	Oakland H. S.	0
20	Olympic Club	5
14	Olympic Club	14
10	California	10

1893

46	Olympic Club	0
34	Reliance Club	0
24	Olympic Club	11
6	California	6
18	Reliance Club	0
48	Tacoma	0
50	Port Townsend	0
40	Seattle	0
18	Multnomah A.C.	0

1894

4	Reliance A.C.	18
14	Santa Cruz	4
6	Reliance A.C.	12
6	Sacramento A.C.	0
20	Reliance A.C.	0
6	California	0
4	Chicago	24
12	Chicago	0
28	Los Angeles A.C.	0

1895

4	Olympic Club	0
8	Reliance A.C.	0
10	Olympic Club	2
6	Olympic Club	0
6	California	6

1896

0	Olympic Club	0
10	Reliance A.C.	0
0	Olympic Club	4
20	California	0

1897

6	Reliance A.C.	4
8	Reliance A.C.	6
12	Reliance A.C.	6
0	Reliance A.C.	10
28	California	0

1898

22	Wash. Vol.	0
10	Kansas Vol.	0
22	Olympic Club	0
15	Kansas Vol.	11
0	Iowa Vol.	6
18	League of the Cross	5
6	Olympic Club	6
0	Olympic Club	12
0	California	22

1899

0	Olympic Club	0
0	Olympic Club	0
5	Olympic Club	6
5	Olympic Club	16
17	Nevada	5
0	Olympic Club	10
0	California	30
6	Multnomah A.C.	11
28	All-Seattle	0

1900

6	Reliance A.C.	0
35	San Jose Normal	0
6	Reliance A.C.	0
24	San Jose Normal	0
0	Alumni	14
44	Reliance A.C.	0
34	Oregon	0
0	Nevada	6
5	California	0
0	Multnomah Club	0

1901

6	Olympic Club	0
0	Reliance A.C.	0
6	Olympic Club	6
10	Reliance A.C.	0
12	Nevada	0
0	California	2
0	Michigan	49

1902

12	Reliance A.C.	0
18	Alumni	0
12	Reliance A.C.	0
11	Nevada	5
23	Reliance A.C.	5
0	California	16
35	Utah	11

1903

0	Reliance A.C.	0
17	Pensacola	0
6	Reliance A. C.	0
34	Pensacola	0
57	Fort Baker	0
0	Nevada	0
33	Chemawa Ind.	0
17	Reliance A.C.	0
11	Multnomah A.C.	0
6	California	6
18	Sherman Indians	0

1904

0	Olympic Club	5
34	Pensacola	0
12	Olympic Club	0
0	Sherman Indians	5
0	Multnomah A.C.	0
17	Nevada	0
35	Oregon	0
57	Utah Aggies	0
18	California	0
33	Colorado	0

353

1905

10	St. Vincent's	0
12	Willamette	0
51	15th Infantry	0
10	Oregon	4
21	Nevada	0
6	Sherman Indians	4
16	Southern California	0
12	California	5

*1906

11	Nevada	0
26	Pomona	0
5	Vancouver	3
16	Vancouver	6
6	California	3
9	Vancouver	11
0	Vancouver	3
3	Vancouver	3
11	Victoria	0

*1907

10	Barbarians	6
15	Castaways	11
16	Barbarians	13
31	Nevada	0
6	Barbarians	13
23	Vancouver	12
5	Vancouver	3
21	California	11
0	Vancouver	3
3	Vancouver	0
5	Vancouver	9
3	Victoria	12

*1908

22	Barbarians	0
28	Olympic Club	0
24	Barbarians	0
12	Olympic Club	3
28	Barbarians	3
14	Nevada	0
26	Nevada	0
3	Vancouver	11
11	Vancouver	3
12	California	3
9	Vancouver	0
10	Vancouver	3
16	Vancouver	0
3	Wallabies	13

*1909

16	Barbarians	0
3	Olympics	0
11	Barbarians	0
15	Olympics	0
41	Castaways	0
59	Reliance	0
56	Vancouver	0
19	Vancouver	3
13	California	19

*1910

14	Olympics	0
21	Barbarians	0
19	Olympics	0
34	Barbarians	0
8	Nevada	0
60	Barbarians	0
27	Olympics	0
6	California	25

*1911

23	Barbarians	3
19	Olympics	0
31	Barbarians	3
16	Olympics	0
41	Nevada	0

*Rugby

6	Southern Calif.	3
39	Olympics	3
27	British Columbia	3
5	British Columbia	6
3	California	21
6	Vancouver	13
10	Vancouver	5
9	Vancouver	0

*1912

12	Barbarians	0
17	Olympics	0
0	Australians	6
13	Australians	12
14	Southern California	0
10	Santa Clara	15
0	Barbarians	6
19	Olympics	0
3	California	3

*1913

3	Olympics	5
8	Barbarians	3
13	U. C. Club	3
18	Barbarians	0
29	Olympics	3
0	All Blacks	54
0	All Blacks	56
21	Barbarians	5
19	Olympics	12
13	California	8
10	Southern Calif.	0

*1914

17	Olympic Club	0
19	Barbarians	4
61	Alumni	8
31	Barbarians	3
19	Olympic Club	5
35	Titans	6
13	Santa Clara	0
31	Alumni	3
36	Olympic Club	6
26	California	8

*1915

0	Olympic Club	0
31	Barbarians	6
18	Titan Club	0
48	Olympic Club	13
80	Barbarians	0
49	Olympic Club	8
28	Palo Alto A.C.	3
36	Palo Alto A.C.	18
21	S. C. All Stars	5
29	Olympic Club	11
30	Santa Clara	0

*1916

9	Olympic Club	8
43	Barbarians	0
38	Olympic Club	16
13	Palo Alto A.C.	8
39	Olympic Club	16
19	Palo Alto A.C.	8
35	Presley Stars	6
26	Palo Alto A.C.	9
29	Olympic Club	0
5	Santa Clara	38

*1917

15	Santa Clara	11

1918

No Official schedule.

354

1919

59	USS Boston	0
0	Olympic Club	13
14	Oregon State	6
34	St. Mary's	0
13	Santa Clara	0
10	California	14
0	Southern Calif.	13

1920

41	St. Mary's	0
7	Olympic Club	10
0	Southern Calif.	10
21	Santa Clara	7
10	Oregon	0
3	Washington	0
0	California	38

1921

41	U. S. Marines	0
10	St. Mary's	7
7	Olympic Club	0
7	Pacific Fleet	27
14	Oregon State	7
0	Washington	0
14	Nevada	14
7	California	42

1922

9	Olympic Club	27
7	Santa Clara	0
9	St. Mary's	0
6	Oregon State	0
17	Nevada	7
0	Southern Calif.	6
8	Washington	12
0	California	28
7	Pittsburgh	16

1923

82	Mare Island	0
27	Nevada	0
55	Santa Clara	6
42	Occidental	0
7	Southern Calif.	14
40	Olympic Club	7
14	Oregon	3
17	Idaho	7
0	California	9

1924

20	Occidental	6
7	Olympic Club	0
28	Oregon	13
3	Idaho	0
20	Santa Clara	0
30	Utah	0
41	Montana	3
20	California	20
10	Notre Dame (Rose Bowl)	27

1925

0	Olympic Club	9
20	Santa Clara	3
28	Occidental	0
13	Southern California	9
26	Oregon State	10
35	Oregon	13
0	Washington	13
82	U.C.L.A.	0
27	California	14

1926

44	Fresno State	7
13	Calif. Tech.	6
19	Occidental	0
7	Olympic Club	3
33	Nevada	9
29	Oregon	12
13	Southern California	12
33	Santa Clara	14
29	Washington	10
41	California	6
7	Alabama (Rose Bowl)	7

1927

33	Fresno State	0
7	Olympic Club	6
0	St. Mary's	16
20	Nevada	2
13	Southern California	13
20	Oregon State	6
19	Oregon	0
13	Washington	7
6	Santa Clara	13
13	California	6
7	Pittsburgh (Rose Bowl)	6

1928

0	Y.M.I.	7
21	West Coast Army	8
6	Olympic Club	12
26	Oregon	12
45	U.C.L.A.	7
47	Idaho	0
47	Fresno State	0
0	Southern California	10
31	Santa Clara	0
12	Washington	0
13	California	13
26	Army	0

1929

45	West Coast Army	0
6	Olympic Club	0
33	Oregon	7
57	U.C.L.A.	0
40	Oregon State	7
0	Southern California	7
39	Calif. Tech.	0
6	Washington	0
7	Santa Clara	13
21	California	6
34	Army	13

1930

32	West Coast Army	0
18	Olympic Club	0
20	Santa Clara	0
0	Minnesota	0
13	Oregon State	7
12	Southern California	41
20	U.C.L.A.	0
25	Washington	7
57	Calif. Tech.	7
41	California	0
14	Dartmouth	7

1931

46	West Coast Army	0
0	Olympic Club	0
6	Santa Clara	0
13	Minnesota	0
25	Oregon State	7
0	Washington	0
12	U.C.L.A.	6
0	Southern California	19
26	Nevada	0
0	California	6
32	Dartmouth	6

1932

6	Olympic Club	0
20	San Francisco	7
27	Oregon State	0
14	Santa Clara	0
26	West Coast Army	0
0	Southern California	13
6	U.C.L.A.	13
13	Washington	18
59	Calif. Aggies	0
0	California	0
0	Pittsburgh	7

1933

27	San Jose State	0
3	U.C.L.A.	0
7	Santa Clara	0
0	Northwestern	0
20	San Francisco	13
0	Washington	6
21	Olympic Club	0
13	Southern California	7
33	Montana	7
7	California	3
0	Columbia (Rose Bowl)	7

1934

48	San Jose State	0
7	Santa Clara	7
17	Oregon State	0
20	Northwestern	0
3	San Francisco	0
16	Southern California	0
27	U.C.L.A.	0
24	Washington	0
40	Olympic Club	0
9	California	7
13	Alabama (Rose Bowl)	29

1935

35	San Jose State	0
10	San Francisco	0
6	U.C.L.A.	7
6	Washington	0
9	Santa Clara	6
3	Southern California	0
32	Montana	0
13	California	0
7	Southern Methodist (Rose Bowl)	0

1936

0	Santa Clara	13
13	Washington State	14
7	Oregon	7
7	Southern California	14
19	U.C.L.A.	6
14	Washington	14
20	Oregon State	14
0	California	20
0	Columbia	7

1937

7	Santa Clara	13
6	Oregon	7
12	U.C.L.A.	7
13	Washington	7
0	Oregon State	0
7	Southern California	6
23	Washington State	0
0	California	13
0	Columbia	0

1938

0	Santa Clara	22
8	Washington State	0
27	Oregon	16
2	Southern California	13
0	U.C.L.A.	6
7	Washington	10
0	Oregon State	6
0	California	6
23	Dartmouth	13

1939

0	Oregon State	12
0	Oregon	10
14	U.C.L.A.	14
5	Washington	8
7	Santa Clara	27
0	Southern California	33
0	Washington State	7
14	California	32
14	Dartmouth	3

1940

27	San Francisco	0
13	Oregon	0
7	Santa Clara	6
26	Washington State	14

21	Southern California	7
20	U.C.L.A.	14
20	Washington	10
28	Oregon State	14
13	California	7
21	Nebraska (Rose Bowl)	13

1941

19	Oregon	15
33	U.C.L.A.	0
0	Oregon State	10
42	San Francisco	26
13	Washington	7
27	Santa Clara	7
13	Southern California	0
13	Washington State	14
0	California	16

1942

0	Washington State	6
6	Santa Clara	14
0	Notre Dame	27
54	Idaho	7
14	Southern California	6
7	U.C.L.A.	21
20	Washington	7
49	Oregon State	13
26	California	7
28	St. Mary's Pre-Flight	13

1943-45

No football—World War II

1946

45	Idaho	0
33	San Francisco	7
6	U.C.L.A.	26
33	Santa Clara	27
20	Southern California	28
0	Oregon State	0
15	Washington	21
27	Washington State	26
25	California	6
18	Hawaii	7

1947

16	Idaho	19
13	Michigan	49
7	Santa Clara	13
6	U.C.L.A.	39
0	Washington	25
7	Oregon State	13
0	Southern California	14
6	Oregon	21
18	California	21

1948

26	San Jose State	20
12	Oregon	20
7	Washington State	14
14	Santa Clara	27
34	U.C.L.A.	14
6	Southern California	7
20	Washington	0
0	Army	43
39	Montana	7
6	California	7

1949

49	San Jose State	0
44	Harvard	0
7	Michigan	27
7	U.C.L.A.	14
40	Washington	0
27	Oregon State	7
7	Santa Clara	7
34	Southern California	13
63	Idaho	0
14	California	33
74	Hawaii	20

1950

33	San Jose State	16
55	San Francisco	7
21	Oregon State	0
23	Santa Clara	13
7	U.C.L.A.	21

356

7	Washington	21
7	Southern California	7
28	Washington State	18
0	Army	7
7	California	7

1951

27	Oregon	20
26	San Jose State	13
23	Michigan	13
21	U.C.L.A.	7
21	Santa Clara	14
14	Washington	7
21	Washington State	13
27	Southern California	20
35	Oregon State	14
7	California	20
7	Illinois (Rose Bowl)	40

1952

28	Santa Clara	13
14	Washington State	13
14	Michigan	7
41	Oregon State	28
14	U.C.L.A.	24
14	Washington	27
35	San Jose State	13
7	Southern California	54
20	Oregon	21
0	California	26

1953

20	College of Pacific	25
7	Oregon	0
21	Illinois	33
21	Oregon State	0
21	U.C.L.A.	20
13	Washington	7
48	Washington State	19
20	Southern California	23
54	San Jose State	0
21	California	21

1954

13	College of Pacific	12
18	Oregon	13
12	Illinois	2
0	Navy	25
0	U.C.L.A.	72
13	Washington	7
26	Washington State	30
7	Southern California	21
14	San Jose State	19
20	California	28

1955

33	College of Pacific	14
0	Oregon State	10
6	Ohio State	0
14	Michigan State	38
13	U.C.L.A.	21
7	Washington	7
34	San Jose State	18
28	Southern California	20
44	Oregon	7
19	California	0

1956

40	Washington State	26
7	Michigan State	21
20	Ohio State	32
40	San Jose State	20
21	Oregon	7
27	Southern California	19
13	U.C.L.A.	14
19	Oregon State	20
13	Washington	34
18	California	20

1957

46	San Jose State	7
26	Northwestern	6
7	Rice	34
18	Washington State	21
21	Washington	14
20	U.C.L.A.	6
26	Oregon	27
35	Southern California	7
14	Oregon State	24
14	California	12

1958

6	Washington State	40
7	Rice	30
0	Northwestern	28
22	Washington	12
0	Air Force	16
21	U.C.L.A.	19
6	Southern California	29
0	Oregon	12
16	Oregon State	24
15	California	16

1959

27	Oregon	28
14	Wisconsin	16
21	College of Pacific	6
0	Washington	10
19	Washington State	36
28	Southern California	30
54	San Jose State	38
13	U.C.L.A.	55
39	Oregon State	22
17	California	20

1960

14	Washington State	15
7	Wisconsin	24
9	Air Force	32
10	Washington	29
20	San Jose State	34
8	U.C.L.A.	26
6	Southern California	21
6	Oregon	27
21	Oregon State	25
10	California	21

1961

9	Tulane	7
34	Oregon State	0
3	Michigan State	31
17	San Jose State	6
0	Washington	13
0	U.C.L.A.	20
7	Oregon	19
15	Southern California	30
0	Washington State	30
20	California	7

1962

6	Tulane	3
16	Michigan State	13
0	Oregon State	27
6	Washington State	21
0	Washington	14
17	U.C.L.A.	7
14	Oregon	28
14	Southern California	39
21	San Jose State	9
30	California	13

1963

29	San Jose State	13
7	Oregon	36
9	U.C.L.A.	10
13	Rice	23
11	Washington	19
24	Notre Dame	14
7	Oregon State	10
11	Southern California	25
15	Washington State	32
28	California	17

1964

23	Washington State	29
10	San Jose State	8
20	U.C.L.A.	27
34	Rice	7
0	Washington	6
6	Notre Dame	28
10	Oregon	8
10	Southern California	15

357

16	Oregon State	7
21	California	3

1965

26	San Jose State	6
7	Navy	7
17	Air Force	16
17	Oregon	14
0	Southern California	14
31	Army	14
8	Washington	41
16	Tulane	0
13	U.C.L.A.	30
9	California	7

1966

25	San Jose State	21
21	Minnesota	35
33	Tulane	14
3	Oregon	7
7	Southern California	21
6	Illinois	3
20	Washington	22
21	Air Force	6
0	U.C.L.A.	10
13	California	7

1967

7	Oregon State	13
21	Kansas	20
28	San Jose State	14
0	Southern California	30
31	Washington State	10
16	U.C.L.A.	21
20	Army	24
14	Washington	7
17	Oregon	14
3	California	26

1968

68	San Jose State	20
28	Oregon	12
24	Air Force	13
24	Southern California	27
21	Washington State	21
17	U.C.L.A.	20
7	Oregon State	29
35	Washington	20
24	Univ. of Pacific	0
20	California	0

1969

63	San Jose State	21
28	Oregon	0
35	Purdue	36
24	Southern California	26
49	Washington State	0
20	U.C.L.A.	20
33	Oregon State	0
21	Washington	7
47	Air Force	34
29	California	28

1970

34	Arkansas	28
34	San Jose State	3
33	Oregon	10
14	Purdue	26
24	Southern California	14
63	Washington State	16
9	U.C.L.A.	7
48	Oregon State	10
29	Washington	22
14	Air Force	31
14	California	22
27	Ohio State (Rose Bowl)	17

1971

19	Missouri	0
38	Army	3
38	Oregon	17
3	Duke	9
17	Washington	6
33	Southern California	18
23	Washington State	24
31	Oregon State	24
20	U.C.L.A.	9
12	San Jose State	13
14	California	0
13	Michigan (Rose Bowl)	12

1972

44	San Jose State	0
10	Duke	6
41	West Virginia	35
21	Southern California	30
24	Washington	0
13	Oregon	15
17	Oregon State	11
23	U.C.L.A.	28
13	Washington State	27
21	California	24
39	Hawaii	7

1973

6	Penn State	20
10	Michigan	47
23	San Jose State	12
24	Illinois	0
13	UCLA	59
23	Washington	14
45	Washington State	14
24	Oregon State	23
26	USC	27
24	Oregon	7
26	California	17

1974

20	Penn State	24
7	Illinois	41
21	San Jose State	21
16	Michigan	27
13	UCLA	13
34	Washington	17
20	Washington State	18
17	Oregon State	13
10	Southern Cal.	34
17	Oregon	0
22	California	20

358

STANFORD LETTERMEN

"A"

Abena, Tim D. 1966, '67, '68
Abraham, Richard P. 1945, '50, '51
Adams, C. C. 1892
Adams, Doug 1971, '72
Adams, Frederic L. 1917, '19, '20
Adams, P. A. 1897
Adams, Woodrow G. 1933, '34, '35
Afflerbaugh, Jack K. 1931, '32, '33
Albert, Frank 1939, '40, '41
Albertson, Kendall 1928, '30, '31
Albertson, Marcellus O. 1929, '30, '32
Alexander, William F. 1969, '70
Allen, Harold K. 1931, '32, '33
Alustiza, Alfonso 1937
Alustiza, Frank 1933, '34, '35
Alustiza, John 1969
Alvarado, Donald R. 1971, '72
Anderson, Gary A. 1973, '74
Anderson, E. Martin, Jr. 1946, '47, '48
Anderson, Ray E. 1973, '74
Anderson, Robert W. 1946, '47
Anderson, Stanley 1937, '38, '39
Anderson, Stanley 1932, '34
Anderson, Todd M. 1973, '74
Andrews, Robert W. 1942
Andrews, Robert B., Jr. 1948, '49
Angove, Jerry C. 1955, '56
Arch, Dennis J. 1966
Armitage, Matthew 1952, '53, '54
Armour, Merrill A. 1925
Armstrong, Eric B. 1940, '41
Arnett, Richard W. 1920
Arrell, James L. 1910 (rugby)
Artman, Corwin W. 1928, '29
Askea, Michael V. 1971, '72
Atkinson, Franklin R. 1961, '62
Atkinson, Herbert D. 1954
Atkinson, Lacy 1974
August, Peter 1942, '46, '47
Austin, Charles A. 1913, '14 (rugby)

"B"

Babajian, Kenneth A. 1961, '62, '63
Backer, Phillip T. 1954
Baker, George H. 1922, '23, '24
Baker, Phil L. 1930, '31
Banducci, Bruno 1940, '41, '42
Bansbach, Louis P. 1900, '02, '03, '04
Barbee, Troy W., Jr. 1956, '57, '58
Bardin, William J. 1929, '30
Barnes, John D. 1947, '48, '49
Barnes, Benny J. 1970, '71
Barnes, Michael E. 1961
Barneson, Harold J. 1917 (rugby)
Barnhisel, Arthur H. 1892
Barnhisel, Walter B. 1901, '02
Bartell, Max J. 1902
Bates, William F. 1931, '32, '33
Baumgaertner, Joe P. 1974
Baumgartner, Edward C. 1910 (rugby)
Beale, Gregory A. 1968
Beatie, Jerome C. 1955, '56
Beck, Braden W. 1963, '64
Beedle, Dale D. 1935
Bell, J. Ainslie 1946, '47
Benjamin, Guy E. 1974
Benson, Boyd H. 1948, '49, '50
Berg, Richard L. 1963, '64
Bergthold, Rudy G. 1973, '74
Bernhard, Harvey H. 1942, '46
Berry, Robert M. 1972
Berryman, Robert P. 1946
Bessey, John D. 1959, '60
Betts, Forrest A. 1917, '19, '21
Bickel, John H. 1951
Bickenbach, Lee P. 1941
Bigelow, Windsor D. 1931
Bigloe, David C. 1898
Bihlman, George H. 1919
    (rugby 1914, '16, '17)
Bittner, Robert B. 1966, '67, '68
Black, Robert H. 1934, '35
Blackstone, Bruce G. 1972, '73
Blanchard, John G. 1972, '73, '74
Blanchard, Marcus 1898
Blase, Roland R. 1913, '14 (rugby)
Blunt, Robert L. 1964, '65, '66
Boensch, Fred M. 1942, '46
Bogue, George R. 1924, '25, '26
Bogue, Harris D. 1929, '30
Bond, John E. 1957, '58, '59
Bonetti, John E. 1950, '51
Bonney, Fred L. 1919

Borda, Richard J. 1952
Boren, Frank H. 1899
Boruck, Holbrook M. 1949
Boryla, Michael J. 1971, '72, '73
Boughton, Robert S. 1972
Boulware, George L. 1919
Bowers, Richard L. 1958, '59
Braden, Joseph R. 1914, '15, '16 (rugby)
Bragonier, Dennis S. 1971, '72
Braheny, J. William 1938, '39
Brandin, Alf E. 1934, '35
Brazel, Charles W. 1952
Breen, Paul 1972, '73
Brenner, John M. 1938
Briggs, Stewart D. 1892
Brigham, Samuel T. J. 1936, '37
Brill, John M. 1965, '66, '67
Broderick, John R. 1950, '51, '52
Brodie, John R. 1954, '55, '56
Bronstein, Howard S. 1933
Brooks, Irving L. 1921
Broome, Richard D. 1949, '50
Broughton, Gregory J. 1966, '67, '68
Brown, David E. 1942, '46
Brown, Delos E. 1964, '65
Brown, Floyd C. 1907, '09, '10, '11 (rugby)
Brown, Isaiah 1968, '69
Brown, Jackie R. 1969, '70, '71
Brown, Mark W. 1969
Brown, Robert L. 1969
Brownson, Lynn J. 1946
Brubaker, E. William 1942
Bryan, Robert E. 1950
Budge, Hamilton W. 1947, '48
Buehler, Charles E. 1960, '61, '62
Buehler, George S. 1966, '67, '68
Bunce, Donald R. 1968, '69, '71
Burford, Christopher W. 1957, '58, '59
Burget, Bill G. 1956
Burke, Edward W., Jr. 1946, '47
Burke, Thomas R. 1961, '63
Burke, William 1929
Burkland, Phil V. 1957, '59
Burnett, Brady F. 1893
Burnett, William W. 1897, '99, '00
Burns, William S. 1914 (rugby)
Bush, Clarence E. 1930
Bush, Ronald J. 1952, '53, '54
Butler, Charles W. 1961
Butler, John R. 1959, '60, '61
Butler, Lawrence A. 1970, '71

Butt, Dale I. 1919
Butterfield, Hayden G. 1904
Byrer, James W. 1957, '58

"C"

Caddel, Ernest W., Jr. 1930, '31, '32
Cadwalder, Theodore R. 1907, '08 (rugby)
Caffall, Mark 1942
Caglieri, Guido G. 1929, '30
Cairns, Walter S. 1899
Calfee, Tsar N., Jr. 1950, '51
Callaway, Claude P. 1933, '34, '35
Calvelli, Anthony 1936, '37, '38
Camera, Paul C. 1955, '56
Campbell, Don L. 1947, '48
Campbell, Floyd P. 1919
Campbell, Gordon 1931, '32, '33
Campbell, Howard F. 1917, '19, '20
Campbell, John D. 1921, '22, '23
Campbell, William E. 1895
Cardinalli, Ray A. 1974
Carle, Nathaniel A. 1895, '96, '97
Carlson, Harry J., Jr. 1935
Carrigan, Andrew J. 1966, '67
Carroll, Daniel B. 1912, '13, '14, '15, '16 (rugby)
Carswell, Donn A. 1954, '55, '56
Carter, Harley R. 1921
Casey, John R. 1940
Cass, Bruce C. 1968
Cass, Louis 1909, '11, '12 (rugby)
Castagnoli, James D. 1948, '49
Castellucci, Davis L. 1951
Caughey, Edgar R. 1919
Chalmers, Alexander J. 1903, '04, '05, '06
Chandler, Lore R. 1917 (rugby)
Chapple, John L. 1962, '63
Cheda, Gilbert E. 1906, '08, '09, '10 (rugby)
Childs, Robert D. 1947
Church, Gerald B. 1973, '74
Clark, George H. 1901, '02, '03, '04
Clark, John B. 1956, '57
Clark, John E. 1934, '36, '38
Clark, John V. 1947
Clark, Philip L. 1919
Clark, William N. 1929, '30
Clay, Roger A. 1965
Cleaveland, Norman 1922, '23, '24

Clemans, Carl L. 1892
Clinton, Edgar M. 1898
Clover, Philip P. 1913, '14 (rugby)
Cochran, Guy H. 1892, '93, '94, '95
Code, Thomas K. 1892 '93, '95
Coffis, James T. 1935, '36, '37
Coker, Charles M. 1947
Colberg, Kent S. 1962, '63
Coldiron, Gene D. 1937, '38, '39
Cole, Alfred W. 1940, '41
Coleman, Richard R. 1916 (rugby)
Colvin, Donald L. 1930, '31, '32
Cone, Jesse A. 1949, '50, '51
Conaway, Carlton D. 1963
Conklin, Roch M. 1956, '58
Connelly, Michael O. 1964, '65
Conrad, Robert L. 1965, '66
Cook, Alex J. 1927, '28, '29
Cook, Archibald B. 1906, '07, '08, '09
  (rugby)
Cook, Hart N. III 1948, '49, '51
Cook, Ronald M. 1951, '52, '53
Cooper, Kenneth F. 1900, '01
Corbus, William 1931, '32, '33
Corbus, William 1971, '72
Cordes, Charles 1971, '72
Cordova, Mike P. 1974
Cottle, Christopher C. 1959, '60, '61
Cotton, S. W. 1894, '95, '96, '97
Cowan, Roger D. 1970, '71, '72
Cox, James E. 1942, '46
Crahan, Jack L. 1947
Craig, Gary H. 1960, '61, '62
Crane, Robert L. 1939, '40, '41
Cravens, Robert I. 1920, '22, '23
Crawford, David P. 1905, '07, '08, '09
Crepeau, Richard A., Jr. 1954
Crist, Frank L., Jr. 1950, '51, '52
Crooks, George A. 1967, '68, '69
Cross, Eric C. 1970, '71, '72
Cross, James K. 1967, '69
Cuddeback, Murray W. 1922, '23, '24
Culin, W. Edward C. 1948
Cummings, Edward A. 1960, '61, '62
Cummings, Irving, Jr. 1937
Curr, Allan M. 1962
Curtice, Aubrey A. 1919

"D"

Daka, Robert E. 1937, '38
Daly, John S. 1897

Dana, I. Ross 1942
Darsie, William P. 1912, '13 (rugby)
Davidson, E. E. 1913 (rugby)
Davidson, Horace H. 1927, '28
Davidson, Harry D. 1947
Davidson, Donald D. 1958
Dawson, Raymond E. 1929, '30, '31
Deems, Howard E. 1920
DeForest, Joseph G. 1899, '00
DeGroot, Dudley S. 1920, '21, '22
De la Forest, John M. 1966, '67, '68
DeLellis, Anthony R. 1961, '62, '63
Dennis, Guy H. 1922, '23
Derby, Richard 1965, '66
DeSylvia, Terry 1964, '65
DeSwarte, David 1946
Devine, Aubrey A., Jr. 1946, '47, '48
DeWeese, Armand J. 1955, '56, '57
deWitt, Wallace W. 1938
De Young, E. William 1948, '49
Dick, Douglas W. 1956, '58
Ditlevsen, Robert F. 1940
Doctor, Stephen D. 1954, '55, '56
Doe, Charles W. 1919
Dole, Alfred R. 1902
Dole, Charles S. 1895, '98
Dole, George E. 1905
Dole, Kenneth L. 1908, '09, '10, '11
  (rugby)
Dole, Norman D. 1922, '23
Dole, Wilfred H. 1902, '03, '04
Donahue, Neil A. 1937, '38, '39
Donohue, William F. 1959
Donovan, Pat E. 1972, '73, '74
Dorn, Ernest F. III 1953, '54, '55
Doster, Guy L. 1952, '53
Doub, William K. 1930, '31, '32
Doughty, R. M. 1921, '22
Douglas, Jon A. 1955, '56, '57
Douglas, Joe G. 1921
Dowd, Bernard G., Jr. 1958, '59, '60
Downing, Claud S. 1892, '93
Downing, Paul M. 1892, '93, '94
Driscoll, Thomas A. 1928, '29
Drown, Jack A. 1933, '34
Dubofsky, Frank N. 1961, '62
Durket, Michael 1947
Dwight, Herbert M. 1923

"E"

Eadie, Ronald E. 1950, '51, '52

361

Eagle, Walter E. 1955
Edwards, LeRoy M. 1906
Ehrhorn, Charles S. 1930, '31
Eldredge, David P. 1952
Eller, Jack R. 1946
Elliott, Richard C. 1955
Enberg, Donald M. 1948, '49, '50
Erb, Arthur L. 1913, '14, '15 (rugby)
Erb, Benjamin E. 1908, '10, '11, '12 (rugby)
Erb, William M. 1899, '00
Erickson, Wayne C. 1946, '47
Essegian, Charles A., Jr. 1950, '51, '52
Evans, Charles B. 1908 (rugby)
Ewing, Terry M. 1968, '69, '70

"F"

Face, William H., Jr. 1958, '59, '60
Fair, Lee P. 1971, '72
Falk, Oliver S. 1917 (rugby)
Faulkner, George C. 1908 (rugby)
Faville, Richard W. 1921, '22, '23
Fawcett, Randall 1941, '42
Fay, Peter 1937, '38
Feldman, Martin 1946, '47
Fenton, K. L. 1906, '07 (rugby)
Ferguson, James J. 1971, '72, '73
Ferko, Leo M. 1936, '37
Fernandes, Ronald A. 1958, '59, '60
Ferris, Harold H. 1947
Fickert, Charles 1894, '95, '96, '97, '98
Field, Julian D. 1947, '48, '49
Fisher, Forrest S. 1896, '97, '98
Fisher, Ralph S. 1899, '00
Fitting, John W. 1909 (rugby)
Fitzmorris, Tyce M. 1961
Fix, Donald R. 1947, '48, '49
Flanagan, Thomas F. 1964, '65
Flatland, Richmond, Jr. 1946, '47
Fleishhacker, Herbert, Jr. 1927, '28, '29
Flood, Randolph G. 1918, '19
Flood, Raymond O. 1924
Flowers, Monteville D., Jr. 1919
Forbes, Frank A., Jr. 1946
Francis, Dan R. 1973, '74
Francis, Jack P. 1940, '41
Frank, Alvin H. 1910, '11 (rugby)
Frankenheimer, Julius J., Jr. 1892, '93, '94, '95
Freeman, Charles G. 1968
Freeman, Christopher 1925, '26, '27

Freeman, Lewis R. 1898
Freis, Joel H. 1956, '57, '58
Frentrup, Ralph L. 1927, '28, '29
Frisbee, Robert D. 1942
Frizell, Porter T. 1905
Fujikawa, Ronald K. 1969
Furlanic, Richard A. 1954, '55

"G"

Gaedtke, Richard J. 1949, '50
Gallarneau, Hugh 1938, '39, '40
Ganong, Carl F. 1907, '08 (rugby)
Gant, Richard A. 1952, '53
Gant, Vernon F. 1968
Garber, Sidney J. 1957, '58, '59
Garcia, Rodrigo F. 1971, '72, '73
Gard, F. J. 1911, '12, '13, '14 (rugby)
Garner, Rodney G. 1950, '51
Garnier, Edward P. 1936, '37
Garrett, Robert D. 1951, '52, '53
Gebert, Jack D. 1953
Geissler, E. D. 1910, '11 (rugby)
Gergen, Robert R. 1954, '55, '56
Ghilotti, Robert V. 1947, '48
Giallonardo, Thomas M. 1967
Gilman, Charles E. 1899
Goldberg, Jerome L. 1952, '53, '54
Goldstein, Max H. 1971, '72, '73
Gordon, Jack S. 1959, '60, '61
Graff, Stanley R. 1938, '39, '40
Grant, John E. 1935, '36
Graves, Jonathan 1968, '69, '70
Grayson, Robert H. 1933, '34, '35
Greer, William L. 1939
Grey, George C. 1930, '31, '32
Gribbin, Franklin P. 1931, '32, '33
Griffin, Robert R., Jr. 1949, '50, '51
Grimm, Trevor A. 1959
Grosh, M. D. 1892
Groves, James L. 1937, '39
Guillory, John L. 1964, '65, '66
Gustafson, Jerry F. 1953, '54, '55

"H"

Hachten, William A. 1946
Haley, Samuel M. 1911 (rugby)
Hall, Efton, Jr. 1970
Hall, Elwin B. 1912, '13, '14 (rugby)
Hall, Robert P. 1942, '46
Halstead, Samuel T. 1915 (rugby)

Hamilton, Glenn H. 1936, '38
Hamilton, Robert A. 1933, '34, '35
Hammett, Raymond M. 1940, '41, '42
Hancock, Ronald C. 1971, '72
Hand, Milton N. 1930, '31
Handley, Robert R. 1963, '64, '65
Hanner, Allen F. 1952
Hansel, Timothy J. 1960, '61, '62
Hanson, Peter A. 1971, '72, '73
Harder, Theodore 1926, '27, '28
Hardy, Arthur C. 1931
Harrelson, William H. 1893, '94
Harrigan, P. F. 1910, '11, '12 (rugby)
Harrington, Al Tauasu 1955, '56, '57
Harris, Leo A. 1925, '26
Harris, Marvin K. 1961, '62, '63
Hartranft, S. Glenn 1921
Hartvickson, Leon M. 1967
Hartwig, Charles M. 1962, '63
Hauser, Henry P. 1917 (rugby)
Hauverman, Cornelius D. 1901, '02, '03
Haygood, John T. 1967, '68
Hazelrigg, Thomas R. 1965, '66, '67
Hazzard, William C. 1894
Head, Gordon E. 1934
Hearney, Richard D. 1960
Heffernan, Robert E. 1966, '67, '68
Heinecke, Walter 1927, '28, '29
Heinly, Donald 1908 (rugby)
Heiser, Peter E. 1929, '30, '31
Helser, Charles W., Jr. 1920
Henry, Wilbur A. 1918
Heron, Ivar C. 1917 (rugby)
Hey, Clifford L. 1924
Hibler, Michael K. 1964, '65, '66
Higgins, John M. 1946
Hildebrand, Alfred P. 1961, '62, '63
Hill, Donald K. 1925, '26, '27
Hill, Harrison W. 1898, '00, '01
Hill, Leroy A. 1973, '74
Hillman, Harry H., Jr. 1929, '30, '31
Hillman, John N. 1931, '32, '33
Hinshaw, Dean S. 1958, '59, '60
Hinshaw, Chester J. 1960
Hoaglin, Mark E. 1974
Hoegn, Robert L. 1951, '52
Hoffman, Clifford P. 1926, '27, '28
Hogg, Charles H. 1892
Hoisch, Alan M. 1942
Hokanson, Charles R. 1949, '51
Holdridge, Jay F. 1936
Holman, John R. 1906, '07, '08, '09

(rugby)
Holt, Preston 1919
Holwerds, Jacob J. 1932, '33
Honore, George L. 1959, '61
Hoos, Earl M. 1933, '36
Horn, Richard H. 1949, '50, '51
Horton, Harry L. 1905, '09
Horowitz, Steven C. 1969, '70
Houck, George M. 1922
Howard, Robert P. 1962, '63, '64
Howe, John M. 1952, '53
Hugasian, Harry 1949, '50, '51
Hulen, Ray J. 1930, '31
Humphreys, Philip M. 1965
Hunt, Albert B. 1930
Hunt, Robert W. 1923, '24
Huss, Jon D. 1966, '68
Hyde, Clarence E. 1904
Hyland, Richard F. 1925, '26, '27

"I"

Inge, Ron E. 1973, '74
Ingham, George W. 1959
Isaacs, Carl E. 1955, '56
Ishman, Reginald E. 1971, '72, '73

"J"

Jacobs, George C. 1903
Jacob, Joseph C. 1949, '50
James, Edwin W. 1898
Janssen, Clayton R. 1922
Jeffs, A. S. 1895, '96, '97
Jena, Douglas K. 1972, '73
Jenke, James A. 1974
Jessen, Christopher F. 1961, '62
Johannessen, Edward L. H. 1939, '41
Johnston, Charles F. 1922, '23, '24
Johnston, Philip F. 1932
Jones, Lawrence C. 1970, '71
Jones, Richard V., Jr. 1954, '55
Jones, Winford M. 1939
Jubb, Stephen W. 1969, '70

"K"

Kadziel, Ronald D. 1968, '69, '70
Kaffen, James P. 1972, '73
Karakozoff, Alex L. 1973, '74
Kauffman, James H. 1968, '69, '70
Kazanjian, John C. 1927

Keblusek, Edward R. 1946
Kegley, Carl S. 1917 (rugby)
Kehl, James A. 1970, '71
Kehrli, Bruce A. 1963, '64, '65
Kellar, William W. 1974
Keller, Richard 1968, '69
Kellner, Stuart L. 1966, '67, '68
Kelly, James B. 1924
Kemper, Steve A. 1973, '74
Kennedy, Martin H. 1892, '93, '94
Kerkorian, Gary R. 1949, '50, '51
Kerman, John R. 1939, '40
Kern, Eugene F. 1911, '12 (rugby)
Kester, Edgar C. 1916 (rugby)
Keusseff, Stephen E. 1938, '39
Kieburitz, Geoffry B. 1974
Kidd, John D. 1956, '57
Killefer, Wade 1969
Kindler, Dorsey B. 1946
King, Leon 1950, '51
Kinney, Paul B. 1918
Kirkland, Alfred D. 1951, '52
Kirsch, William B. 1937, '38
Kirtman, Nathaniel 1967
Kite, Walter E. 1932
Klabau, Theodore A. 1927, '28, '29
Klein, Bud D. 1948, '49
Klippert, L. Younger 1970, '71, '72
Kloos, Michael A. 1971
Kolesnikow, Andy M. 1974
Kmetovic, Peter G. 1939, '40, '41
Knight, Courtland W. 1913, '15 (rugby)
Knight, Robert B. 1901
Koehn, John P. 1970
Koerner, William 1905, '06, '07, '08
Kraft, Warren H. 1921
Krickeberg, Roy W. 1953, '54

"L"

Laakso, Albert M. 1948, '49
Laborlle, Henri J. 1932
Lacey, Laurence A. 1958, '59
Lachmund, Otto G. 1913, '14 (rugby)
La Combe, Emile A. 1931
Laird, William H. 1930
Laidlaw, Scott R. 1972, '73, '74
Lamanuzzi, Victor 1971, '72
Lambert, Thomas B. 1930, '31
Langford, Mike J. 1974
La Prade, Loren H. 1941, '42
Larsen, Niels T. 1934, '35

Lasater, Richard W. II 1968, '69, '70
Lathan, Robert M. 1951
Laubscher, Wesley F. 1951
Laumeister, Clarence F. 1906 (rugby)
Laverty, Roger M. 1942
Lawson, James W. 1922, '23, '24
Lazetich, Peter G. 1969, '70, '71
Leahy, John G. 1959
Ledeboer, Frederick B. 1937, '38
Lee, Howard S. 1899, '00, '01, '02
Leeuwenburg, Richard P. 1962, '63
Lettinich, Edward B. 1934
Levy, David N. 1919, '20
Lewis, David R. 1964, '65, '66
Lewis, John K. 1955
Lewis, Laurence D. 1926, '27, '28
Lightfoot, Dan R. 1968, '69, '70
Liljenwall, Theodore J. 1947, '48
Lilly, John K. 1917 (rugby)
Lindskog, Stanley V. 1960, '61, '62
Lindskog, Victor, J. 1940, '41
Lodato, Jack D. 1962, '63, '64
Long, Joe E. 1955
Long, Robert W. 1954, '55, '56
Longinotti, John F. 1965
Loomis, Frederick C. 1923
Lorimer, Delmar B. 1972, '73
Lucas, Richard M. 1949, '50
Luckett, William E. 1936, '37
Ludeke, Frederick S. 1921, '22, '23
Ladeke, John M. 1954
Lynn, Tom M. 1974
Lyons, Willard E. 1905

"M"

Mac Alpine, Archibald, B. 1920
Mac Donald, John W. 1956
Madigan, Richard B. 1946
Maentz, Robert C. 1933, '34, '35
Mangan, Robert T. 1936
Mannon, William H. 1942
Manoogian, Norman V. 1950, '51, '53
Manoukian, Donald J. 1954, '55, '57
Margala, Kenneth J. 1971
Marks, William P. 1930, '31
Marquess, Mark E. 1966, '67, '68
Marriott, Joseph S. 1916 (rugby)
Marshall, Robert G. II 1954, '55
Martin, Forest S. 1972, '73, '74
Martin, Joseph C. 1972, '73
Martin, Eugene B. 1946, '47, '48

Mason, John F. 1964, '65, '66
Massey, Thomas J. 1967, '68
Mastin, Robert H. 1941
Mathias, Robert B. 1951, '52
Matthews, Robert E. 1935, '36, '37
Mayers, Frank B. 1907 (rugby)
Mayrhofer, Leonhard F. 1952
McCain, Warren E. 1940, '41
McCamant, James D. 1954
McClintock, Colin H. 1939
McClure, Timothy J. 1968, '69, '70
McCloud, Charles E. 1970, '71, '72
McColl, Duncan B. 1974
McColl, William F. 1949, '50, '51
McCormick, Charles T. 1961, '63
McCreery, John H. 1925, '26, '27
McDonough, John T. 1939
McGovern, Larry D. 1974
McElroy, William D. 1937, '38
McFadden, Ralph J. 1900, '01, '02
McFadden, Thomas L. 1899, '00
McGilvray, A. B. 1902
McKay, Charles W. 1951
McKenna, John F. 1956
McKenna, Thomas J. 1955
McKenzie, Douglas B. 1967, '68
McKettrick, Jack W. 1947, '48
McMillan, Donald C. 1936
McMillan, Frank L. 1937
McMillan, George 1893
McMillen, Roderick E., Jr. 1957, '58, '59
McMillen, Jeri L. 1955, '56, '57
Medved, Anton J. 1942
Meiners, Arnold W. J. 1939, '40, '41
Melloway, Marvin L. 1949
Merlo, James L. 1971, '72
Merlo, Richard M. 1974
Merrill, James A. 1970
Merriman, Lloyd A. 1946
Mertz, Laurence L. 1921, '22
Mervin, Daniel D. 1947, '48, '49
Messer, Philip H. 1966, '67, '68
Meyer, Frederick D. 1939, '40, '41
Meyers, Robert E., Jr. 1950, '51
Meyers, William J. 1971, '72
Middlekauff, Peter D. 1964
Middleton, Joel D. 1923, '24, '25
Millage, James H. 1926
Miller, John D. 1907, '08 (rugby)
Miller, Michael R. 1967
Milligan, Robert F. 1931
Mills, James M. 1965, '66

Minturn, LeRoy 1906, '07, '09, '10
(rugby)
Mitchell, Emery F. III 1948, '49
Mitchell, Howard L. 1923, '24, '25
Mitchell, Mowatt M. 1907, '08, '09
(rugby)
Mitchell, Robert S. 1941
Mitchell, Standish L. 1909, '10 (rugby)
Moffatt, Philip J. 1929, '30, '31
Moffett, Eugene V. 1966
Mohrman, Allen M., Jr. 1965, '66
Molfino, Albert A. 1905, '06
Monmouth, Reuben L., Jr. 1972
Monteith, Richard J. 1952, '53
Monsalve, Carlos A. 1934
Moore, Dennis J. 1968, '69, '70
Moore, Francis J. 1925
Moore, Miles N. 1969, '70, '71
Moore, Patrick S. 1970, '71, '72
Moore, Robert R. 1968, '69, '70
Morehouse, Charles J. 1960
Morley, Samuel R. 1951, '52, '53
Morley, Vivirn A. 1927
Morris, Allyn E. 1947
Morrison, Benjamin F. 1942
Moscrip, James H. 1933, '34, '35
Mosich, Anthony J. 1954, '55
Muller, Donald F. 1927, '28, '29
Muller, Westley C. 1933, '34, '35
Mullin, Jack W. 1939
Munger, John R. 1936
Murphy, Chester G. 1896, '97, '98, '99
Murphy, Michael 1925, '26, '27
Murray Gary S. 1970, '71, '72
Murray, Paul C. 1922, '23
Myers, Glenn C. 1963, '64, '65

"N"

Nafziger, James 1947, '48
Nagel, Otto A. 1918 (rugby)
Natcher, Stanlus Z. 1926
Neal, Joe F. 1962, '63, '64
Neff, John R. 1954, '55
Neill, Philip S. 1929, '30, '31
Neill, William C., Jr. 1923, '24
Nelson, David E. 1965, '66, '67
Nevers, Ernest A. 1923, '24, '25
Nichols, Robert G., Jr. 1962, '63, '64
Nicholson, William H. 1967, '68
Nicolet, Robert A. 1957, '58
Nikolai, Irvin 1957, '58, '59

365

Norberg, Henry F., Jr. 1940, '41, '42
Norgard, Alvar A. 1931, '33
Norman, Richard M. 1958, '59, '60
Nye, Blaine F. 1965, '66, '67

"O"

O'Connor, Robert C. 1933
Ogle, William A. 1964, '65, '66
Olenchalk, John H. 1974
Oliver, Richard E. 1967, '68, '69
Olmsted, Clarence E. 1910 (rugby)
Olson, Robert W. 1973, '74
Orme, Charles H., Jr. 1938, '39, '40
Ostrander, Dale H. 1960
Ostrander, William R. 1965
Ostrom, Sig R. 1973, '74
Ottmar, David A. 1972, '73
Owen, Chauncey C. 1906, '07 (rugby)

"P"

Packard, David 1933
Palamountain, Bennett H. 1932, '33
Palin, W. Drew 1973, '74
Pallette, Charles W., Jr. 1919
Palmer, Richard A. 1940
Pape, Terry E. 1972, '73, '74
Pappas, Ted A. 1973, '74
Parish, Don E. 1967, '68, '69
Parker, Garth 1897, '98, '99
Parker, Melvin F. 1918, '19
Parker, Roderick J. 1938, '40
Patchett, Ernest L. 1925, '26
Patitucci, Frank M. 1961, '62, '63
Patrick, John C. 1919, '20, '21
Patterson, David E. 1939, '42
Patton, Chester G. 1939
Paulman, William H. 1935, '36, '38
Pavko, Michael R. 1965, '66
Pavlic, John W. 1961, '63
Page, John P. 1962
Peck, Edward L. 1913 (rugby)
Peck, Kendall R. 1947, '49
Pelouze, Robert F. 1916 (rugby), '19, '20
Pemberton, John R. 1906, '07, '09 (rugby)
Pershing, Richard S. 1919, '20, '21
Peter, Donald G. 1959, '60
Peterson, Dennis W. 1971, '72
Peterson, Robert L. 1956, '57, '58

Peterson, Thor J. 1938, '39, '40
Pettigrew, Gary L. 1963, '64, '65
Pettingill, Henry S., Jr. 1914, '15, '16, '17 (rugby)
Phelps, Robert C. 1947
Pheney, William D. 1922
Phleger, Atherton M. 1946, '47, '48
Pike, Gary E. 1958, '59
Plain, Louis C. III 1956, '58
Plate, Horatio R. 1898
Player, Stephen W. 1960, '61
Plunkett, James W. 1968, '69, '70
Polich, Tyrone T. 1956
Poltl, Randall P. 1971, '72, '73
Pomeroy, Russell A. 1949, '50
Pool, Hampton J. 1938, '39
Post, Ellis 1926
Post, Seraphin T. 1927, '28
Poulson, Charles W. 1949, '50
Poulson, Ward E. 1924, '25, '26
Powell, Owen M. 1950, '51
Prelsnik, Charles J. 1931
Presley, George J. 1906 (rugby)
Preston, A. E. 1901
Preston, John B. 1927, '28, '29
Preston, Patrick P. 1967, '68, '69
Price, Fred V. 1925
Price, Robert L. 1960, '61, '62
Protiva, Eric V. 1956, '57, '58
Ptacek, Edward D. 1963
Purkitt, Claude H. 1940
Pursell, Frank D. 1958, '59, '60
Pursell, Stephen W. 1960, '61, '62
Pyle, H. Carter, Jr. 1951, '52

"Q"

Quist, George 1946, '47

"R"

Raffetto, Estral J. 1925
Raftery, Michael R. 1955, '56
Ragsdale, Richard A. 1962, '63, '64
Raitt, C. B. 1899, '00, '01
Rannells, Roland J. 1957
Rasmussen, Neil, Jr. 1936, '37
Rath, Robert R. 1964, '65
Rau, Allan F., Jr. 1946, '47, '48
Read, John M. 1964, '65, '66
Reed, Harold E. 1907
Reeves, Frank W. 1910, '13, '14 (rugby)

Rehm, Francis E. 1914, '15 (rugby)
Reid, William J. 1972, '73
Reinhard, Robert R. 1967, '68, '69
Reisner, John A. 1933, '34
Renwick, Donn C. 1965, '66, '67
Repath, Charles J. 1918, '19
Revak, Paul A. 1952
Reynolds, Barry R. 1971, '72
Reynolds, Jackson E. 1894, '95
Reynolds, James M. 1919
Reynolds, Kenneth M. 1931
Reynolds, Robert C. 1933, '34, '35
Rhyne, Homer 1907 (rugby)
Rice, Arthur H. 1898, '99
Rice, Gordon 1949, '51
Rice, J. Bermingham 1896, '97
Rich, Ellsworth L. 1892
Riegel, Gordon S. 1972, '73, '74
Righter, Cornelius E. 1917 (rugby), '19, '20
Rinker, Robert L. 1967
Rintala, Rudolph A. 1930, '31
Ritchey, Craig S. 1963, '64, '65
Robesky, Donald A. 1926, '27, '28
Robesky, Kenneth L. 1939, '40, '41
Robinson, Benjamin B. 1956, '57, '59
Robinson, Noel J. 1955, '56, '57
Robnett, Timothy L. 1970, '71
Rodolph, Frank E., Jr. 1899
Rogers, Charles O. 1932
Rogers, William B., Jr. 1952, '53
Rohrer, Robert L. 1947, '48
Roosevelt, William K. 1901, '04
Root, John P. 1965, '66, '67
Rose, Kenneth C. 1948, '49
Rosekrans, John N. 1948
Ross, Thomas L. 1963, '64, '65
Roth, A. Edwards 1909 (rugby)
Rothert, Harlow P. 1928, '29, '30
Rouble, Lawrence E. 1933, '34, '35
Rounds, George S. 1960
Rounsaville, Guy, Jr. 1962, '63, '64
Rowen, Keith L. 1972, '73, '74
Royse, Larry L. 1960, '61
Rubin, Dale F. 1965
Rush, John P. 1898
Rye, H. John G. 1949, '50, '51
Ryska, Tom A. 1974

"S"

Sadler, James D. 1938

Saibel, Charles M. 1969
St. Geme, Joseph W., Jr. 1950, '51, '52
Sampson, Ralph G. 1969, '70, '71
Sandborn, Thomas 1909 (rugby)
Sande, John P. III 1968, '69, '70
Sanderman, Fred A. 1942
Sanders, Donald L. 1951
Sanderson, Reginald J. 1970, '71, '72
Sappenfield, Joel W. 1954, '55
Sargent, Gary A. 1960, '61, '62
Satre, Philip G. 1969, '70, '71
Schallich, Timothy R. 1970, '71
Scheidecker, William R. 1953
Schmitt, Lawrence E. 1959, '60
Schneider, Philip D. 1965, '67
Scholfield, William R. 1903
Schott, Carl V. 1934, '35, '36
Schrader, Carl F. 1962, '63, '64
Schultz, Jack G. 1968, '69, '70
Schwarzenbek, Francis 1917 (rugby)
Scott, Errol G. 1959, '60, '61
Scott, Joseph K. 1947
Scott, Leland S. 1909 (rugby)
Scott, Robert E. 1950
Scott, William D. 1970, '71, '72
Scribner, Frederick F. 1931
Searight, Benjamin F. 1896
Sears, Roger G. 1959, '60, '61
Seeley, Carrol C. 1900
Sellman, Roland 1926, '27, '28
Seymour, Peter M. 1967, '68, '69
Seymour, Robert J. 1955
Sharp, David B. 1968, '69
Shaw, Thomas L. 1948, '49, '50
Shea, Charles A. III 1956, '57
Sheehan, Dennis J. 1969, '70, '71
Sheehan, Timothy G. 1965, '66
Sheldon, Willard H. 1919
Sheller, Willard N. 1941, '42
Shields, Harvey H. 1903, '04
Shipkey, Arthur H. 1942
Shipkey, Harry H. 1922, '23, '24
Shipkey, Theodore E. 1924, '25, '26
Shlaudeman, Karl W. 1919, '20
Shlaudeman, Robert 1919, '20, '21
Shockley, Hillary E. 1969, '70, '71
Shoemaker, William B. 1966, '67, '68
Shore, Robert A. 1966, '67, '68
Shroyer, James L. 1961, '62, '63
Siemens, Jeffrey S. 1974
Siemon, Jeffrey G. 1969, '70, '71
Sim, William C. 1932, '33

367

Simkins, William J. 1928, '29, '30
Simone, Michael A. 1970, '71
Simons, Carlton B. 1960, '61, '62
Sims, Robert F. 1926, '27, '28
Single, Douglas W. 1972
Singler, Bill D. 1973, '74
Sinnerud, James A. 1958
Skrabo, Paul M. 1974
Slaker, Frank L. 1900, '01
Slusher, Dale 1905
Smalling, Charles O. 1928, '29
Smiley, Arthur C. 1970
Smith, Barrett C. 1951, '52, '53
Smith, Edward A. 1899, '00, '01, '02
Smith, G. W. 1903
Smith, James Z. 1959, '61
Smith, Lyle W. 1933
Smith, Rea E. 1896, '97, '98
Smith, Sidney B. 1947
Smith, Ferrell W. 1968, '69, '70
Smitherum, Edgar 1915 (rugby)
Smith, Warren L. 1910, '11, '12 (rugby)
Smythe, James J. 1974
Snider, John E. 1972, '73, '74
Snider, Malcolm P. 1966, '67, '68
Solomon, Fred F. 1923, '24, '25
Sones, Thomas H. 1970, '71
Soper, Harold C. 1914, '15 (rugby)
Sorensen, Loren R. 1953
South, Glenn E. 1938, '40
Southwood, Eric J. 1949, '51
Spalding, Alfred B. 1894, '95
Spence, Daniel H. 1961, '62
Sprott, Walter K. 1902, '03, '04
Sproull, Henry F. 1921
Stahle, Douglas C. 1939, '40, '41
Stamm, Edward A. 1940, '41, '42
Standlee, Norman S. 1938, '39, '40
Stanford, J. N. 1905, '06
Stanton, John G. 1952, '53, '55
Steele, Russell B. 1956, '57, '58
Stein, Richard B. 1957
Steinberg, John C., Jr. 1951, '52, '53
Stephen, Roy A. 1957, '58
Steuber, Harold A. 1959, '60, '61
Stevenson, Don V. 1974
Stewart, James R. 1952
Stewart, John K., Jr. 1953, '54, '55
Stice, Robert H. 1919, '20, '21
Stillwell, Roger H. 1972, '73, '74
Stojkovich, Andrew 1938, '39
Stone, Glen J. 1971, '72, '73

Stone, Grant B. 1936, '37
Storum, William A. 1950, '51, '52
Stott, Edmund P. 1904, '05, '06
Straight, Herbert R. 1896
Sturgeon, John B. 1939
Sundell, Alfred L. 1910 (rugby)
Sundheim, George M. 1973, '74
Supple, Frederick E., Jr. 1946
Sutton, Richard X. 1937
Swan, Frederick H. 1924, '25, '26
Swanson, Peter L. 1957, '58
Swarts, Clifton R. 1917 (rugby)
Swartz, Donald E. 1966, '67
Swigart, Theodore E. 1915, '16 (rugby)
Symonds, Nathaniel M. 1926

"T"

Tandy, Ray E. 1928, '29, '30
Tanner, Edwin S. 1951, '52, '53
Targhetta, Paul 1931, '32, '33
Tarpey, Paul A. 1901, '02
Tarr, William H. 1953, '54, '55
Taylor, Albert W. 1921
Taylor, Charles A. 1940, '41, '42
Taylor, Edwin D. 1950
Taylor, Jack R. 1955, '56, '57
Taylor, Perry N. 1929, '30
Taylor, Wilbur R. 1949, '50
Templeton, Robert L. 1915, '16, '17 (rugby), '19, '20
Templeton, Robert M. 1939
TenBruggencate, Al J. 1974
Tenn, David T. 1973, '74
Tennefoss, Marvin 1950, '51, '52
Terriell, Chester C. 1908 (rugby)
Test, Eric B. 1973, '74
Thoburn, James H. 1910, '12, '13 (rugby)
Thomas, Arthur B. 1922, '23, '24
Thomas, Benjamin A. 1896, '97
Thomas, John M. 1957, '59
Thompson, James G. 1929
Thompson, John M. 1940
Thompson, Robert A. 1901, '03, '04, '05
Thompson, Robert N. 1951, '52
Thorpe, Charles A. 1906, '07, '09 (rugby)
Thurlow, Stephen C. 1961, '62, '63
Tilton, Lloyd I. 1913 (rugby)
Tipton, David L. 1969, '70
Tipton, Tom E. 1974

368

Titus, Michael G. 1946, '47
Tobin, Donald J. 1951
Tod, Jay K. 1931, '32, '33
Todd, Raymond W. 1934, '35
Tomerlin, Clemens 1940
Tomlinson, Daniel J. 1971
Toorvald, Philip S. 1960
Topping, William K. 1933, '34, '35
Traeger, William J. 1899, '00, '01
Trombetta, Julius C. 1926
Trompas, Alexander G. 1934, '35
Trout, William W., Jr. 1939
Tsoutsouvas, Louis S. 1936, '37
Turriziani, Alfred L. 1948

"U"

Ukropina, James R. 1957, '58
Urban, Joseph C. 1912, '13, '14, '15
    (rugby)

"V"

Vahan, Randolph K. 1960, '61, '62
Vail, Stanley M. 1907 (rugby)
Valli, Louis P. 1955, '56, '57
Van Alstyne, Bruce E. 1949, '50
Van Dellen, Elzo L., Jr. 1933, '34
Vanderlip, Manford 1955
Van Dervoort, Theodore, Jr. 1905, '07
Van Galder, Gary C. 1955, '56, '57
Van Hook, Stuart G. 1924, '25
Vataha, Randall E. 1969, '70
Vigby, Jack 1917 (rugby)
Verdieck, James E. 1939, '40
Vermilya, Robert H. 1928
Vick, James A. 1950, '51, '52
Vigna, Joseph A. 1935, '36
Vincenti, Louis R. 1927
Volmert, Lawrence E. 1964, '65, '66
Vucinich, Milton C. 1940, '41, '42

"W"

Wakefield, Charles 1942, '46
Waldo, John H. 1918
Waldvogel, Jerry A. 1974
Walker, David B. 1972, '73, '74
Walker, Edgar L. 1924, '25, '26
Walker, Frank F. 1915, '16 (rugby)
Walker, Harold L. 1947
Walker, Kelly J. 1973, '74
Walsh, Thomas J. 1959, '60, '61

Walton, H. A. 1892, '93
Walton, Jackson 1934, '37
Wark, Thomas L. 1916, '17, (rugby)
    '19
Warnecke, John C. 1939, '40
Washington, Demea G. 1968, '69, '70
Washington, Gene A. 1966, '67, '68
Waters, Ruch A. 1974
Watkins, Frederick B. 1911, '13 (rugby)
Watson, Donald R. 1957, '58
Watson, Jarvis P. 1952, '53
Watts, Frank A. 1918, '19
Weaver, Clark E. 1962, '63
Wedge, Wesley E. 1954
Wedge, Winfred E. 1952, '53, '54
Weingartner, Thomas A. 1966, '67, '68
Weller, Milo J. 1903, '04
Wentworth, William A. 1953
West, Byron F. 1937, '38
West, R. F. 1904
Wheat, Gilbert C. 1923
Whipple, John H. 1947
White, Charles H. 1934
White, Gordon W. 1948, '49, '50
White, Robert W. 1948, '49, '50
White, Stephen F. 1972, '73
Whitehouse, Louis M. 1893
Whittemore, John R. 1892
Wiggin, Paul D. 1954, '55, '56
Wilbur, John L. 1963, '64, '65
Wilburn, Albert T. 1964, '65, '66
Wilcox, Chester A. 1920, '21, '22
Wiley, William M. 1972
Wilkin, John S. 1963
Wilkins, Earl B. 1916 (rugby)
Willard, Michael R. 1967
Willard, William C. 1937, '38, '40
Williams, Brad B. 1973, '74
Williams, Charles R. 1966, '67
Williams, Fred L. 1934, '35, '36
Williams, Howard L. 1967, '68, '69
Williams, Lewis I. 1971
Williams, Thomas N. 1958
Williams, Thomas M. 1895, '96
Wilson, Elwood J. 1929
Wilson Gerald E. 1973, '74
Wilson, John H. 1892 '93
Wilson, Philip L. 1898
Wilson, Philip L., Jr. 1931
Wilson, Philip C. 1952, '53
Wilson, William A. 1941
Wilton, Frank S., Jr. 1926, '27, '28

Winesberry, John C. 1971, '72, '73
Wylie, James T. 1914, '15 (rugby)
Wylie, Robert M. 1959, '60
Wines, Blaine L. 1913, '14 (rugby)
Winham, William P. 1916, '17 (rugby)
Winnek, Phil S. 1929
Winters, Jerry E. 1960
Wittenau, Carl 1929
Woodcock, Elbert C. 1911 (rugby)
Woodward, Tyleve F. 1921, '22, '23
Woollomes, James P. 1920
Worden, Richard C. 1927, '28
Worley, David E. 1951

"Y"

Young, Gordon A. 1954, '55, '56
Young, William B. 1942

"Z"

Zager, Peter G. 1936, '37, '38
Zaltosky, Craig R. 1972, '73
Zappettini, Donald M. 1942, '46

ACKNOWLEDGMENTS

The author gratefully acknowledges assistance from the following for the items indicated:

The Wow Boys—Cyclone Covey
The Color Of Life Is Red—Don E. Liebendorfer
The Tournament Of Roses—Joe Hendrickson
The History Of American Football—Allison Danzig
Football-Facts And Figures—Dr. L. H. Baker
Football's Greatest Coaches—Edwin Pope
Great Moments In Stanford Sports—Stanford Press
Stanford Quad